HOME ECONOMICS
OCR CHILD DEVELOPMENT FOR GCSE

Carolyn Meggitt

HODDER EDUCATION

AN HACHETTE UK COMPANY

Orders: please contact Bookpoint Ltd, 130 Milton Park, Abingdon, Oxon OX14 4SB. Telephone: (44) 01235 827720. Fax: (44) 01235 400454. Lines are open from 9.00–5.00, Monday to Saturday, with a 24-hour message answering service. You can also order through our website www.hoddereducation.co.uk

If you have any comments to make about this, or any of our other titles, please send them to educationenquiries@hodder.co.uk

British Library Cataloguing in Publication Data
A catalogue record for this title is available from the British Library

ISBN: 978 0 340 97506 0

First Edition Published 2009

Impression number   10 9 8 7 6 5 4 3 2
Year   2012 2011 2010

Hachette UK's policy is to use papers that are natural, renewable and recyclable products and made from wood grown in sustainable forests. The logging and manufacturing processes are expected to conform to the environmental regulations of the country of origin.

Cover photo © Goodshoot/Corbis
Illustrations by Kate Nardoni/Cactus Design and Illustration
Typeset by Fakenham Photosetting Ltd, Fakenham, Norfolk NR21 8NN
Printed in Italy for Hodder Education, an Hachette UK Company, 338 Euston Road, London NW1 3BH

CONTENTS

ACKNOWLEDGEMENTS

The author and publishers would like to thank the following people for the photographs used in the book:

David Meggitt for his photography; all the staff, children and parents at Bushy Park Nursery; the children and parents of friends and neighbours; the Shooting Star Children's Hospice for permission to photograph the toys in part five, and Laura Meggitt for taking the photographs.

The author would like to thank the publishing team at Hodder Education for their help and support.

INTRODUCTION

This book has been written primarily to support the specification requirements for the OCR GCSE Home Economics: Child Development, although it also supports the GCSE courses of other examining boards, as well as other courses with a child development component.

How the book is organised

The book is concerned with the growth and development of children from conception to the age of five. It is divided into seven parts. Parts one to six cover the content requirements of the specification. You will find everything you need to know to gain the GCSE within this book. Part seven includes information on how the course is assessed, guidance on completing the coursework, examination techniques and practice exam questions.

Part one	Family and parenting
Part two	Preparation for pregnancy and birth
Part three	Physical development
Part four	Nutrition and health
Part five	Intellectual, social and emotional development
Part six	Community support
Part seven	Coursework and exam preparation

Throughout the text, key terms and definitions are highlighted and there is also a comprehensive glossary at the end of the book. Revision questions, ideas for further research and child study activities are included at the end of sections within each part or chapter of the book.

The book is supported by a teacher's resource, which contains resource sheets and activities for use in coursework, and more advice on how to be successful in the examination.

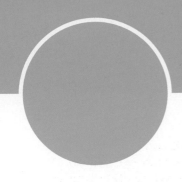

CREDITS

The author and publishers would like to thank the following for permission to reproduce material in this book:

page 2 top left Valentine-Fotolia.com; page 2 top right Monkey Businass-Fotolia.com; page 2 bottom left Alamy/Celia Mannings; page 2 bottom right Vitaliy Hrabar-Fotolia.com; page 5 left Corbis/Sipley/Classic Stock; page 5 right Alamy/Jaubert Bernard; page 8 Alamy/Image Source Pink; page 48 FASawareUK; page 66 Science Photo Library/BSIP, Astier; page 72 Mother & Baby PL/Ruth Jenkinson; page 73 Mother & baby PL/Ruth Jenkinson; page 74 Alamy/Shout; page 75 Alamy/Shout; page 76 Mother & Baby PL/Ruth Jenkinson; pages 78 & 79 Alamy/Radek Detinsky; page 83 top Getty/Stockbyte; page 83 middle Stephen Coburn-Fotolia.com; page 83 bottom Mother & Baby PL/Ruth Jenkinson; page 83 right Julian Rovagni-Fotolia.com; page 84 Alamy/Stockbyte; page 86 Alamy/fStop; page 87 Melissa Schalke-Fotolia.com; page 94 Alamy/Gary Roebuck; page 95 rooting reflex: Babyarchive.com; grasp reflex: Alamy/Larry Lilac; stepping or walking reflex: Science Photo Library/BSIP Bajande; startle reflex: Alamy/Reagan Pannell; asymmetric tonic neck reflex: Getty/Stephanie Rausser; page 100 Anyka-Fotolia.com; page 102 Alamy/Syner-Comm; page 103 top Alamy/Petr Bonek; page 103 bottom Alamy/Jacky Chapman; page 104 top Alamy/Peter Usbeck; page 104 bottom Alamy/Petr Bonek ; page 106 David Meggitt; page 112 top David Meggitt; page 112 bottom Getty/Richard Elliott; page 113 top Gary Roebuck; page 113 middle David Meggitt; page 113 David Meggitt; page 114 top Science Photo Library/Johnny Greig; page 114 middle David Meggitt; page 114 bottom David Meggitt; page 115 top David Meggitt; page 115 middle David Meggitt; page 115 bottom David Meggitt; page 116 top David Meggitt; page 116 bottom David Meggitt; page 117 David Meggitt; page 137 David Meggitt; page 143 Getty/Ghislaine & Marie David de Lossy; page 152 left Alamy/Shout; page 152 right Alamy/Jack Sullivan; page 159 Vitaliy Hrabar-Fotolia.com; page 161 David Meggitt; page 190 Jose Manuel Gelpi/© Jose Manuel Gelpi-Fotolia.com; page 200 Science Photo Library/Gusto Images; page 208 left Science Photo Library/Ian Hooton; page 208 right Science Photo Library/Carolyn A Mckeone; page 214 Justin O'Hanlon; page 218 David Meggitt; page 219 top Science Photo Library/Ian Boddy; page 219 bottom David Meggitt; page 220 top Corbis/Laura Dwight; page 220 middle Justin O'Hanlon; page 220 bottom David Meggitt; page 228 David Meggitt; page 229 left Bookstart; page 229 right Bookstart; page 230 Carolyn Meggitt; page 233 David Meggitt; page 242 David Meggitt; page 253 top David Meggitt; page 253 bottom David Meggitt; page 254 top Corbis/Somos Images; page 254 bottom David Meggitt; page 256 Science Photo Library/Ian Boddy; page 257 top David Meggitt; page 257 bottom David Meggitt; pages 258–262 Carolyn Meggitt; page 265 David Meggitt

Every effort has been made to obtain necessary permission with reference to copyright material. The publishers apologise if inadvertently any sources remain unacknowledged and will be glad to make the necessary arrangements at the earliest opportunity.

FAMILY AND PARENTING

1 Family structures in the UK

What is a family?

The nature of the family has changed in the UK. It has become more complex, mainly due to changes in society – such as moral attitudes towards marriage and changes to the laws concerning divorce. The word 'family' means different things to different people, depending on who you are – your own beliefs and attitudes – and your experiences of family life.

Even social scientists disagree on what defines a family, but a useful definition for the twenty-first century in the UK is as follows:

> A family is a 'small social group, consisting of at least one adult and child, usually living together, related by blood, marriage or adoption' (Alan Yeo and Tina Lovell, 2002, *Sociology and Social Policy*, 2nd edn, London: Hodder & Stoughton, p. 75).

The family can include all or some of the following individuals:

- grandparents, uncles and aunts and other relations
- foster parents, step-parents, stepchildren, or only one parent
- two parents living separately
- parents who have chosen to marry or those who are cohabiting
- parents of the same sex bringing up children.

Types of family

In today's society there are many different types of family structure and children are likely to come from a wide range of home backgrounds. Many children will live with parents who cohabit (live together) but are not legally married. These children may have been given either one or both of the parents' surnames as their own.

 KEY TERMS

Sibling: A brother or sister.

Stepfamily: Stepfamilies consist of married or cohabiting (living together) couples who, between them, have at least one child from a previous relationship who either visits or lives with them.

Step-parent (stepmother or stepfather): The individual who is not the biological parent of the child or children is referred to as the step-parent.

Stepbrother or stepsister: A child who has brothers or sisters through the remarriage of a parent to somebody who has children.

Half-brother or half-sister: A sibling with one shared biological or adoptive parent.

The nuclear family

The nuclear family is the most common family type in the UK today. It is made up of no more than two generations (parents and children): a father, a mother and their 'joint' biological children all live together. They may be married or cohabiting. Often the nuclear family live away from the rest of the family and need to make more effort to maintain links with other family members.

The nuclear family

The extended family

The extended family is a nuclear family 'extended' by other relations. It is usually a large group, which may include grandparents, parents, aunts and uncles, brothers, sisters and cousins living in the main family home. Pakistani and Bangladeshi households are the largest – often containing three generations, with grandparents living with a married couple and their children.

The extended family

The reconstituted family

The reconstituted family (or stepfamily) is one that has two parents, each of whom may have children from previous relationships, and that has reformed into a single unit. In a reconstituted family, children live with one natural parent and one step-parent. Families may also include stepsisters and stepbrothers and/or half-sisters and half-brothers.

The reconstituted family

The lone-parent family

The lone-parent family is one in which there is only one parent living with the children. It is often assumed that this is the mother, but in many instances it is the father. It is sometimes referred to as a 'broken nuclear family' because it often – but not always – arises out of the break-up of a nuclear family. In a lone-parent family, a single parent takes care of children, either through choice or for other reasons. This may be, for instance, because of divorce or separation, or the death of a partner.

The lone-parent family

Table 1.1 Types of family in the UK

The adoptive family	The foster family	Residential care home
The adoptive family is one in which a child has been adopted, resulting in the parents having assumed legal responsibility for the child.	The foster family is one that is temporarily caring for a child or children who may or may not have their own families. Foster parents may or may not have 'parental responsibility.'	Children without parents, or children whose parents are unable to look after them, are looked after in residential homes by people who are not their parents. Residential care homes are usually run by social services.

Table 1.1 Contin.

The types of family in table 1.1 represent patterns of family life that are commonly found in the UK, but within any of them there will be variations. For example:

- A reconstituted family may have not only step-parents and stepchildren, but also children from the new adult partnership who become half-siblings (half-brothers or half-sisters) to the existing children. This is also known as a blended family.
- In lone-parent families the absent parent may remain in contact with and have access to the children, but may have formed new relationships and had more children. This means that the original children are part of both a lone-parent family and a stepfamily.

Other family types that are less common include:

- The nomadic family – one that has no permanent town or village. A nomadic family may live in a mobile home and travel to different sites, settling in one place only for a short period of time – for example, traveller families.
- The communal family – one in which children live in a commune where, in addition to their parent or parents, they are cared for by other people who share the home.

There is no 'correct' model for a family structure, just as there is no 'best' way of bringing up children. However, certain things do seem to be important for all families. Always remember that every family is different.

Why is marriage less popular?

Sociologists put forward several ideas to try to explain the rise in cohabitation and the decline in marriage. These include:

- financial factors: marriage is expensive
- more secular society (secularisation is the process in modern societies in which religious ideas and organisations tend to lose influence when faced with science and other forms of knowledge)
- economic independence of women
- insecurity of employment
- awareness of divorce.

Cohabitation

This involves adults living together as if they were married, but without a legally binding contract. There has been a marked increase in the number of cohabiting couples in the UK. Cohabitation can take different forms, including:

- a trial before marriage

- raising children in long-term relationships
- one or both parties are divorced.

 QUICK FACTS

- One in ten children in the UK now lives with one birth parent and one step-parent.
- Two in five marriages in the UK end in divorce.
- Two-fifths of all marriages are remarriages.
- Seventy per cent of fathers who do not live with their children have contact with them.
- A quarter of children have experienced their parents' divorce. Over half of them will find themselves members of a stepfamily when their mothers and fathers go on to find new partners.
- Half of these stepfamilies will have a new child belonging to the step-couple.

2 Roles, responsibilities and values of the family

Roles within the family are changing. They also vary from culture to culture. The nuclear family remains the most common type of family in the UK today, but the roles of parents and children within the family have changed. Table 1.2 shows the main changes that have taken place over the last century.

	Early twentieth century	Early twenty-first century
	A typical family in the early twentieth century	A typical family in the early twenty-first century
Family size	**Families were larger:** The average family size in 1909 was 3.5, but many families had 8 or 9 children, although not all survived.	**Families are smaller:** The average family size in 2006 was 1.8 children.
	Infant mortality rate: In 1911, 10% of babies born in the UK had died before their first birthday.	**Infant mortality rate:** In 2006, 0.4% of babies born in the UK had died before their first birthday.
	Family planning: Due to a lack of contraceptive methods, couples were unable to plan when to have children.	**Family planning:** From the second half of the twentieth century, various contraceptive methods – particularly the birth control pill – have enabled couples to plan when to have children.
The role of men	Men were the chief providers for the family. They did not do domestic chores as these were seen as 'women's work'. Fathers were often authoritarian figures who controlled every aspect of family life. Physical violence towards women and children was fairly common.	In most families with dependent children, the father is still the main wage earner and the mother often works part-time. Fathers are seen as less authoritarian. They are more involved in home-based tasks and in rearing their children. Some fathers opt to care for the children at home while the mother works – this is known as **role reversal**.
The role of women	Traditionally, women looked after the children and did all the domestic chores. Women in wealthy families employed other women to cook, clean and care for their children. Until the 1950s, a woman was expected to give up her job to look after her husband and the house. There were few labour-saving gadgets and little leisure time.	Women increasingly work outside the home – either from necessity or by choice. They have certain legal rights in employment, such as equal pay and maternity rights; it is also illegal to discriminate against a person on the grounds of their gender or marital status. Women still do the bulk of household chores, but family responsibilities are often shared.

Table 1.2 Family life and parents' roles in the early twentieth and twenty-first centuries

Conjugal roles	These were unequal – or **segregated** – roles. The man did the paid work and the woman looked after the home and children.	These are now shared – or **joint** – roles, with men and women spending a more equal amount of time on tasks in the home (although research shows that women still perform the majority of home-based tasks).
The family home	Most of the UK population were working class (they mainly did manual jobs) and lived in towns and cities. Poor housing conditions were common, with overcrowding and poor sanitation. Children shared bedrooms and possessions. Many people lived in 'back-to-back' terraced houses, and until the 1930s children played in the street. Children had very few clothes or toys and family holidays were rare.	Most of the UK population live in homes which have a piped water supply, electricity and flush toilets. Most children have a space to call their own, even in shared bedrooms. Most homes have televisions, a telephone, a car and a computer. Over 60% of homes now have an internet connection. Children have their own toys and organised leisure activities. Longer holidays – often abroad – are taken frequently.
Marriage	A man and woman started courting in their late teens or early twenties, married after a few years and then started a family. Often the newly-weds lived with one set of parents until they could afford their own home. This meant that many families were **extended families**, with grandparents and older siblings helping with finances and with childcare.	In the 1980s, couples started living together (cohabiting), whether or not they were to be married. Illegitimacy ceased to be a social stigma. Marriage continued to be important, however, and figures for remarriage were high. Most families today consist of parents and their children – the **nuclear family**. The Civil Partnership Act 2004 enables a same-sex couple to register as partners of each other.
Divorce	Divorce was rare in the early twentieth century. Then the only legal basis for divorce was adultery, and it was difficult to gain social acceptance as a divorced person, because of attitudes towards those who had sex outside marriage. Divorced women had no rights to property or to financial support.	Divorce increased throughout the second half of the twentieth century, and by the 1990s as many as one-third of marriages ended in divorce. Now, for every three marriages in the UK there are two divorces – the highest rate in Europe. There is no longer a social stigma in being divorced, and women have legal rights to property and financial support.
Children	In poorer families, young children were often obliged to work. (It was legal for children to start full-time work at just 12 years old.) Childhood ended at 14 or 15, with an apprenticeship in a trade or office. Apprentices worked long hours for little pay. In wealthy families, boys as young as seven were sent away to boarding schools, where they often suffered cold dormitories, poor food and bullying. Poor families were commonplace and it was believed that 4% of people lived in poverty.	All children in the UK starting secondary school from September 2008 must receive full-time education until the age of 17 and the great majority of them are educated in state schools. The welfare state provides a range of benefits to help parents with childcare costs, and social workers have the powers to intervene in families where children are believed to be at risk. A quarter of families with children under five years now live in **poverty**. Lack of employment is an important factor, together with the high cost of housing, nutritious food, clothing and transport.

Table 1.2 Contin.

KEY TERMS

Infant mortality: Babies dying in the first year of life.

Childhood mortality: Children dying between 1 and 14 years.

Conjugal roles: The roles of the man and woman (husband and wife) in the home.

Shared roles: Where men and women contribute equally to the housework, but not necessarily in the same way.

The functions of the family

The responsibilities of the family are as follows:

1. Meeting the primary needs of food, clothing, shelter, warmth and opportunities for rest and sleep.
2. Providing love and nurture – children need to feel loved and to learn to love; this means they need some reliable people in their lives who show them affection and warmth, and who enjoy receiving their love and warmth in return.
3. Teaching socialisation – families introduce children to their culture (the way this comes about varies in different parts of the world, and will differ even between families within one culture); this means that through their family children learn about:
   - social behaviour – the sort of behaviour that people expect of them
   - customs – things which people always do or always do in a particular way, by tradition
   - values – the accepted principles or standards of an individual or a group.

In addition, all children and their families need:

- good-quality core public services, such as health and education
- safe places to play
- decent housing
- leisure opportunities
- an inclusive community, free of crime, antisocial behaviour and racial harassment.

Parental responsibility

The Children Act (1989) is an important piece of legislation.-The Act identifies the needs of children as paramount (i.e. of the greatest importance) and attempts to support them in the family by giving 'parental responsibility' to one, or more, appropriate person(s).

- Parental responsibility is *automatically* given to married parents or to the natural mother, if unmarried.
- In cases of parents cohabiting, the natural father can be made a legal guardian by applying through the courts.
- Divorced parents may have joint parental responsibility or, in some circumstances, adults other than the parents may be given parental responsibility – perhaps grandparents or foster parents.
- Where a child is the subject of a care order (there are many reasons for this – e.g. risk of abuse, parental ill health) the local authority has parental responsibility.
- An unmarried father does not have parental responsibility, but does have a financial responsibility for his children.

Parental responsibility under the Act includes:

- naming and registering the child at birth
- deciding where the child should live
- making decisions about the child's education (how and where) and making sure the child receives education from 5 to 17 years
- consenting to medical care and treatment
- choosing the faith/religion in which the child will be raised
- maintaining the child
- protecting the child
- applying for a passport for the child.

Family customs and values

Regardless of family structure, all families develop their own customs and practices, even in small daily events such as mealtimes. For some, it is always a 'sit at the table' affair; for others, it is always 'eat on your lap'; for many it is a mixture of formal and informal, depending on the time and occasion. Similarly, some regular family activities, like walking the dog or going shopping, often follow a pattern, and a routine is developed that will be very different from another family's routine. Special occasions (such as birthday celebrations, weddings or other cultural festivals) often have highly developed routines which are followed every time; as they are passed down through families these routines become traditions or even rituals.

Figure 1.1 Celebrating a wedding

REVISION QUESTIONS

1. Give a brief description of four types of family structure found in the UK today.
2. Why is marriage less popular now than it was in the early twentieth century?
3. What is a reconstituted family?
4. Which is the most common family structure in the UK today?
5. Give a brief description of four ways in which family life has changed over the last thirty years.

RESEARCH ACTIVITY

1. **Child study activity:** Describe the child's family:
   - If possible, draw up a simple family tree – extending from the child's grandparents downwards and outwards, to include great-aunts, uncles, siblings and cousins. (Remember to observe confidentiality by using only first names or initials.)
   - Describe the family's customs and note any cultural differences from your own family – for example, the family's eating habits and mealtimes, leisure activities and parental roles.

2. **Family support groups:** Using the internet or a reference library, find out about the different support groups for:
   - lone-parent families
   - families with a child with special needs.

Write a short paragraph about the type of support provided for each family group.

Useful organisations include: Gingerbread (www.gingerbread.org.uk), Contact a Family (www.cafamily.org.uk) and National Parent Partnership Network (www.parentpartnership.org.uk).

(See also 'Guidelines for research using the internet' in part seven, page 295.)

3 Changing patterns in parenting and family life

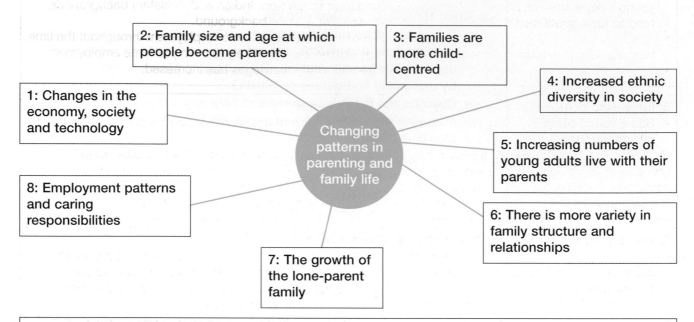

1: Changes in the economy, society and technology

- **Opportunities:** Children and young people today have more opportunities than previous generations and most take full advantage of them; however, children from lower socio-economic backgrounds are still more likely to experience a range of obstacles to success. While these factors can be overcome, they put poorer children at a disadvantage.
- **Studying:** More children and young people work hard and succeed at school, going on either to study at college or university or to find a job.
- **Communication:** The internet and mobile phones have had a huge impact on the way young people live and the way in which they communicate and obtain information.
- **Freedom of choice:** Families have more choice in many areas of their lives – from what they eat to how they spend their leisure time. The majority of children and young people have good relationships with their parents, who remain the strongest influence on their lives and the choices they make.

2: Family size and age at which people become parents

- **First-time mothers are older:** The average age of giving birth to the first child has gone up from 23.7 years in 1971 to 29.1 years in 2007.
- **Families are smaller:** Parents are having fewer children when they do decide to start a family. During the 1960s there was a 'baby boom' in the UK, with 2.94 children per woman in 1964. In 2007, this rate had decreased to 1.84 children per woman.
- **Teenage mothers:** Britain has the highest teenage pregnancy rate in western Europe and the second-highest in the world after the USA.

3: Families are more child-centred

- **Families are smaller:** With fewer children to care for, more individual care and attention can be given to each child.
- **More leisure time:** Today's parents work fewer hours, are relatively more affluent and have a higher standard of living. More time and money can be spent on children and on their leisure activities.
- **TV programmes and books:** There are many books and programmes which instruct parents on the best ways to bring up their children.
- **Consumer society:** Children are targeted by large businesses to encourage them to want the latest toys and gadgets. Parents often feel the need to satisfy their children's 'pester power' demands.

4: Increased ethnic diversity in society
- **Marriage trends in different ethnic groups:** Young Muslim adults are more likely to be married than young people from any other cultural background, and those from Indian and Pakistani backgrounds tend to have significantly larger families than those from a white background.
- **Ethnicity and employment trends:** Black women often remain in full-time employment throughout the time they are having children, whereas white and Indian women are more likely to be in part-time employment.
- **Mixed-ethnicity marriages:** The number of mixed-ethnicity marriages has increased.

5: Increasing numbers of young adults live with their parents
- Some young people may be delaying leaving home because of economic necessity, such as difficulties in entering the housing market.

(Against this trend, there is an increase in homelessness. Some young people from disadvantaged groups live apart from their parents at a young age – including teenage mothers and young people estranged from their parents and homeless. Despite recent improvements, too many young people leave the care system at too young an age and without the right support to live independently.)

6: There is more variety in family structure and relationships
- **Changes in divorce patterns:** There has been a long-term increase in the divorce rate. It has been estimated that in England and Wales, 28 per cent of children living in married-couple families will experience divorce in their family before reaching the age of 16, and of the 12.5 million dependent children, 2.5 million are living in stepfamilies. (See table 1.1 on pages 2–3.)
- **More parents are cohabiting:** It has become increasingly common for parents to live together without marrying. The number of cohabiting-couple families in the UK increased by 65 per cent between 1996 and 2006. The number of married-couple families fell by 4 per cent over the same period.
- **Cohabiting-couple families are much younger than married-couple families:** In 2001, half of cohabiting-couple families in the UK were headed by a person aged under 35, compared with one in every ten married couples.
- **Reconstituted or stepfamilies:** A stepfamily is formed when a parent takes a new partner. In the past they were almost always created as a result of the death of a parent. Now they are usually formed after separation or divorce.

7: The growth of the lone-parent family
- **There are more children living in lone-parent families:** The proportion of children living in lone-parent families has more than tripled since 1971 to 26 per cent in 2006. (See table 1.1 on pages 2–3.)
- **Lone parents are more likely to be poor than other families:** Fifty per cent of lone-parent families live on low incomes.
- **Teenage mothers often have fragile relationships with their partners:** In fact, fifty per cent of such relationships have ended by the time the baby is one year old.
- **It is becoming easier for lone parents to work:** They are helped by the introduction of tax credits and the New Deal for Lone Parents, along with the huge increase in childcare places.

8: Employment patterns and caring responsibilities
- **Mothers are working more** (either by necessity or by choice): Since the 1970s, the proportion of women working has increased from 56 to 70 per cent.
- **Fathers are spending more time with their children:** In the late 1990s, fathers of children under five were spending an average of two hours per day on child-related activities, compared to less than a quarter of an hour per day in the mid-1970s.
- **More childcare services are available** to fit in with the family where both parents work; these include nannies, childminders, workplace crèches, nurseries, preschools, day nurseries and Sure Start centres.
- **New legal rights for working parents:** Extended maternity leave rights, and rights to paternity leave, coupled with rights to request flexible working arrangements when their children are young, have all enabled more mothers and fathers to find a work–life balance which better suits their family's needs.

The effects of divorce and separation on children

United Kingdom
Thousands

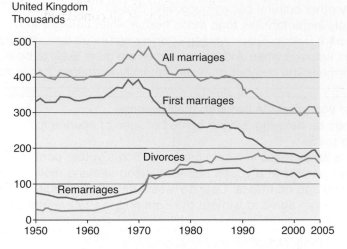

Figure 1.2 **Marriages and divorces (Source: Social Trends, 2007)**

Divorce and separation are on the increase. It is now probable that more than a third of all new marriages will end within 20 years, and four out of ten will ultimately end in divorce. All children will be affected in some way when parents separate and/or become divorced. How a child reacts to this depends on various factors:

- their age
- their ability to understand what is happening
- the way they are treated
- the reasons for the divorce.

Children may experience a variety of feelings about their parents' divorce. These include the following:

- Feeling insecure: Because of the loss of daily routine and because of the loss of the familiar presence of two parents.
- Being in denial: Children may deny that it is really happening; they may pretend that what is going on is temporary and that soon everything will go back to normal.
- Feeling relieved: Children may welcome the certainty that separation brings, particularly if there have been constant rows or violence between their parents.
- Feeling emotionally stressed: This is more likely when parents are involved in lengthy battles over which parent gets custody and where the children should live.
- Feeling sad and apathetic: Some children experience frequent mood swings, and changes in behaviour and eating habits. They may also experience depression.
- Feeling anger: Some children feel anger towards their parents, possibly more so towards the one they think is responsible. They might also become angry with themselves, believing that the divorce is their fault.
- Feeling anxious or afraid: Children may worry about what the future might hold; this includes fears about where they might live, whether they will be allowed to see one parent or another, and the worry that if one parent can go, perhaps the other one will leave too.
- Feeling guilty: Some children feel they are in some way responsible for the break-up and they may feel torn between two parents.

Even if the marriage or partnership has been very tense, or even violent, children may still have mixed feelings about the separation. Much will depend on the ways in which the parents handle the situation, how many children are affected and the ages and temperaments of all concerned.

Lone-parent families

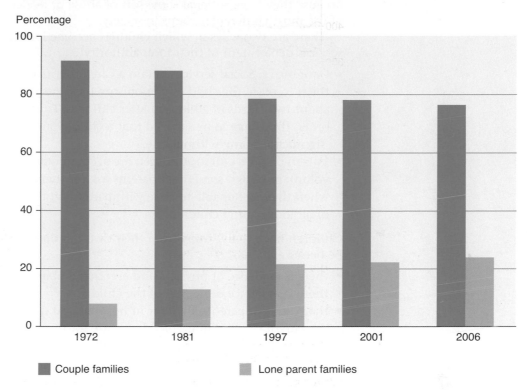

Figure 1.3 **The proportion of dependent children living in families: by family type, Great Britain (Source: Social Trends, 2007)**

The growth of families headed by one parent has been one of the biggest changes in family life. Britain now has one of the highest proportions of lone-parent families in Europe, and the number has tripled since 1971. Nine out of ten lone parents are women. The most common reason for lone-parent families is still separation and divorce, but there are other factors which have led to there being more lone parents with dependent children; these include:

- the death of a partner (bereavement)
- one partner working abroad
- one partner in prison or in long-term hospital care
- making a positive choice to be a lone parent
- surrogate motherhood and the availability of treatments such as IVF (in vitro fertilisation), which enable women to have children without a male partner
- changed social attitudes – there is no longer a stigma attached to lone parenthood and men feel less pressure to marry women when they become pregnant.

4 The reasons why children may be in local authority care

The term looked-after children refers to children who are in the care of local authorities. The majority of children who stay in long-term care are there because they have suffered some sort of abuse or neglect; these children are one of the most vulnerable groups in society.

There are two ways in which children become looked after by the social services department of their local authority:

- Care order: Social services obtain a care order from the courts which enables them to place the child in compulsory local authority care. This applies to about two-thirds of all looked-after children. For the courts to grant a care order, they have to be satisfied that a child is suffering or would suffer 'significant harm' without one.
- Voluntary agreement: Children are accommodated by the local authority on a voluntary basis – sometimes parents ask for their children to be taken into care when they feel unable to cope with parenting; this applies to about one-third of all looked-after children.

Children have to live away from their own families for all sorts of reasons. It may be because:

- there is evidence of physical and emotional abuse
- there is evidence of neglect of the child
- the parent or parents are ill or in hospital and unable to care for their child
- the parent or parents are unable to care for their child because of their own substance abuse or poor parenting skills
- the family is in acute stress and the child needs to spend some time away from home
- the child needs a short time away from their birth family while a package of support is put in place to try to rebuild family relationships
- the child has complex disabilities and needs to live in a specialist residential establishment
- the child's parent or parents have made a voluntary agreement with the local authority.

Where children are looked after by the local authority

Most of the children looked after by local authorities when their own families are unable to care for them are placed in foster families. There are currently over 80,000 children looked after by local authorities in the UK; 62 per cent of these children are in foster homes.

Others live in residential children's homes, and some with their parents (usually as part of the transition from public care back to living with their families). It is only when foster care is either not possible or not desirable that residential care is chosen.

Residential children's homes

Children's homes exist to ensure that the needs of children are met when they cannot live with their own family. They offer a safe place for children to develop and grow, as well as providing food, shelter and space for play and leisure in a caring environment. All children who live in a children's home must have a care plan. A care plan states:

- why a child is living in a home

- what is supposed to happen while they are living there
- what is supposed to happen at the end of their stay.

Most children *will* go home, but a few go to live with other families and a few go to live in other homes.

It is considered very important that children and young people stay in touch with their family and friends. It is only when they might be hurt, or when a court order states that contact is not allowed, that some children will not be able to visit or have visits from their family.

Foster care

Foster care is arranged through local social services departments or through independent fostering agencies. There are different types of foster care, depending on the needs of both the child and their family. These include short-term care for just a few days or weeks, and long-term placements, as well as care for disabled children or children with behavioural problems.

The main categories of foster care are as follow:

- Emergency: When children at risk of abuse need somewhere safe to stay for a few nights.
- Short term: When carers look after children for a few weeks or months, while plans are made for the child's future.
- Short breaks: When disabled children, children with special needs or children with behavioural difficulties regularly stay for a short time with a family, so that their parents or usual foster carers can have a break.
- Long term: Not all children who need to permanently live away from their birth family want to be adopted, so instead they go into long-term foster care until they are adults.
- Specialist therapeutic: For children and young people with very complex needs and/or challenging behaviour.
- Family and friends or kinship: A child who is the responsibility of the local authority goes to live with someone they already know, which usually means family members such as grandparents, aunts and uncles or their brother or sister.

Anyone can apply to be a foster carer, provided that they have the qualities needed to look after children who cannot live with their parents. The advantages to children of being in a foster family include the following:

- Children have the opportunity to experience family life, and to develop a relationship with members of the foster carer's family.
- Links between children and their natural or birth parents are encouraged, unless inappropriate or where the child would be considered at risk from continued contact.
- It is usually easier for children to relate to a foster family than to have to get to know and trust a number of different care workers in a residential home.

Adoption

Adoption is a way of providing a new family for children who cannot be brought up by their own parents. It is a legal procedure in which all the parental responsibility is transferred to the adopters. Once an adoption order has been granted it cannot be reversed, except in extremely rare circumstances. An adopted child loses all legal ties with their first mother and father (the birth parents) and becomes a full member of the new family, usually taking the family's name.

The majority of adoption agencies are part of the local authority social services (in England and Wales) or social work department (in Scotland). Some are voluntary societies – for example, Barnardo's.

Every year, National Adoption Week is held to encourage more families to come forward to adopt the children who wait the longest – older children, children with disabilities, brothers and sisters, and children from some black and minority ethnic backgrounds.

Many of the children waiting for new families are of school age, and over half of them are in groups of brothers and sisters who need to be placed together. There are disabled children and children whose future development is uncertain; some children will have been abused and/or neglected and all will have experienced moves and uncertainty, and their resulting behaviour may be challenging.

In order to adopt a child, individuals must be:

- over 21
- happy to make space in their life and home for a child
- patient, flexible and energetic
- determined to make a real difference to a child's life, for a lifetime.

It usually takes at least six months for social workers from an adoption agency to get to know prospective adopters, assess them and help to prepare them for the task ahead.

- Confidential enquiries will be made of the local social services or social work department and the police.
- Applicants will be examined by their GP and will be asked to provide personal references from at least two friends.
- The adoption agency's independent adoption panel will consider a report on the application and recommend whether or not applicants should be approved as adopters. In Scotland, prospective adopters must be given the opportunity to meet the panel.

	Adoption	Foster care
Rights	An adoptive parent has full legal rights over the child.	A foster carer has no legal rights over the child.
Responsibility	An adoptive parent has *permanent* responsibility for the child.	Foster carers share *temporary* responsibility for the child with a local authority and the child's parents.
Costs	An adoptive parent – just like a birth parent – must cover all the financial costs of looking after the child.	Foster carers receive an allowance to cover the costs of looking after the child.

Table 1.3 The differences between adoption and fostering

REVISION QUESTIONS

1. List six possible reactions or emotions that children may have when their parents are separated or divorced.

2. Give four reasons why children may have to be looked after away from their family home.

3. Briefly describe the main differences between foster care and adoption. Why are there very few babies available for adoption today?

4. Why is foster care considered a better option for looked-after children than residential children's homes?

 DISCUSSION TOPIC

In groups, discuss what sort of family group you belong to. How do you think your own family type has contributed to your personality and overall development?

5 Preconceptual health and care

What is preconceptual care?

Preconceptual care means that both partners work to reduce known risks before trying to conceive, in order to create the best conditions for an embryo to grow and develop into a healthy baby – in other words, actively planning for a healthy baby. Caring for the *woman's* health is particularly important because in the very early weeks of pregnancy she may not even know she is pregnant, but the first 12 weeks of life in the womb (or uterus) are the most crucial, as this is when all the essential organs are formed.

Guidelines for preconceptual care

Use barrier methods of contraception

It is advisable to discontinue the pill so that the woman's natural hormonal pattern can be re-established. It is best to wait three months after stopping taking the pill before trying to conceive. During those three months, a condom or diaphragm should be used – this will reduce the risk of miscarriage. It is also a good idea for the woman to keep a record of her menstrual periods, so that her due date can be calculated more accurately after pregnancy is confirmed.

Stop smoking

Stopping smoking is probably the single most important thing that a woman and her partner can do towards having a healthy baby. Smoking cuts the amount of oxygen supplied to the baby through the placenta and can result in miscarriage or low birthweight. If a woman smokes 20 cigarettes per day, she reduces her natural fertility by over 20 per cent. Some men who smoke are less fertile because they produce less sperm. It is also important to continue not smoking after the baby is born, as babies born into a household where there is a smoker are more at risk of cot death, chest infections and asthma.

Eat a healthy, nutritious diet

A balanced diet allows a woman to build up reserves of the nutrients vital to the unborn baby in the first three months. Some basic guidelines are set out below:

- Eat something from the four main food groups every day (potato and cereals, fruit and vegetables, milk and milk products, and high-protein foods).
- Cut down on sugary foods and eat fresh foods where possible.
- Avoid pre-packed foods and any foods that carry the risk of salmonella or listeria – such as soft or blue-veined cheeses, pâté, liver and raw meat.
- Do not go on a slimming diet – follow your appetite and do not eat more than you need.
- Vegetarian diets which include milk, cheese and eggs provide the vital protein the baby needs.
- Vegans should eat soya products and nuts and pulses to supply protein; vitamin B12 may need to be taken as a supplement.
- Folic acid tablets and a diet rich in folic acid, taken both preconceptually and in pregnancy, help the development of the brain and spinal cord, and also help to prevent defects such as spina bifida. Sources of folic acid include broccoli, nuts and wholegrain cereals.

Genetic counselling

Couples with a close family history of, or a previous child with, any disorder that is inherited (such as cystic fibrosis or sickle-cell disease) should seek medical advice regarding the chances of a subsequent child having the same disorder. A specialist in genetic counselling may help such couples to decide whether or not to go ahead with a pregnancy. Tests may be carried out to try to diagnose any problem prenatally (i.e. before the birth), but all such tests carry some element of risk in themselves.

Avoid hazards at work

Some chemicals and gases may increase the risk of miscarriage or birth defects. Women should be aware of the risks and take precautions, after discussion with the environmental health officer.

Sexually transmitted infections (STIs)

STIs should be treated. If either partner thinks there is any risk of syphilis, gonorrhoea, genital herpes or HIV infection, then both partners should attend a special clinic for advice and tests. STIs can cause miscarriage, stillbirth or birth defects.

The use and misuse of drugs

No drugs should be taken unless prescribed by a doctor. Existing conditions such as epilepsy or diabetes will need to be controlled before and during pregnancy. The use of recreational and illegal drugs, such as cannabis, amphetamines and cocaine, can put the baby at risk of miscarriage, premature birth and poor development. Such drugs should not be taken during pregnancy or in the month prior to conception. Many addictive drugs cross the placental barrier and can damage the unborn baby.

Check for rubella (German measles) immunity

Rubella (or German measles) is usually a mild illness in adults and children and causes no long-term side effects. However, if a pregnant woman contracts rubella – particularly in the early stages of pregnancy – it can cause damage to the baby, including deafness, blindness and heart defects. Most women will be immune to rubella because they will have been given the rubella vaccine at school. However, some may have missed the vaccine and some women may lose immunity as the years go by. If the woman is found not to be immune, the immunisation cannot be given while pregnant, and she is at risk if she comes into contact with someone who has the illness.

Cut down on alcohol

Advice from the Department of Health is that pregnant women or women trying to conceive should avoid drinking alcohol. Heavy drinking is harmful both to the woman and (if she is pregnant) to the unborn child. Even moderate drinking (1–2 glasses of wine or beer a day) increases the risk of miscarriage, and babies are born smaller and more vulnerable. Heavy drinking, especially in the first few weeks of pregnancy, can cause foetal alcohol syndrome, which causes serious damage to the baby. If a pregnant woman does choose to drink, to minimise the risk to the baby she should not drink more than 1–2 units once or twice a week and should not get drunk.

Exercise

Regular exercise is recommended in the preconceptual period – just as it is for normal living. Pregnancy and labour are physically demanding and therefore it makes sense to be as fit as possible before becoming pregnant.

6 The roles and responsibilities of parenthood

The most important factor in deciding to start a family is to ensure that the baby is wanted. There are so many forms of contraception available to people in the UK today that, ideally, every baby brought into the world should be wanted by both parents. This does not mean that unplanned babies are necessarily unwanted, however – they may end up being just as wanted as those who have been longed for – for example, when a couple have experienced fertility problems.

Factors which affect the decision to have children

Starting a family is a huge responsibility for both parents. A baby tends to take over all aspects of a couple's life together. While the birth of a baby is normally a momentous and rewarding experience, a child will continue to demand a lot of the parents' time and energy for some time to come, particularly if they go on to have more children.

Relationship between partners

- A secure, stable, loving relationship: This is the ideal starting point for beginning a family. Couples also need to be mature enough to consider how to provide for their children's needs and to take decisions together about discipline and education.
- Changing relationships: Any relationship – however stable – will be affected when there is a new family member. For example, fathers can feel left out or neglected when the mother is breastfeeding or concentrating on caring for a very young baby. Mothers often find the responsibility of full-time baby care an anxious and tiring time. Couples find they have less time to be alone together and there may be periods of sleepless nights for both partners.
- Problems in the relationship: Some couples who are experiencing difficulties in their relationship sometimes decide to have a baby in the hope that it may improve their own relationship – this rarely works out for the best.

Money

- Financial support: Apart from having enough money to put a roof over their heads, studies show that parents can expect to spend approximately 20 per cent of their income on a child. This includes clothing, food, equipment, nappies – and infant formula milks if the mother is not breastfeeding.
- Cost of childcare: This needs to be considered if both partners continue to work outside the home. As the child grows older, extra expenses, such as holidays, presents, parties and leisure activities, also need to be planned for.

Parental age

- Women and men: Women have less choice than men over *when* to plan a family. This is because as they get older their ability to conceive diminishes and the quality of their eggs deteriorates. Once a woman has been through the menopause she is no longer able to have children. Men, however, are physically capable of fathering children well into old age.
- Biological urge: Many women feel a strong biological urge to become mothers – this is often referred to as the 'body clock' ticking, and it usually occurs in a woman's late twenties and early thirties. Female fertility falls off quite dramatically after the age of 40, whereas there is no such pressure for men. Men might find this 'ticking clock' difficult to understand and be

genuinely fearful of the extra responsibilities that fatherhood brings. They may also fear 'losing' their partner to the baby.

- Older parents: Couples are increasingly choosing to start their families later in life. The average age of a first-time mother in 2007 was 29 years. The number of women choosing to start families in their late thirties and early forties has also risen sharply since the late 1990s. This trend towards later maternity is strongest among women with better educational qualifications, with some postponing child-rearing in order to pursue their careers – and to achieve financial security. In addition, some women who have already raised a family might want to have another child with a new partner, while others simply do not meet the 'right' partner until later in life.

Changes in lifestyle

- Roles of mother and father: Becoming a parent for the first time brings about considerable changes to a couple's lifestyle. Apart from financial constraints, there will be less freedom to do as they please, as babies need constant care until they reach independence. Decisions need to be made concerning childcare; it is still usually the mother who gives up work to look after the baby – often returning part-time at a later stage.

Peer pressure/social expectations

- Romantic ideal: Young women may have a friend with a cute baby and this might give them an idealised vision of motherhood.
- Grandparents: Some women feel pressure from their own parents, who drop hints about longing to be grandparents.
- Work: Women who are unhappy at work might find the prospect of motherhood appealing.

7 Methods of contraception

Contraception means 'against conception'. When a man and a woman have sexual intercourse, there is always a chance that the woman will become pregnant. The only 100 per cent effective method of contraception is abstention – that is, abstaining from sex, or 'saying no'.

Method of contraception	How it works – reliability and effectiveness	Advantages	Disadvantages
Barrier methods of contraception: These three methods all help to protect against sexually transmitted infections, as well as preventing conception.			
Male condom A sheath made from very thin latex (rubber)	The male condom is worn on the penis to stop sperm from entering the woman's vagina. It needs to be put on when the penis is erect, and before the penis comes into contact with the vagina. **Effectiveness:** 98% effective – if used correctly and consistently.	• Helps protect against many sexually transmitted infections (STIs), including HIV • The man can take responsibility for contraception • Condoms are available free from family planning clinics and are sold in many pubs, supermarkets, chemists and petrol garages	• Putting one on can interrupt or impair the enjoyment of sex • Can only be used once and must be discarded immediately after use • If not used properly, male condoms can slip off or split • Some people are sensitive to latex, but if this is a problem polyurethane condoms can be used
Female condom A soft sheath made from polyurethane	The female condom is worn inside the vagina to stop sperm getting to the womb. It needs to be put in the vagina before there is any contact between the vagina and penis. **Effectiveness:** 95% effective – if used correctly and consistently.	• Helps protect against many sexually transmitted infections (STIs), including HIV • The woman can take responsibility for contraception • Available free from most family planning clinics and sold widely	• Putting one in can interrupt the enjoyment of sex • Female condoms can get pushed too far into the vagina • They are expensive to buy

Table 1.4 Methods of contraception

Method of contraception	How it works – reliability and effectiveness	Advantages	Disadvantages
Diaphragm or cap A circular dome made of thin, soft latex (rubber) or silicone 	A diaphragm or cap is inserted into the vagina before sex to cover the cervix, so that sperm cannot get into the womb. It needs to be used with a *spermicidal* gel or cream (spermicides kill sperm). After sex, the diaphragm or cap needs to be removed and washed. They are reusable. **Effectiveness:** 92–96% effective – if used correctly with spermicidal gel or cream.	• Helps protect against some sexually transmitted infections (STIs), including HIV • There are no serious health risks, and it is only necessary to think about it when having sex • It can be put in several hours before having sex	• It can take time to learn how to use them • Some women suffer from cystitis when using them • Weight loss or gain, or having a baby, a miscarriage or an abortion may mean a new diaphragm or cap will need to be fitted
Non-barrier methods of contraception: If a couple are not in a monogamous – that is, faithful – relationship, they can help to protect themselves against sexually transmitted infections (STIs) by using condoms as well as the methods outlined below, even though they do not need the condoms for contraception.			
Combined pill A tablet containing the hormones oestrogen and progestogen that a woman takes daily for 21 days. After 21 days, there are seven days without a pill, then the process starts again	The hormones prevent ovulation (release of an egg). They also make it difficult for sperm to reach an egg, or for an egg to implant itself in the lining of the womb. **Effectiveness:** Over 99% effective – if used correctly. This means that fewer than 1 woman in 100 will get pregnant in a year.	• Does not interfere with the sex act • Can prevent heavy, painful periods • Can protect against cancers of the ovary, womb and colon, plus some pelvic infections	• It must be taken at the same time every day and on the correct days to be effective • If a pill is forgotten or the woman experiences any vomiting or severe diarrhoea, then she could get pregnant • There may be unwanted side effects, such as mood swings, headaches and breast tenderness (there is no evidence that it causes weight gain)

Table 1.4 Contin.

Method of contraception	How it works – reliability and effectiveness	Advantages	Disadvantages
Progestogen-only pill (POP) Sometimes called the mini-pill, it contains the hormone progestogen, but does not contain oestrogen; it is taken every day within a specific three-hour period	The POP thickens the mucus in the cervix, which stops sperm getting to an egg. It also thins the lining of the womb so that an egg cannot implant itself there. In some women, it stops ovulation too. **Effectiveness:** 99% effective – if used correctly and consistently.	• The POP can be taken by women with a medical history which means they cannot take oestrogen • It can be taken when breastfeeding	• Not reliable if not taken at the same time each day or within three hours of that time • Reliability may be affected by sickness or severe diarrhoea, as well as some medicines • Periods may become irregular • Temporary side effects may include spotty skin and breast tenderness
Intrauterine device (IUD) A small, T-shaped, plastic and copper device that is inserted into the womb by a specially trained health professional	An IUD prevents sperm from surviving in the cervix, womb or Fallopian tubes. It may also prevent a fertilised egg from implanting in the womb. **Effectiveness:** Over 99% effective.	• An IUD is effective as soon as it is put in and it can stay in the womb for up to ten years • It is not necessary to think about contraception every day or at every instance of sexual intercourse • It can be removed at any time by a trained health professional, and normal levels of fertility will return quickly	• It can make periods heavier, longer or more painful • There is a very small chance of getting an infection within 20 days of the IUD being fitted • There is a risk of the body spontaneously expelling it

Table 1.4 Contin.

Method of contraception	How it works – reliability and effectiveness	Advantages	Disadvantages
Intrauterine system (IUS) Mirena® A small, T-shaped, plastic device that is inserted into the womb by a specially trained health professional Reservoir containing slow-release progestogen hormone	The IUS slowly-releases a progestogen hormone into the womb which: • thickens the womb lining so it is less likely to accept a fertilised egg • thickens the mucus from the cervix so it is difficult for sperm to move through and reach an egg. **Effectiveness:** Over 99% effective.	• Once the IUS is in place, it is no longer necessary to think about contraception every day or at every instance of sexual intercourse • Like the IUD, it can be removed at any time by a trained health professional, and fertility quickly returns to normal • It can also make periods lighter, shorter or stop them altogether	• Some women may experience mood swings, skin problems or breast tenderness • There is a slight risk of getting an infection after having it inserted; the fitting can be uncomfortable
Contraceptive injection An injection given every few weeks, the most common of which is Depo-Provera , which lasts for 12 weeks	The injection contains progestogen, which: • thickens the mucus in the cervix, and stops sperm reaching an egg • thins the lining of the womb so that an egg cannot implant there. In some women it also stops ovulation (the release of an egg). **Effectiveness:** Over 99% effective if used correctly.	• Only needs to be given every 12 weeks • Can be useful for women who might forget to take the pill every day • May provide some protection against cancer of the womb and pelvic inflammatory disease	• Side effects can include weight gain, headaches, mood swings and breast tenderness • Periods may also become more irregular or longer, or may stop altogether • It can take up to a year for fertility levels to get back to normal after an injection, so it may not be suitable for women who want to have a baby in the near future

Table 1.4 Contin.

Method of contraception	How it works – reliability and effectiveness	Advantages	Disadvantages
Contraceptive patch A sticky patch, a bit like a nicotine patch, that delivers oestrogen and progestogen into the skin; each patch lasts for one week (a new patch is used each week for three weeks, followed by a week off)	The patch works like the combined pill, as it contains the same hormones. The patch: • prevents ovulation (the release of an egg) • thickens cervical mucus, making it harder for sperm to travel through the cervix • thins the womb lining, making it unlikely that an egg will implant itself there. **Effectiveness:** Over 99% effective when used correctly.	• No need to think about it every day, and it is still effective even if the woman experiences vomiting or diarrhoea • Because ovulation is prevented, there is a monthly 'withdrawal bleed', which can be lighter and shorter than a period • The patch can be worn in the bath, in the swimming pool and while playing sports • It can also protect against cancers of the ovary, womb and colon, and some pelvic infections	• The patch must be changed every week • It can increase blood pressure and some women experience temporary side effects such as headaches • A small number of women develop a blood clot when using the patch, but this is not common
Contraceptive implant A small, flexible tube (containing progestogen) which is inserted under the skin of the upper arm by a trained professional	The implant, which is called Implanon® in the UK: • slowly releases progestogen into the body and works to stop the release of an egg from the ovary • thickens cervical mucus and thins the womb lining, which make it harder for sperm to move through the cervix, and make it less likely that the womb will accept a fertilised egg • lasts for three years. **Effectiveness:** Over 99% effective when used correctly.	• Once in place, there is no need to think about contraception for three years • It can be useful for women who cannot use contraception containing oestrogen • Once removed, fertility levels return to normal immediately	• Possible side effects include some initial bruising, tenderness or swelling where the implant was inserted • Some women may find that their periods change, becoming either lighter or heavier and longer • Some prescribed medicines or homeopathic remedies may reduce its effectiveness

Table 1.4 Contin.

Method of contraception	How it works – reliability and effectiveness	Advantages	Disadvantages
Natural family planning A method that teaches you when it is possible to have sex without getting pregnant 	Natural family planning plots the times of the month (menstrual cycle) when a woman is fertile and when she is infertile. The woman learns how to note and record fertility signals, such as body temperature and cervical secretions, to identify when it is safer to have sex. **Effectiveness:** Up to 98% effective, depending on what method is used and if it is used according to the teaching and instructions.	• There are no physical side effects, and it can also be used to plan a pregnancy • No chemical or physical devices are necessary • It is acceptable in all faiths and cultures	• The need for keeping records every day of fertility signals, such as temperature and cervical secretions • It takes three to six menstrual cycles to learn the method effectively • Condoms must be used to have sex during fertile times (which last around eight days per month) • It does not protect against sexually transmitted infections (STIs)

Table 1.4 Contin.

Withdrawal method (or coitus interruptus – interrupted intercourse)

This method of natural contraception (sometimes called 'being careful') is widely used by people who may not want to be bothered with 'medical' methods of contraception. The man pulls his penis out of the vagina before the semen is ejaculated. This is a *very* unreliable method of contraception, as a small amount of semen can escape before ejaculation. It is also very frustrating for both partners. However, it is much better in situations of spontaneous sexual intercourse than not using any form of contraception at all.

Emergency contraception

If a woman has had unprotected sex or thinks that her usual contraceptive method might not have worked, she can use either of the following emergency methods to prevent pregnancy:

• the emergency contraceptive pill (sometimes called the morning-after pill)
• the IUD (intrauterine device).

Both the emergency pill and the IUD may be obtained free of charge from any of the following:

- a GP surgery that provides contraception
- a contraception clinic
- a sexual health clinic
- some genito-urinary medicine (GUM) clinics
- a young person's clinic
- some pharmacies
- most NHS walk-in centres and minor injuries units
- some accident and emergency departments.

It is also possible to buy the emergency pill from most pharmacies (for those aged 16 and over), and from some privately run clinics such as the British Pregnancy Advisory Service (BPAS) or Marie Stopes.

How emergency contraception works

The emergency contraceptive pill needs to be taken within 72 hours of unprotected sex. It is more effective the sooner it is taken. It contains progestogen and works by delaying or preventing ovulation. If taken within 24 hours of unprotected sex, the emergency pill will prevent up to 95 per cent of pregnancies that could be expected to occur if no emergency contraception was used. This drops to 58 per cent if it is taken 72 hours after unprotected sex.

The IUD can be inserted up to five days after unprotected sex, or up to five days after the earliest time you could have ovulated. It may prevent an egg being fertilised or may prevent an egg implanting in the womb. The IUD will prevent 99 per cent of pregnancies that could be expected to occur.

There are no serious side effects from using the emergency pill, but it could cause sickness, dizziness, tiredness, headaches, tender breasts or abdominal pain. It could also make the woman's next period earlier or later than usual.

 KEY TERMS

Barrier method: A device that will not allow semen or sperm to come into contact with the cervix.

Contraception: The prevention of conception by the use of birth control devices.

Preconceptual care: When both partners work to reduce known risks before trying to conceive, in order to create the best conditions for an embryo to grow and develop into a healthy baby.

 REVISION QUESTIONS

1. What is preconceptual care, and why is it important?
2. Why is it important not to smoke during pregnancy? List the effects that parental smoking can have on the unborn baby (the foetus) and on the child when born.
3. Select three different methods of contraception and list the advantages and disadvantages for each one.

RESEARCH ACTIVITY

Using the internet or a library, research the possible effects on the foetus of the mother drinking alcohol or taking drugs such as cocaine, heroin or ecstasy. Prepare a fact sheet which includes the following information:

● how prenatal exposure to alcohol affects the unborn baby

● a brief description of foetal alcohol syndrome

● how the use of drugs such as cocaine, heroin and ecstasy affects the unborn baby.

PREPARATION FOR PREGNANCY AND BIRTH

1 Reproduction

Understanding how a baby is conceived

The human reproductive system contains all the organs needed for reproduction, or producing babies. Conception occurs in the Fallopian tube when a male sperm meets a female egg (the ovum) and fertilises it. The fertilised ovum then contains genetic material from both mother and father – a total of 46 chromosomes (23 pairs) – and conception has taken place – or a new life begins.

The male reproductive system

The male reproductive system consists of the following:

- Testes: There are two testes, which are contained in a bag of skin called the scrotum. They have two functions: (1) to make male sex hormones – including testosterone – which affect the way a man's body develops, and (2) to produce millions of male sex cells called sperm.
- Sperm duct system: This is made up of the epididymis (where the sperm are stored) and the vasa deferentia (sperm ducts). The sperm can pass through the sperm ducts and mix with fluids produced by the glands. The fluids provide the sperm cells with nutrients. This mixture of sperm and fluids is called semen.
- Urethra: The urethra is the tube inside the penis that can carry urine and semen. A ring of muscle ensures that the urine and semen do not get mixed up.

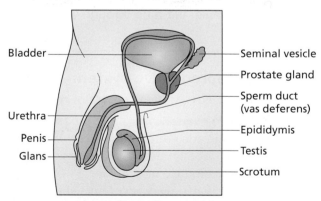

Figure 2.1 **The male reproductive system**

- **Penis**: The penis has two functions: (1) to pass urine out of the man's body, and (2) to pass semen into the vagina of a woman during sexual intercourse. It is made up of two parts: the shaft and the glans. The shaft is the main part of the penis, and the glans is the tip (or head). At the end of the glans is a small slit or opening, which is where semen and urine exit the body through the urethra.

🔑 KEY TERMS

Epididymis: A storage chamber in the male's body, which is attached to each testicle. This is where sperm cells are nourished and mature.

Penis: The male reproductive organ, involved in sexual intercourse and elimination of urine.

Semen: The milky white fluid discharged from the penis during ejaculation. It consists of seminal fluid produced by the seminal vesicles mixed with sperm cells.

Sperm: The microscopic cells produced by a male that contain the genes from the father. A sperm cell from the father must join with an egg cell from the mother for a baby to be created.

Sperm duct (vas deferens; plural = vasa deferentia): A muscular tube that passes upward, alongside the testicles, and transports the sperm-containing semen.

Testes (singular = testis): The medical name for testicles – the main male reproductive glands in which sperm are produced. The testicles also produce the main male hormone testosterone.

Testosterone: The hormone that causes boys to develop deeper voices, bigger muscles, and body and facial hair; it also stimulates the production of sperm.

Urethra: In the male: the tube through which urine and semen exit the body.

The female reproductive system

The female reproductive system consists of the following:

- **Ovaries**: The two ovaries control the production of the hormones oestrogen and progesterone and contain hundreds of undeveloped female sex cells called egg cells or ova. Women have these cells in their bodies from birth – whereas men continually produce new sperm.
- **Fallopian tubes**: Each ovary is connected to the uterus by a Fallopian tube (or egg duct). The tube is lined with cilia, which are tiny hairs on cells. Every month, an egg develops and becomes mature, and is released from an ovary into the tube. The cilia waft the egg along inside the egg tube and into the uterus.
- **Uterus**: The uterus (also called the womb) is a pear-shaped, hollow, muscular bag with a soft lining. The uterus is where a baby develops until its birth.
- **Cervix**: The cervix is a strong ring of muscle between the lower end of the uterus and the vagina. It keeps the baby in place while the woman is pregnant.
- **Vagina**: The vagina is a muscular tube that leads from the cervix to the outside of the woman's body. A man's penis enters the woman's vagina during sexual

intercourse. The opening to the vagina has folds of skin called labia which meet to form a vulva. The urethra also opens into the vulva, but it is separate from the vagina, and – as with the male urethra – is used for passing urine from the body.

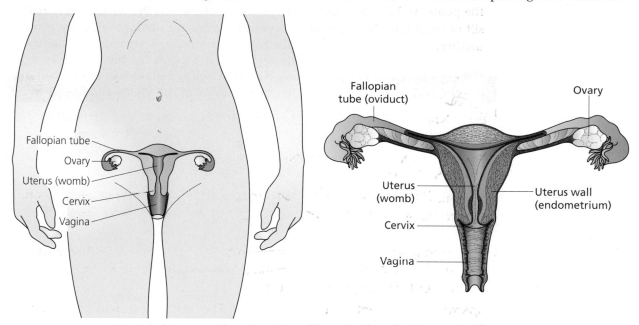

Figure 2.2 (a) and (b) The female reproductive system

> ### 🔑 KEY TERMS
>
> **Cervix:** The lower end, or neck, of the uterus, which leads into the vagina and gradually opens during labour.
>
> **Fallopian tubes:** There are two Fallopian tubes – one each side of the uterus – that lead from the area of the ovaries into the uterine cavity. When an ovary releases an egg, the nearest Fallopian tube draws it in and transports it down to the uterus.
>
> **Ovary:** The female sex gland.
>
> **Uterus:** Another name for the womb.
>
> **Vagina:** The vagina is a muscular, hollow tube that extends from the vaginal opening to the uterus.

The menstrual cycle

Menstruation – or having periods – is part of the female reproductive cycle. This cycle starts when girls become sexually mature at the time of puberty. Menstrual cycles vary in length from three to seven days – the average length is approximately 29 days.

Menstruation: The menstrual cycle starts with a menstrual period when a woman bleeds from her uterus (womb) via the vagina. This blood flows for an average period of five days. Gradually a new egg develops in one of the ovaries.

Ovulation: About 14 days after menstruation starts an ovum (or ripened egg) is released from one of the ovaries – this is called ovulation. The egg travels down the **Fallopian tube**, and then into the **uterus**. The endometrium – or lining – of the uterus has repaired itself and 'thickened up' again just in case the egg is now fertilised by a sperm and is ready to grow into a baby. If her body detects at the end of the cycle that the egg was not fertilised, it flushes out the blood, uterus lining and the egg, and prepares to start again.

Fertilisation

Fertilisation occurs when an egg cell meets with a sperm cell and joins with it. This happens after sexual intercourse. During sexual intercourse the man's penis becomes hard and erect. This is so it can be placed inside the woman's vagina. The release of semen from the man's penis is called ejaculation. Sperm cells travel in semen from the penis and into the top of the vagina. They enter the uterus through the cervix and travel to the egg tubes. If a sperm cell meets with an egg cell there, fertilisation can take place. The fertilised egg divides to form a ball of cells called an embryo. This attaches to the lining of the uterus and begins to develop into a foetus, and finally a baby.

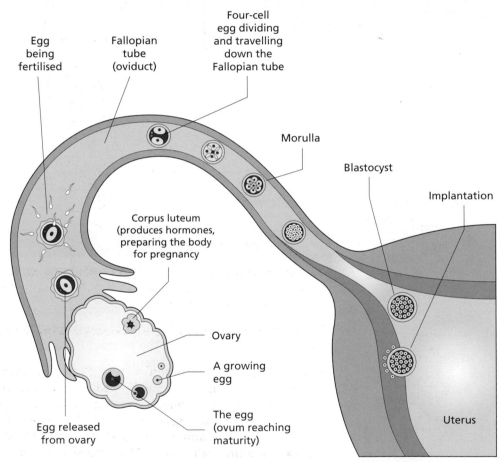

Figure 2.3 Ovulation, conception and implantation

Genes and inheritance

Each cell in the human body contains 23 pairs of **chromosomes** – i.e. 46 chromosomes in total (except the sex cells – sperm and ova – which have 23 chromosomes). When fertilisation takes place, the male and female chromosomes from these sex cells join together to form a new cell, called a **zygote**, which has its full 23 pairs.

Girl or boy?

In humans, sex is determined by the male. Sperm cells contain an X or a Y chromosome but egg cells contain only X chromosomes. If a sperm cell carrying an X chromosome fertilises the egg the resulting baby will be female; if the sperm cell is carrying a Y chromosome then the baby will be male.

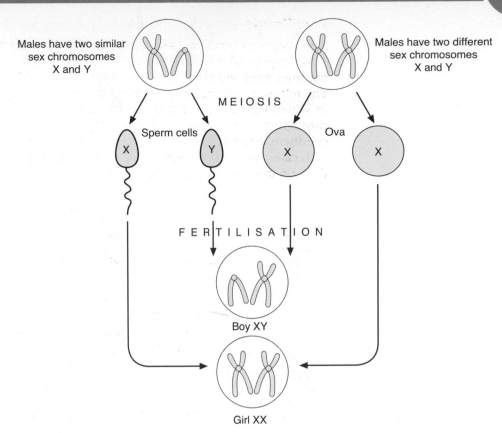

Figure 2.4 **Sex determination**

Each chromosome contains thousands of **genes**. Each gene is responsible for certain individual characteristics inherited from the parents, including eye colour, hair colour and height.

The development of the embryo and foetus: the early days of life

Within about 30 hours of fertilisation, the egg divides into two cells, then four, and so on (see figure 2.5); after five days it has reached the 16-cell stage and has arrived in the uterus (womb). Sometimes a mistake happens and the ovum implants in the wrong place, such as in the Fallopian tube – this is called an ectopic pregnancy and it is not sustainable. By about the tenth day, the cell mass forms a tiny ball of new tissue called a blastocyst and has embedded itself entirely in the **endometrium**, and the complex process of development and growth begins. The outer cells of the blastocyst go on to form:

- the placenta (or afterbirth; called chorionic villi during early development), which provides the foetus with oxygen and nourishment from the mother via the umbilical cord and removes the foetal waste products; it also acts as a barrier to certain microorganisms, but some may cross this barrier and cause damage to the embryo or foetus
- the amniotic sac (or membranes), which is filled with amniotic fluid (mostly composed of water) and provides a protective cushion for the foetus as it develops and becomes more mobile
- the embryo proper, which is formed from the inner cell mass – until eight weeks after conception, the developing baby is called an embryo; from eight weeks until birth, the developing baby is called a foetus; the embryonic cells are divided into three layers:

Fertilisation: only one sperm can fertilise the egg

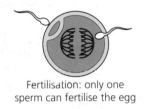

Two-cell stage

Four-cell stage

Blastocyst

Figure 2.5 **The early days of life**

1. ectoderm – forms the outer layer of the baby, the skin, nails and hair; it also folds inwards to form the nervous system (brain, spinal cord and nerves)
2. endoderm – forms all the organs inside the baby
3. mesoderm – develops into the heart, muscles, blood and bones.

Development of the embryo

- At 4–5 weeks, the embryo is the size of a pea (5 mm), but the rudimentary heart has begun to beat and the arms and legs appear as buds growing out of the sides of the body (see figure 2.6).
- At 6–7 weeks, the embryo is 8 mm long and the limb buds are beginning to look like real arms and legs; the heart can be seen beating on an ultrasound scan (see figure 2.7).
- At 8–9 weeks, the unborn baby is called a foetus and measures about 2 cm. Toes and fingers are starting to form and the major internal organs (brain, lungs, kidneys, liver and intestines) are all developing rapidly (see figure 2.8).
- At 10–14 weeks, the foetus measures about 7 cm and all the organs are complete. By 12 weeks, the unborn baby is fully formed and just needs to grow and develop. The top of the mother's uterus (the fundus) can usually be felt above the pelvic bones (see figure 2.9).
- At 15–22 weeks, the foetus is large enough for the mother to feel its movements. A mother who has had a child before may be able to identify the fluttering sensations that can be felt earlier. At 22 weeks, the greasy, white, protective film called vernix caseosa has begun to form, and the foetus is covered with a fine, downy hair called lanugo (see figure 2.10).
- At 23–30 weeks, the foetus is covered in vernix and the lanugo has usually disappeared. From 28 weeks, the foetus is said to be viable – that is, if born now, s/he has a good chance of surviving, although babies have survived from as early as 23 weeks. The mother may be aware of the foetus's response to

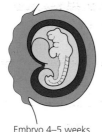

Embryo 4–5 weeks

Figure 2.6 Embryo: 4–5 weeks

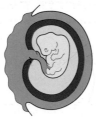

Embryo 6–7 weeks

Figure 2.7 Embryo: 6–7 weeks

Foetus 8–9 weeks

Figure 2.8 Foetus: 8–9 weeks

Foetus 10–14 weeks

Figure 2.9 Foetus: 10–14 weeks

Foetus 15–22 weeks

Figure 2.10 Foetus: 15–22 weeks

Foetus 23–30 weeks

Figure 2.11 Foetus: 23–30 weeks

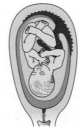

Foetus 31–40 weeks

Figure 2.12 Foetus: 31–40 weeks

sudden or loud noises, and s/he will be used to the pitch and rhythm of the mother's voice. At 30 weeks, the foetus measures 42 cm (see figure 2.11).
- At **31–40 weeks**, the foetus begins to fill out and become plumper; the vernix and lanugo disappear and the foetus usually settles into the head-down position, ready to be born. If the head moves down into the pelvis it is said to be 'engaged', but this may not happen until the onset of labour (see figure 2.12).

 KEY TERMS

Amniotic sac: Often called 'membranes' or the 'bag of waters', the amniotic sac is the bag of amniotic fluid that surrounds and cushions the foetus.

Blastocyst: The rapidly dividing fertilised egg when it enters the woman's uterus.

Embryo: The unborn child during the first eight weeks after conception.

Endometrium: The lining of the womb which grows and sheds during a normal menstrual cycle and which supports a foetus if a pregnancy occurs.

Fertilisation: Fertilisation is the moment when sperm and egg meet, join and form a single cell. It usually takes place in the Fallopian tubes. The fertilised egg then travels into the uterus, where it implants in the lining before developing into an embryo and then a foetus.

Foetus: The unborn child from the end of the eighth week after conception until birth.

Lanugo: Downy, fine hair on a foetus. Lanugo can appear as early as 15 weeks of gestation, and typically begins to disappear sometime before birth.

Umbilical cord: The cord connecting the foetus to the maternal placenta. It contains blood vessels that carry nutrients to the placenta and remove waste substances.

Vernix: A protective, white, greasy substance that often covers the skin of the newborn baby.

Viable: Able to maintain an independent existence – to live after birth.

REVISION QUESTIONS

1. What is the function of the ovaries?
2. What is the usual length of the menstrual cycle in human females?
3. What happens to the lining of the uterus (womb) during menstruation?
4. Where in the female reproductive system does fertilisation take place?
5. After about how many days into the menstrual cycle does a woman release an egg from an ovary (or ovulate)?
6. Where are sperm made and where are they stored?
7. What is the placenta?
8. What substances need to cross the placenta from the mother to the foetus in order to keep the foetus alive?
9. What is the function of the amniotic sac (or membranes)?
10. When does the embryo become a foetus?

ACTIVITY

1. Draw and label a diagram of:
   - the **male reproductive system**, showing the position of: sperm duct, testis, scrotum, penis and seminal vesicle
   - the **female reproductive** system, showing the position of: ovary, Fallopian tube, uterus, vagina, cervix and endometrium.
2. Look at the chart showing a typical 28-day menstrual cycle.

1 2 3 4 5 6 7	8 9 10 11 12	13 14 15
Stage 1: Menstruation	Stage 2: Repair	Stage 3: Ovulation

16 17 18 19 20 21 22	23 24 25 26 27 28
Stage 4: Receptive	Stage 5: Premenstrual

   - At which stage is the woman *most* likely to conceive?
   - At which stage is the woman *least* likely to conceive?

2 The problems of infertility

Infertility means that a couple are unable to conceive. Doctors usually define infertility as the inability to achieve a successful pregnancy after one year of well-timed, unprotected intercourse. For many couples, it could take six months or longer to become pregnant, although on average, 25 per cent of women will conceive within the first month of having unprotected sexual intercourse, and 60 per cent will conceive within six months. Infertility may be **primary**, meaning the couple have never achieved a pregnancy, or **secondary**, which means they have conceived in the past but are having difficulties conceiving again. Infertility in women is also linked to age. Women in their early twenties are about twice as fertile as women in their late thirties. The biggest decrease in fertility begins during the mid thirties.

Being infertile is a major cause of stress and unhappiness for couples who desperately want to start a family, but fortunately there are now a number of treatments available to assist conception.

What causes infertility?

There are a number of factors which can affect fertility; in 30 per cent of couples who have problems trying to conceive, a cause cannot be identified. Table 2.1 lists causes of infertility in both males and females, along with treatment options. Fertility may be improved generally by following the guidelines for good preconceptual care:

- eating a healthy diet
- keeping fit and avoiding being overweight
- avoiding stress – severe stress can affect female ovulation and can also limit sperm production
- avoiding drugs – including marijuana, cocaine, alcohol and smoking
- checking for and treating sexually transmitted diseases
- the man wearing loose boxer shorts rather than close-fitting pants – this helps to lower the temperature around the testes and so increase healthy sperm production; he should also avoid taking saunas and hot baths.

Female		Male	
Condition	**Possible symptoms and treatment**	**Condition**	**Possible symptoms and treatment**
Endometriosis: Patches of endometrial tissue (the uterine lining that sheds with each monthly period) grows outside the uterus (e.g. in the Fallopian tubes or the pelvis)	Painful menstrual periods, irregular or heavy bleeding and possibly repeated miscarriages Laparoscopic (or keyhole) surgery to remove abnormal tissue or unblock tubes, and other treatments to aid conception	Male tube blockages: A blockage in one or both of the vasa deferentia – the tubes which carry the sperm; varicose veins in the testicles are the most common cause of male tube blockages; sexually transmitted diseases, such as **chlamydia** or gonorrhoea, are also linked to tube blockage	No symptoms Surgery to repair the varicose veins or other obstruction

Table 2.1 Causes of infertility

Female		Male	
Condition	**Possible symptoms and treatment**	**Condition**	**Possible symptoms and treatment**
Ovulation problems: Any condition (usually hormonal) which prevents the release of a mature egg from an ovary	Absent or infrequent periods and excessively heavy or light bleeding Fertility drugs which stimulate the ovaries to produce and release eggs, and in vitro fertilisation (IVF) using these drugs	**Very low or no sperm count;** also poor sperm motility (the ability to move) and abnormally shaped sperm can all cause infertility	No symptoms Fertility drugs may boost sperm production; other options include donor sperm and injecting sperm directly into the egg
Poor egg quality: Eggs which become damaged or develop chromosomal abnormalities cannot sustain a pregnancy; this problem is usually age-related – egg quality declines considerably when a woman is in her late 30s and early 40s	No symptoms *Egg donation*: Eggs are taken from a donor and fertilised with the man's sperm, so the baby has the genes from the father but not the birth mother *Surrogacy*: Another woman carries a couple's or a donor's embryo and bears the child for them	**Other rare conditions affecting male fertility** • Damaged testicles: This can happen either through injury or as a result of having mumps • Testicular cancer and testicular surgery • Ejaculation disorders: Some men have a condition which makes it difficult for them to ejaculate (e.g. retrograde ejaculation, which causes a man to ejaculate semen into the bladder)	
Polycystic ovary syndrome (PCOS): Ovaries contain many small cysts, have hormone imbalances and do not ovulate regularly	Irregular menstrual periods, excessive body and facial hair growth, acne and weight gain Fertility drugs which stimulate the ovaries to produce and release eggs, and in vitro fertilisation (IVF) using these drugs		
Blocked or damaged Fallopian tubes: This prevents eggs from getting to the uterus and sperm from getting to the egg; main causes include pelvic inflammatory disease (PID), sexually transmitted diseases such as chlamydia and previous sterilisation surgery	No symptoms Surgery to open the tubes, if possible (small area of blockage); if surgery fails, in vitro fertilisation (IVF) is an option		

Table 2.1 Contin.

Other possible causes of infertility in couples

- **Unexplained infertility:** This term is used when doctors are unable to find a cause for infertility after a full series of tests and assessments; couples with unexplained infertility who have been trying for less than five years have about a 15–30 per cent chance of becoming pregnant in a given year

- **Combination infertility:** The term used to describe couples who have both male and female infertility problems, or when one partner has more than one fertility problem; symptoms and treatment methods vary, depending on the causes

Table 2.1 Contin.

IVF (in vitro fertilisation)

This is probably the best-known assisted conception treatment. 'In vitro' is Latin for 'in glass', and refers to the glass dish in which fertilisation takes place. IVF involves the following treatment:

- a woman's eggs are collected and fertilised with her partner's (or donated) sperm in a laboratory
- two to five days after the eggs (embryos) are fertilised, the healthiest ones are selected to be put back into the woman's womb
- it is hoped that at least one embryo will implant and the woman will become pregnant.

This treatment is especially suitable for women with unexplained infertility, blocked Fallopian tubes, or where other treatments, such as fertility drugs or IUI (intrauterine insemination), have been unsuccessful. A clinic may recommend using donated eggs for women who are over 40.

GIFT (gamete intra-Fallopian transfer)

GIFT is similar to IVF. Eggs and sperm are both collected, as for IVF, and they are screened to find the healthiest specimens. The sperm and eggs are then mixed together and placed in one of the woman's Fallopian tubes. Fertilisation can then occur naturally.

ICSI (intra-cytoplasmic sperm injection)

ICSI is the biggest advance in fertility treatment since IVF. It is not a stand-alone treatment, but is used in combination with IVF. ICSI involves injecting a single sperm into the centre of an egg, to give it the best chance of fertilising. After fertilisation, up to three embryos are replaced in the uterus. ICSI is often recommended if the male partner has a very low sperm count, or if other problems with the sperm have been identified. It can also be used if there are very few eggs collected from the woman that appear to be capable of being fertilised.

IVM (in vitro maturation)

IVM is a new technique in which eggs are matured in the laboratory before being fertilised with sperm. Fertilisation is, therefore, still in vitro. The difference between IVM and 'standard' IVF is that the eggs are immature when they are collected. This process means that the woman does not need to take as many drugs before the eggs can be collected as she might if using the standard IVF process, when mature eggs are collected.

Surrogacy

Surrogacy is where another woman carries an embryo for an infertile couple. A surrogate mother carries and gives birth to a baby for a couple who are unable to have a baby. She hands the baby over to the couple after the birth. There are two types of surrogacy, partial and full:

- **Partial surrogacy:** The surrogate mother conceives a baby using her own egg, fertilised with the intended father's sperm. This is done by **artificial insemination**, using a syringe.
- **Full surrogacy:** The surrogate mother carries the intended parents' genetic child, conceived through **IVF**, for which specialist doctors are needed. (For this treatment, the infertile woman must still have working ovaries.)

There are several reasons why a couple may choose to use a surrogate mother. These include when the woman:

- is infertile and fertility treatments have failed
- is unable to carry a child herself because of abnormalities in her uterus
- has a health condition which means it is dangerous for her to be pregnant or to give birth.

Infertility treatments and multiple pregnancies

Fertility drugs work by stimulating follicle ripening and ovulation; sometimes they work *too* well and result in the ripening of more than one egg at a time. Women who are treated with fertility drugs are, therefore, more likely to conceive more than one child at a time.

 REVISION QUESTIONS

1. What is the difference between primary infertility and secondary infertility?
2. Give two possible reasons for male infertility.
3. Give two possible reasons for female infertility.
4. Briefly describe what is involved in IVF (in vitro fertilisation) and ICSI (intra-cytoplasmic sperm injection).

 RESEARCH ACTIVITY

On your own or as a group, use the internet or a reference library to research and produce a fact sheet about the following aspects of surrogacy:

- types of surrogacy
- reasons why women may choose surrogacy rather than adoption or fostering
- the law in the UK relating to surrogacy
- the legal status of the child.

3 Pregnancy

The signs and symptoms of pregnancy occur after the fertilised ovum has implanted in the lining of the uterus. All women then start to produce a hormone, HCG (human chorionic gonadotrophin), which can be detected in the blood or the urine.

Testing for pregnancy

A pregnancy is usually confirmed by a simple urine test, which detects the presence of HCG in the urine.

Home pregnancy testing kits are widely available in large supermarkets and chemist shops; they almost always give an accurate result.

Signs and symptoms of pregnancy

- **Missed period (amenorrhoea):** Missing a period is a very reliable symptom of pregnancy if the woman has no other reason to experience a change in her menstrual cycle; occasionally, periods may be missed because of illness, severe weight loss or emotional upset.

- **Breast changes:** Sometimes the breasts will tingle and feel heavier or fuller immediately; surface veins become visible and the primary areola (the ring around the nipple), will become darker. This is more noticeable on fair-skinned women. As pregnancy continues (at about 16 weeks), colostrum can be expressed from the nipple.

- **Passing urine frequently:** The effect of hormones and the enlarging uterus result in women having to pass urine more often than usual.

- **Tiredness:** This can be noticeable in the first three months of pregnancy, but usually lifts as the pregnancy progresses.

- **Sickness:** Nausea (feeling sick) or vomiting can occur at any time of the day or night, but is usually referred to as 'morning sickness'. Some unlucky women experience nausea throughout pregnancy.

4 Diet during pregnancy and lactation

Every pregnant woman hears about 'eating for two', but the best information available today suggests that this is not good advice. Research shows that the quality (not the quantity) of a baby's nutrition before birth lays the foundation for good health in later life. Therefore, during pregnancy, women should eat a well-balanced diet.

Guidelines for a healthy diet in pregnancy

- Lean meat, fish, eggs, cheese, beans and lentils are all good sources of nutrients. Eat some every day.
- Starchy foods like bread, potatoes, rice, pasta and breakfast cereals should form the main part of any meal (along with vegetables).
- Dairy products, such as milk, cheese and yoghurt, are important as they contain calcium and other nutrients needed for the baby's development.
- Citrus fruit, tomatoes, broccoli, blackcurrants and potatoes are good sources of vitamin C, which is needed to help the absorption of iron from non-meat sources.
- Cut down on sugar and sugary foods like sweets, biscuits and cakes, and sugary drinks like cola.
- Eat plenty of fruit and vegetables that provide vitamins, minerals and fibre. Eat them lightly cooked or raw.
- Green, leafy vegetables, lean meat, dried fruit and nuts contain iron, which is important for preventing anaemia.
- Dairy products, fish with edible bones like sardines, bread, nuts and green vegetables are rich in calcium, which is vital for making bones and teeth.
- Margarine or oily fish (e.g. tinned sardines) contain vitamin D to keep bones healthy.
- Include plenty of fibre in the daily diet; this will prevent constipation, and help to keep the calorie intake down.
- Cut down on fat and fatty foods. Reducing fat has the effect of reducing energy intake; it is important that these calories are replaced in the form of carbohydrate. Fat should not be avoided completely, however, as certain types are essential for body functioning, as well as containing fat-soluble vitamins.
- Folic acid is a B vitamin, which is very important throughout pregnancy, but especially in the first 12 weeks when the baby's systems are being formed. (Most doctors recommend that pregnant women take a folic acid supplement every day, as more folic acid is required than is available from a normal diet.)
- Department of Health advice is to eat according to appetite, with only a small increase in energy intake for the last three months of the pregnancy (200 kcal a day).

Foods to avoid	Reasons
• **Soft and blue-veined cheese,** such as Camembert, Brie, stilton and chèvre, goat's cheese • **Pâté** (any type, including liver pâté and vegetable pâté) • **Prepared salads** (such as potato salad and coleslaw) • **Ready-prepared meals** or reheated food, *unless* they are piping hot all the way through	**Listeria** High levels of the listeria bacteria are occasionally found in prepared foods. Some ready-prepared meals are not always heated at a high enough temperature to destroy the bacteria. **Listeriosis** (infection with listeria bacteria) can cause problems for the unborn child, such as: • miscarriage • stillbirth • meningitis • pneumonia.
• **Raw or partially cooked eggs,** such as home-made mayonnaise, and some mousses and sauces • **Unpasteurised milk** (both goat's and cow's milks)	**Salmonella** Salmonella is found in unpasteurised milk, raw eggs and raw egg products, raw poultry and raw meat. Eggs should only be eaten if they are cooked until both the white and the yolk are solid. Salmonella food poisoning could cause: • miscarriage • premature birth.
• **Some types of fish,** such as shark, swordfish and marlin, must be avoided altogether	**High levels of mercury** High levels of mercury can harm a baby's developing nervous system. Women should eat no more than two tuna steaks a week (or four cans of tinned tuna). High levels of mercury can cross the placenta and may cause delayed development.
• **Unwashed raw fruit and vegetables** • **Raw or undercooked meat** • **Unpasteurised goat's milk or goat's cheese**	**Toxoplasmosis** Toxoplasmosis is an infection caused by a parasite found in cat faeces. It can also be present in raw or undercooked meat, and in soil left on unwashed fruit and vegetables. Although rare, the infection can occasionally be passed to the unborn baby, which can cause serious problems, such as: • miscarriage • stillbirth • eye damage • hydrocephalus.
• **Liver and liver products** (e.g. liver pâté)	**Too much vitamin A** Women should avoid eating liver and liver products such as pâté and avoid taking supplements containing vitamin A or fish liver oils (which contain high levels of vitamin A). If high levels of vitamin A build up in the body it can cause serious problems, including birth defects.
• **Peanuts** and foods that contain peanuts	**Peanut allergy** Avoiding foods like peanuts – and foods that contain peanuts – may reduce the baby's chances of developing a potentially serious peanut allergy. This is especially true if there is a history of allergies, such as hay fever or asthma, in the family.

Table 2.2 Foods to avoid during pregnancy

Foods to avoid during pregnancy

During pregnancy, women should avoid certain foods. Sometimes this is because they cause problems such as food poisoning. At other times, certain foods contain harmful bacteria and toxins which can cause serious problems for the unborn baby.

Women at risk from poor nutrition

Some women are at risk from poor nutrition during pregnancy. Any woman who restricts her diet for personal, religious or cultural reasons may have to take care, although well-balanced vegetarian and vegan diets should be safe. The following groups of women are potentially at risk:

- adolescents who have an increased nutritional requirement for their own growth, as well as providing for the foetus
- women with closely spaced pregnancies
- recent immigrants
- women on low incomes
- women who are very underweight or overweight
- women with restricted and poorly balanced diets
- women with pre-existing medical conditions, such as diabetes mellitus and food allergies
- women who have had a previous low-birthweight baby.

Diet for mothers who are breastfeeding

If the mother is going to breastfeed her baby, she should follow the principles for the healthy diet in pregnancy. Both calcium and energy requirements increase dramatically when the woman is lactating, and most women find that breastfeeding is also one of the most effective ways of regaining their pre-pregnancy weight. The mother should have at least 0.5 litres of milk and a pot of yoghurt or some cheese every day to satisfy her body's need for extra calcium, and she should try to drink 1.5–2 litres of water each day. The Food Standards Agency recommends that breastfeeding mothers should take supplements containing ten micrograms (mcg) of vitamin D each day.

 REVISION QUESTIONS

1. List the signs and symptoms of pregnancy.
2. Why is folic acid an important part of the diet during pregnancy?
3. List **five** foods that should be avoided during pregnancy and explain the reasons why.

5 Making choices for health and wellbeing during pregnancy

The midwife, doctor and health visitor are available throughout a pregnancy to give advice on diet, rest, exercise or any issue that may be causing concern; they can also offer advice on the current maternity benefits and how to apply for them.

Health factors to consider are as follows:

- **Eating a healthy diet**: During pregnancy the body uses up a lot of energy. Following the guidelines on page 44 will ensure that the baby receives the best start in life.
- **Rest and relaxation**: High levels of progesterone in the bloodstream often cause extreme tiredness – especially during the first few weeks of pregnancy. During the last few weeks, women are often very tired because of the extra weight they are carrying. Learning some relaxation techniques can be helpful, and women should take every opportunity to get some extra sleep during the day.
- **Exercise and posture**: Regular exercise keeps the joints and muscles supple, which helps to prepare the body for the demands of both pregnancy and labour. Swimming, walking and cycling are all suitable exercises during pregnancy. Some areas have special aqua-natal classes, held in local swimming pools and led by trained midwives or obstetric physiotherapists. Backache can be a problem in pregnancy, as the hormones cause muscles and ligaments to relax in preparation for childbirth. Women should always squat or kneel when picking up something from the floor and should protect their back by avoiding sudden movements.
- **Pelvic floor exercises**: Pelvic floor muscles are made up of a 'sling' of muscles which support the bowel, bladder and uterus. These muscles become weaker with the pressure of the baby as it grows. A useful exercise – ideally performed three or four times a day – is to tighten and pull in the muscles, as if stopping the flow of urine. Think of the pelvic floor as a lift and move it up the floors, holding for about ten seconds at each 'floor', and then slowly bring it back down again.
- **Avoid harmful substances**: The risks to the unborn child are described on pages 48–49. Avoid the following:
  a. smoking and passive smoking (breathing in the smoke from other people's cigarettes)
  b. alcohol
  c. prescribed drugs – unless advised by the doctor
  d. illegal drugs.

Factors affecting physical development of the foetus

Various factors affect the growth and development of the foetus, as explored below.

The mother's age

The best age to have a baby from a purely *physical* point of view is probably between 18 and 30 years. Complications of pregnancy and labour are slightly more likely above and below these ages.

- **Younger mothers**: Under the age of 16 years there is a higher risk of having a small or premature baby, of becoming anaemic and suffering from high blood pressure. In addition, very young teenagers are likely to find pregnancy and motherhood hard to cope with, emotionally and socially, and they will need a great deal of support.

- **Older first-time mothers:** First-time mothers over the age of 35 run an increased risk of having a baby with a chromosomal abnormality. The most common abnormality associated with age is Down's syndrome. A woman in her twenties has a chance of only one in several thousand of having an affected baby, but by 40 years the risk is about 1 in every 110 births, and at 45 the risk is about 1 in every 30. Amniocentesis can detect the extra chromosome which results in Down's syndrome; it is usually offered routinely to women who are 37 or over.

Number of pregnancies

Some problems occur more frequently in the first pregnancy than in later ones – for example, breech presentation, pre-eclampsia (see page 58), low birthweight and neural tube defects. First babies represent a slightly higher risk than second and third babies. The risks begin to rise again with the fourth and successive pregnancies; this is partly because the uterine muscles are less efficient, but it also depends to a certain extent on age and on the social factors associated with larger families.

The use of drugs

Most drugs taken by the mother during pregnancy will cross the placenta and enter the foetal circulation. Some of these may cause harm, particularly during the first three months after conception. Drugs that adversely affect the development of the foetus are known as teratogenic.

For foetus sake,
don't drink any
alcohol when
you're pregnant.

FASawareUK
For more information on
Foetal Alcohol Spectrum Disorder
go to fasaware.co.uk

Figure 2.13 Foetal alcohol syndrome poster

- **Prescription drugs**: Drugs are sometimes prescribed by the woman's doctor to safeguard her health during pregnancy – for example, antibiotics or anti-epilepsy treatment; they have to be very carefully monitored to minimise any possible effects on the unborn child.
- **Non-prescription drugs**, such as aspirin and other painkillers, should be checked for safety during pregnancy.
- **Alcohol** can harm the foetus if taken in excess. Babies born to mothers who drink large amounts of alcohol throughout their pregnancy may be born with **foetal alcohol syndrome**. These babies have characteristic facial deformities, stunted growth and mental retardation. More moderate drinking may increase the risk of miscarriage, but many women continue to drink small amounts of alcohol throughout their pregnancy, with no ill effects.
- **Illegal drugs** such as cocaine, crack and heroin are teratogenic and may cause the foetus to grow more slowly. Babies born to heroin addicts are addicted themselves and suffer painful withdrawal symptoms. They are likely to be underweight and may even die.
- **Smoking** during pregnancy reduces placental blood flow and, therefore, the amount of oxygen the foetus receives. Babies born to mothers who smoke are more likely to be born prematurely or to have a low birthweight.

Infection

Viruses and small bacteria can cross the placenta from the mother to the foetus and may interfere with normal growth and development. During the **first three months** (the first trimester) of a pregnancy, the foetus is particularly vulnerable. The most common problematic infections are:

- **Rubella** (German measles): This is a viral infection that is especially harmful to the developing foetus, as it can cause congenital defects such as blindness, deafness and mental retardation. All girls in the UK are now immunised against rubella before they reach childbearing age, and this measure has drastically reduced the incidence of rubella-damaged babies.
- **Cytomegalovirus** (CMV): This virus causes vague aches and pains, and sometimes a fever. It poses similar risks to the rubella virus – that is, blindness, deafness and mental retardation – but as yet there is no preventive vaccine. It is thought to infect as many as 1 per cent of unborn babies, and of those infected babies about 10 per cent may suffer permanent damage.
- **Toxoplasmosis**: This is an infection caused by a tiny parasite. It may be caught from eating anything infected with the parasite, including:
  a. raw or undercooked meat, including raw cured meat such as Parma ham or salami
  b. unwashed, uncooked fruit and vegetables
  c. cat faeces and soil contaminated with cat faeces
  d. unpasteurised goat's milk and dairy products made from such milk.

In about one-third of cases, toxoplasmosis is transmitted to the foetus and may cause blindness, hydrocephalus or mental retardation. Infection in late pregnancy usually has no ill effects.

- **Syphilis**: This is a bacterial sexually transmitted infection (STI). It can only be transmitted across the placenta after the twentieth week of pregnancy. It causes the baby to develop congenital syphilis, and can even lead to the death of the foetus. If the woman is diagnosed as having the disease at the beginning of the pregnancy, it can be treated satisfactorily before the twentieth week.

REVISION QUESTIONS

1. What effects can smoking during pregnancy have on the baby?
2. What effects can drinking alcohol during pregnancy have on the baby?

 RESEARCH ACTIVITY

'Foetal alcohol syndrome is the biggest cause of non-genetic mental handicap in the western world and the only one that is 100% preventable' (Foetal Alcohol Syndrome Aware UK).

Visit www.fasaware.co.uk to find out about foetal alcohol syndrome. In groups, prepare a poster that highlights the problems associated with heavy drinking during pregnancy.

6 The roles of the different health professionals supporting the pregnant mother

The first decision to be made by the prospective parents is *where* the birth will take place. Facilities and policies vary a great deal around the UK and some people have more choices than others. The options are:

- Home: Some doctors do not agree with home births in any circumstances, as they are concerned about the lack of hospital facilities if anything should go wrong during labour; the woman is entitled to register with another doctor if she wishes to have a home birth. Antenatal care is shared between the community midwife, who visits the woman in her own home or at a health centre, and the GP.
- Hospital: A full stay in hospital is usually seven or eight days, but there are often options to stay only 48 hours or even six hours. Antenatal care is shared between the hospital, the GP and the community midwife.
- GP unit: This type of unit is run by GPs and community midwives, often using beds within a district hospital or in a separate building near the hospital.
- Midwife unit: This type of unit is run entirely by midwives, who undertake all the antenatal care, delivery and post-natal care. The mother and baby usually stay in the unit for between six hours and three days after the birth. Midwife units are not widely available.
- Domino scheme: Domino is an abbreviation of 'domiciliary-in-out'. Care is shared between the community midwife and the GP.

Professionals involved in antenatal care and childbirth

Midwife

Midwives are registered nurses who have had further training in the care of women during pregnancy and labour. They can work in hospitals, clinics or in the community. Most routine antenatal care is carried out by midwives, and a midwife delivers most babies born in the UK. In the community, midwives have a statutory responsibility to care for both mother and baby for ten days after delivery.

Obstetrician

Obstetricians are doctors who have specialised in the care of pregnant women and childbirth. Most of their work is carried out in hospital maternity units, and they care for women who have complications in pregnancy or who need a Caesarean section or forceps delivery.

General practitioner (GP) or family doctor

This is a doctor who has taken further training in general practice. Many GP group practices also have a doctor who has taken further training in obstetrics.

Gynaecologist

This is a doctor who has specialised in the female reproductive system.

Paediatrician

This is a doctor who has specialised in the care of children up to the age of 16. Paediatricians attend all difficult births, in case the baby needs resuscitation.

Health visitor

This is a qualified nurse who has taken further training for the care of people in the community, including midwifery experience. They work exclusively in the community, and can be approached either directly or via the family doctor. They work primarily with mothers, and with children up to the age of five years. Their main role is health education and preventive care.

Private services relating to antenatal care

There are many options available to the woman who can afford to pay for private antenatal and post-natal care. She may choose a home birth with a private or independent midwife. The midwife will undertake all antenatal and post-natal care, and will also deliver the baby. Another option is to have the baby in a private hospital or maternity unit, attended by an obstetrician. Many district hospitals also offer private facilities for paying patients.

7 Antenatal care

The main aim of antenatal care is to help the mother to deliver a live healthy infant. Women are encouraged to see their family doctor (GP) as soon as they think they may be pregnant. The team of professionals – midwife, doctor, health visitor and obstetrician – will discuss with the mother the options for antenatal care, delivery and post-natal care. Antenatal care has the following principles or aims:

- a safe pregnancy and delivery, resulting in a healthy mother and baby
- the identification and management of any deviation from normal
- preparation of both parents for labour and parenthood
- an emotionally satisfying experience
- promotion of a healthy lifestyle and breastfeeding.

The women most at risk of developing complications during pregnancy are those in poor housing, on a poor diet or whose attendance at antenatal clinics is infrequent or non-existent. The midwife and health visitor will be aware of the risks that such factors pose for both mother and baby, and will target these individuals to ensure that preventive healthcare, such as surveillance and immunisation, reaches them.

Early antenatal care (first 12 weeks or first trimester)

The booking appointment

Wherever the woman decides to give birth, early in her pregnancy she will attend a lengthy interview with the midwife, and the medical team will perform various tests. If necessary, a bed is booked for a hospital delivery for around the time the baby is due. Recognition of cultural differences and personal preferences, such as a woman's wish to be seen by a female doctor, are important and most antenatal clinics try to meet such needs. Relatives are encouraged to act as interpreters for women who understand or speak little English, and leaflets explaining common antenatal procedures are usually available in different languages.

1. Taking a medical and obstetric history
   This is usually carried out by the midwife and covers the following areas:
   - details of the menstrual cycle and the date of the last period; the expected delivery date (EDD) is then calculated (see below)
   - details of any previous pregnancies, miscarriages or births
   - medical history – diabetes, high blood pressure or heart disease can all influence the pregnancy
   - family history – any serious illness, inherited disorders or history of twins
   - social history – the need for support at home and the quality of housing will be assessed, especially if the woman has requested a home or domino delivery.
2. Medical examination
   A doctor will need to carry out the following physical examinations:
   - listening to the heart and lungs
   - examining breasts for any lumps, or for inverted nipples which might cause difficulties with breastfeeding
   - noting the presence of varicose veins in the legs and any swelling of legs or fingers
   - internal examination to assess the timing of the pregnancy – a cervical smear may be offered.

3. Clinical tests

- **Height**: This can give a guide to the ideal weight; small women (under 1.5 m or 5 ft) will be more carefully monitored, in case the pelvis is too narrow for the baby to be delivered vaginally.
- **Weight**: This will be recorded at every antenatal appointment – weight gain should be steady (the average gain during pregnancy is 12–15 kg.
- **Blood pressure**: Readings are recorded at every antenatal appointment, as hypertension or high blood pressure in pregnancy can interfere with the blood supply to the placenta and may mean a risk of pre-eclampsia (see below).
- **Urine tests**: Urine is tested at every antenatal appointment for:
  a. sugar (glucose): occasionally present in the urine during pregnancy, but if it persists it may be an early sign of diabetes
  b. protein (albumen): traces may indicate an infection or be an early sign of pre-eclampsia – a special condition only associated with pregnancy, for which one of the main signs is high blood pressure
  c. ketones: these are produced when fats are broken down; the cause may be constant vomiting or dieting, or there may be some kidney damage.
- **Blood tests**: A blood sample will be taken and screened for:
  a. blood group: in case transfusion is necessary; everyone belongs to one of four groups: A, AB, B or O
  b. rhesus factor: positive or negative (see page 59)
  c. syphilis: can damage the baby if left untreated
  d. rubella immunity: if not immune, the mother should avoid contact with the virus and will be offered the vaccination after birth to safeguard future pregnancies
  e. sickle-cell disease: a form of inherited anaemia which affects people of African, West Indian and Asian descent
  f. thalassaemia: a condition similar to sickle-cell disease, which mostly affects people from Mediterranean countries
  g. haemoglobin levels: the iron content of the blood is checked regularly to exclude anaemia.

Calculating when the baby will be born (EDD – estimated date of delivery)

The average length of pregnancy, or gestation, is calculated as 40 weeks. This is because pregnancy is counted from the first day of the woman's last period, not the date of conception – which generally occurs two weeks later. Since some women are unsure of the date of their last menstruation (perhaps due to period irregularities), a pregnancy is considered full-term if birth falls between 37 and 42 weeks of the estimated due date.

A simple method to calculate the due date is to add seven days to the date of the first day of the last period, then add nine months. For example, if the first day of the last period was 1 February, add seven days (8 February), and then add nine months, for an EDD of 8 November.

If the woman has not had at least three cycles following a previous pregnancy, miscarriage, abortion or stopping an oral contraceptive pill, the first date of her last period cannot be relied on to predict her expected date of delivery. In these circumstances, the date will normally be calculated by an examination of the size of her uterus or an ultrasound scan of the foetus – known as the dating scan.

Dating scan

Women are offered an ultrasound scan called the dating scan between 10 and 13 weeks, to estimate when the baby is due. This is known as the estimated date of delivery (EDD). The scan also determines whether she is expecting more than one baby.

Antenatal notes

A record of antenatal care and appointments will be made, and these are known as the antenatal notes (or Cooperation Card). It will usually be the woman's responsibility to look after these notes, and she should bring them with her to each appointment. They should also be carried on her person throughout the pregnancy, so that, should she fall ill while away from home, all the up-to-date medical information is available to other medical personnel. The hospital or midwife keeps duplicate copies of scans and routine tests.

Antenatal care from 13 to 28 weeks (second trimester)

Visits to the antenatal clinic, GP or community midwife will be monthly during this stage of pregnancy, or more often if problems are detected. On each occasion the following checks are made and recorded on the antenatal notes:

- **Weight**: The average weight gain at this stage is 0.5 kg per week.
- **Blood pressure**: A rise in blood pressure could mean there is risk of pre-eclampsia.
- **Foetal heart**: This is heard through a portable ear trumpet or using electronic equipment (a **Sonicaid**). The normal foetal heart rate is 100–115 beats per minute).
- **Urine test**: A sample of urine is tested routinely for glucose (sugar), albumen (protein) and **ketones**.
- **Fundal height** (the size of the uterus): This is checked by feeling the 'bump' and seeing whether the size corresponds to the EDD.
- **Checking for signs of oedema** (swelling) of ankles and fingers: This is an early warning sign of pre-eclampsia.
- **Ultrasound** screening test: This is usually offered at around 11–13 weeks.

By 28 weeks, the hospital will expect to have the mother booked in for a hospital delivery.

Antenatal care from 29 weeks to the birth (the third trimester)

Although this is the shortest trimester, it can often seem to go slowly, as the woman feels heavier and less mobile.

- The unborn baby or foetus is now **viable**, which means that if s/he is born early, there is a very good chance of survival.
- Visits to the antenatal clinic, GP or midwife are fortnightly from 28 weeks, and once a week in the final month of pregnancy.
- The same tests are carried out as in the second trimester. By **palpating** (or lightly pressing) the surface of the woman's abdomen to feel the uterus underneath, the doctor or midwife can now predict the baby's weight and its position in the uterus.
- An ultrasound screening test is usually offered at around 18–22 weeks.

Screening tests in pregnancy

Screening tests estimate the risk of the baby being born with certain conditions, such as Down's syndrome or spina bifida. They aim to detect a disease or condition in the early stages, before it causes significant problems, and when treatment can be offered. These tests are very safe, painless and do not affect the unborn baby in any way.

The main screening tests offered during pregnancy are set out below.

Ultrasound scan

How does it work?

The operator slowly scans across the abdomen with a hand-held transducer that detects sound waves bounced off the uterus and the baby's body. These are transmitted to a computerised monitor for a visual interpretation. Parents are often offered the first photo of their baby while in the womb.

When and why is it used?

An ultrasound scan may be used at any stage of pregnancy, as follows:

- *At 8 weeks*: In this early stage of pregnancy, as well as checking the size of the foetus and looking for more than one baby, ultrasound is used to diagnose early complications such as miscarriage.
- *At 11–13 weeks*: It is now possible to determine the sex of the baby. The same checks are carried out as at 8 weeks and may also be used with the nuchal fold translucency test (see below).
- *At 18–22 weeks*: Most women have a more detailed ultrasound scan. Checks are made to ensure that the right amount of fluid surrounds the baby, and the baby's head, heart, spine, limbs and internal organs are examined in detail. The position, size and function of the placenta are also checked. (The placenta joins the mother and the foetus and allows for the exchange of nutrients and waste products between them.) This scan can also identify some physical abnormalities, such as cleft lip or skeletal abnormalities, and can confirm spina bifida if blood tests have shown the baby is at high risk.

Nuchal fold translucency test

This is a screening test for Down's syndrome which is usually offered at 11–14 weeks. It involves an ultrasound scan to measure the thickness of the layer of fluid at the back of the baby's neck. Babies with Down's syndrome have a thicker layer. If it is thicker than average, women are usually offered a further test for diagnosis, such as amniocentesis or CVS (chorionic villus sampling).

AFP (alpha-fetoprotein) test

This is a blood test offered at around 15–18 weeks which measures the amount of alpha-fetoprotein (AFP) in the woman's blood. (AFP is a protein made by all unborn babies.) Low levels of AFP can mean that the developing baby has an increased chance of having Down's syndrome, while high levels may indicate that there is more than one baby or, rarely, an increased chance of neural tube defects such as spina bifida.

Maternal serum screening (MSS)

This simple blood test is offered to women at about 15–16 weeks into pregnancy. It is also sometimes called the Bart's, double or triple test. The sample is tested for certain hormones and proteins, including AFP (alpha-fetoprotein) and HCG (human chorionic gonadotrophin) ,with or without oestriol. The measurements are analysed in combination with the mother's age, weight and exact gestation (length of pregnancy), to assess the chance, or risk, of the baby having Down's syndrome. The results of the test are expressed either as a risk value (e.g. 1 in 300), or as a positive or negative screening. Having a positive screening (increased risk) does not mean that the baby will definitely have Down's syndrome. Having a negative screening (low risk) is not a guarantee that the baby will not have Down's syndrome. Women with a positive result will be offered amniocentesis.

Diagnostic tests in pregnancy

Diagnostic tests confirm whether a baby has a certain condition and are offered if the screening tests predict an increased risk of a problem. These tests carry a slight risk of miscarriage.

Amniocentesis

Amniocentesis is a diagnostic test which is usually used between 15 and 19 weeks of pregnancy. It is offered to any woman who has a higher risk of carrying a baby with Down's syndrome – either because she is in the higher age group (over 35) or because prior tests (such as the MSS) have detected a higher risk of abnormality. A fine needle is inserted into the amniotic fluid surrounding the baby. Ultrasound is used to guide the positioning of the needle. The amniotic fluid contains some cells from the baby that are cultured in the laboratory and then analysed in detail. Full results can take up to four weeks.

This is an accurate way of finding out whether the baby has a number of genetic or inherited disorders, such as Down's syndrome or cystic fibrosis. Amniocentesis carries a slight risk of harming the baby or causing a miscarriage. It is usually only offered to women when screening tests show they may be at a higher risk of having a baby with a genetic disorder, or to women over 37 years old.

 KEY TERMS

Alpha-fetoprotein: A protein, produced by the foetus's liver, which can be detected in the mother's blood most accurately between the 16th and 18th weeks of pregnancy. High levels of AFP may be associated with **spina bifida**; low levels may be associated with **Down's syndrome**.

Cystic fibrosis: A condition that affects certain organs in the body, especially the lungs and pancreas, by clogging them with thick, sticky mucus. New treatments mean that people with cystic fibrosis can live relatively healthy lives.

Down's syndrome: A genetic disorder resulting from the presence of an extra chromosome; children usually, but not always, have learning difficulties.

Neural tube defects: This term includes anencephaly, encephalocoele and spina bifida. These conditions occur if the brain and/or spinal cord, together with the protecting skull and spinal column, fail to develop properly during the first month of embryonic life.

Spina bifida: This occurs when the spinal canal in the vertebral columns is not closed (although it may be covered with skin). Individuals with spina bifida can have a wide range of physical disabilities. In the more severe forms, the spinal cord bulges out of the back, the legs and bladder may be paralysed, and obstruction to the fluid surrounding the brain causes hydrocephalus.

Chorionic villus sampling (CVS)

For CVS, a fine instrument is inserted through the woman's cervix, into the uterus, and a sample of the chorionic villi (tiny, finger-like projections found in the placenta) is removed. These have the same genetic material as the baby. This test looks for similar problems as amniocentesis, although it does not test for neural tube defects. CVS is performed earlier – usually between 10 and 12 weeks of pregnancy – and the results are usually available within a few days. The results are not quite as accurate as with amniocentesis; the procedure is technically quite difficult and it is not always successful. There is a slightly higher risk of miscarriage with CVS than with amniocentesis.

Problems during pregnancy

The majority of pregnancies proceed without any major problems. Women often experience minor physical problems, but these do not affect their own health or their baby's development. Common, relatively minor problems can be dealt with by the midwife or GP; these include:

- backache
- morning sickness
- feeling faint
- frequent urination
- swollen ankles
- thrush (a fungal infection of the vagina)
- heartburn or indigestion
- varicose veins
- constipation
- moodiness or tearfulness.

The following conditions are potentially more serious and will need medical treatment and supervision during pregnancy and around the time of the birth:

- pre-eclampsia
- premature birth
- rhesus factor
- multiple pregnancies
- placental problems
- diabetes
- breech presentation.

Pre-eclampsia

Pre-eclampsia is a complication of later pregnancy that can have serious implications for the wellbeing of both mother and baby. The oxygen supply to the baby may be reduced and early delivery may be necessary. It is characterised by:

- a rise in blood pressure
- oedema (swelling) of hands, feet, body or face, due to fluid accumulating in the tissues
- protein in the urine.

In severe cases, pre-eclampsia may lead to eclampsia, in which convulsions (seizures) can occur. This can occasionally threaten the life of both mother and baby. If pre-eclampsia is diagnosed, the woman is admitted to hospital for rest and further tests.

Premature birth

Babies who are born before the 37th week of pregnancy are called **preterm** babies. Around 4 per cent of babies are born preterm and most of them weigh less than 2500 g (5.5 lbs). They are, therefore, also described as **low-birthweight** babies. The main problems for preterm infants are:

- **Temperature control**: Heat production is low and heat loss is high, because the surface area is large in proportion to the baby's weight and there is little insulation from subcutaneous fat.
- **Breathing**: The respiratory system is immature and the baby may have difficulty breathing by him/herself – a condition called **respiratory distress syndrome** (RDS). This is caused by a deficiency in **surfactant**, a fatty substance which coats the baby's lungs and is only produced from about 22 weeks of pregnancy.
- **Infection**: Resistance to infection is poor because the baby has not had enough time in the uterus to acquire antibodies from the mother to protect against infection.
- **Jaundice**: Due to immaturity of the liver function.

Rhesus factor (Rh)

As well as belonging to one of four different blood groups (A, B, AB and O), your blood can be rhesus (Rh) positive or rhesus negative. Most people are rhesus positive, and if both partners have the same rhesus factor there is no problem.

However, problems may result if the mother is rhesus negative and the baby inherits the father's rhesus positive gene.

- If the baby's blood enters the mother's bloodstream during delivery, the mother's body reacts to these foreign blood cells by producing **antibodies** to fight them.
- These antibody molecules are able to cross the placenta and go back into the baby, resulting in **anaemia** or, more seriously, **haemolytic disease of the newborn**, which may require several blood transfusions in pregnancy and sometimes also after birth.
- Usually the level of antibodies is not high enough to do serious damage in a *first pregnancy*, but the antibodies remain in the mother's blood and may cause serious problems in subsequent pregnancies.
- Prevention of this situation is by regular tests to assess the **antibodies** in the maternal blood, and by giving an injection of anti-D globulin (anti-rhesus factor) within 72 hours of the first delivery to prevent further formation of antibodies.

Multiple pregnancies

Multiple pregnancies – where there is more than one baby – always need special care and supervision. Twins are the most common multiple birth, occurring in about 1 in 87–100 pregnancies.

Identical (uniovular) twins

Identical twins develop after one sperm has fertilised *one egg*; the egg splits into two and each half becomes a separate baby. Identical twins are *always* the same sex and they share the same placenta.

Non-identical (binovular) twins

Non-identical twins develop when two sperms fertilise *two different eggs*, the mother's ovaries having, for some reason, produced two eggs at ovulation. They grow together in one womb, with two separate placentas. Such twins are sometimes called fraternal twins and can be the same sex or different sexes; they can be as alike or as unlike as any brothers and sisters.

The chances of a woman having non-identical twins increases if she herself is such a twin, or if there is a history of twins in her family.

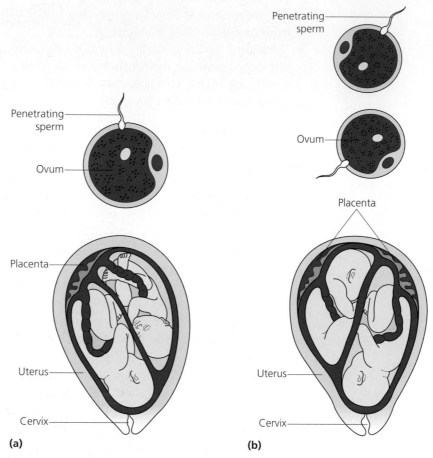

(a)   **(b)**

Figure 2.14 Two types of twins – identical and non-identical

A woman expecting more than one baby is likely to be larger than her dates would suggest and will put on more weight. Routine ultrasound scanning can usually diagnose the presence of more than one baby, unless one baby is 'hiding' behind the other.

The main risk when there is more than one baby is that they will be born too early (be premature), and this risk rises with the number of babies. Usually, women expecting twins or more babies are admitted to hospital for the birth; twins may be delivered vaginally provided both babies are in the head-down position, but triplets and quadruplets are usually born by Caesarean section.

Placental problems

Any vaginal bleeding after about 28 weeks of pregnancy can indicate that there is a problem with the baby's life support system – the placenta.

• Placenta praevia: The placenta lies across the cervix, where pressure from the baby may cause vaginal bleeding. Ultrasound scanning will confirm the position of the placenta and the woman will be hospitalised and the situation monitored. Usually a Caesarean section will be necessary.

- **Placenta abruption**: This is a very serious condition where the placenta is beginning to separate from the wall of the uterus. The woman will be admitted to hospital urgently and may need induction of labour before a Caesarean section.

Diabetes

The way that the kidneys process sugar changes during pregnancy and women may show traces of sugar in their routine urine samples. This 'latent' diabetes disappears after the birth of the baby and does not usually require treatment. Women with pre-existing diabetes need more careful supervision, because their insulin needs may change and their doses may need to be altered. Babies born to mothers with diabetes tend to be large and may need induction of delivery and/or a Caesarean section.

Breech presentation

A baby is said to be breech presentation, or breech position, when it is 'bottom-down' rather than 'head-down' in the uterus just before birth. This means that either the baby's bottom or feet would be born first. (Around 3–4 per cent of full-term babies are positioned this way.) Before full-term, which is defined as 37 weeks, it does not matter if the baby is breech, as there is always a good chance that s/he will turn spontaneously. Women are often offered ECV (or external cephalic version) if their baby is in a breech position after 37 weeks. ECV involves a doctor turning the baby so that it will present 'head-first' when the woman goes into labour. The majority of babies who are in the breech position when labour starts will be delivered by Caesarean section, rather than the more usual vaginal delivery.

 KEY TERMS

Caesarean section: A Caesarean or C-section is when the baby is delivered through an incision in the mother's abdomen and uterus. It is used when a woman cannot give birth vaginally, or if the baby is in distress or danger.

Diabetes: A condition in which the body does not produce enough **insulin** (the hormone which converts sugars into energy), resulting in too much sugar in the bloodstream. It can usually be controlled with appropriate treatment, diet and exercise.

Pre-eclampsia: A condition which a mother may develop late in pregnancy, marked by sudden oedema, high blood pressure and protein in the urine. It can lead to **eclampsia**, where the mother has convulsions, so antenatal care staff monitor women carefully for the warning signs.

Premature (or preterm) baby: A premature baby is one who is born before 37 weeks of gestation.

 REVISION QUESTIONS

1. What is antenatal care?
2. What is the role of the midwife during the antenatal period?
3. List the routine blood tests carried out on pregnant women when they attend the booking clinic, and give reasons for each.
3. What is an ultrasound scan? What information can be gained by using ultrasound scanning at different stages of pregnancy?

8 The importance of antenatal or parentcraft classes

Childbirth preparation classes are offered, usually in later pregnancy, and are held in hospitals, health centres, community halls and private homes. Most classes are free and last for about six weeks. They are normally run by midwives and health visitors. They usually welcome couples to attend and aim to cover:

- **all aspects of pregnancy** – diet and exercise; sexual activity; how to cope with problems such as nausea, tiredness and heartburn
- **labour** – what to expect; pain control methods; breathing and relaxation exercises
- **birth** – what happens at each stage and the different methods of delivery
- **the new baby** – what to expect and how to care for a newborn; common problems, including postnatal depression.

The classes usually include a tour of the maternity unit at the hospital or birthing centre.

They are also valuable meeting places for discussion with other parents-to-be about all the emotional changes involved in becoming a parent. Separate classes may also be held for women with **special needs** – for example, expectant mothers who are schoolgirls, or in one-parent families, or whose first language is not English. Some areas provide classes earlier in pregnancy (from 8 to 20 weeks), or aqua-natal classes, where women can practise special exercises standing in shoulder-high water.

Some organisations, such as the National Childbirth Trust (NCT), also offer parent education classes. These are usually held in small groups in the tutor's home. Fees vary according to circumstances.

The father's role during pregnancy

The father's role is very different from the mother's, but it is important for a balanced family life. It is easy for a father to feel alienated – or excluded – from the pregnancy, as his partner is likely to have her healthcare professionals, friends and relatives gathering round, and sometimes pushing him out. During the pregnancy, a father can support his partner in the following ways:

- **Active involvement:** Being as actively involved as possible – for example, taking time to go to antenatal appointments with his partner, and discussing with her what she would like his role to be in the birth.
- **Antenatal classes:** Attending parentcraft or antenatal classes together and learning all he can about pregnancy and labour. (Most hospitals encourage fathers to visit the labour ward or delivery suite, so that they feel more at ease when their time comes.)
- **The birth plan:** Helping his partner with her birth plan and finding out ways in which he can make pregnancy a pleasurable, relaxing time.
- **Rest and relaxation:** Giving his partner opportunities to rest and relax, by taking on more of the household chores – especially those which involve heavy lifting.
- **Gaining knowledge:** Learning about how the baby is developing in the womb and how these changes affect his partner.
- **Sympathy:** Being sympathetic when his partner suffers the inevitable discomforts during pregnancy.
- **Practical help:** Doing practical things as a team effort – for example, preparing a room for the baby.

- **Packing and preparation**: Making sure he knows what to pack for his partner for hospital, in case of an emergency; ensuring he can be contacted at all times as the time for birth approaches.

9 Preparation for the birth of the new baby

Making a birth plan

Although it is impossible to know ahead what sort of a birth she will have, it is worthwhile for a pregnant woman to think about some of the options she might face in labour. The birth plan is a written plan of *how* the woman would like to give birth. It allows her to make decisions about the management of her childbirth experience, so that she need not think about them during labour. The plan need not be written all in one go – it can be added to or amended as the woman learns more about the childbirth experience from antenatal classes, books or from talking to other mothers. It is also useful to talk ideas through with the midwife and with whoever is destined to be her birthing partner.

The main points to include are:

- place – where she would like to give birth (home birth, at hospital, birth centre if available)
- delivery – what kind of delivery she would like (in bed, in water, a Caesarean section)
- birthing partner – who she would like to be present at the birth (e.g. husband, partner, parent, friend)
- delivery position – what delivery position she would like to be in (sitting, standing, squatting)
- pain relief – what pain relief methods she would prefer (e.g. pethidine, epidural, or just gas and air).

Other questions to answer include the following:

- Would you like music to be played?
- Would you like a natural delivery of the placenta – that is, without an injection?
- If things do not go to plan, how do you feel about an assisted birth (e.g. forceps delivery) or Caesarean section?
- If a Caesarean section is needed, would you prefer to be asleep (general anaesthetic) or awake (epidural or spinal anaesthetic)?
- How do you feel about induction of pregnancy if the baby is overdue?
- Where would you prefer your birthing partner to stand (at your head, at your feet, etc.)?
- Who would you like to cut the umbilical cord?
- Would you like the baby to be placed on your stomach after birth?
- Would you prefer your baby to be breastfed or bottle-fed?
- Do you give consent to have student nurses, midwives or doctors present at the birth (if in a teaching hospital or centre)?
- Do you have any particular religious needs?
- Do you require a special diet while in hospital?

A copy of the birth plan can be placed in the antenatal notes, so that it is available when the woman is in labour.

Packing the bag for a hospital birth

As no woman can be sure of when she is going to go into labour, she is advised to pack a bag about a month before her EDD, with all the essentials for a hospital stay. These include:

- the birth plan
- nightwear that will allow for easy breastfeeding, and a dressing gown

- slippers or warm socks
- money to phone friends from a hospital payphone (mobiles are not allowed in hospital)
- an old nightdress or T-shirt to wear in labour
- massage oils or lotions
- lip balm
- a change of clothes for going home
- maternity sanitary towels
- maternity bras
- digital camera or camcorder (check with hospital first)
- relaxation materials: books, crosswords, magazines, etc.
- music to listen to (some hospitals provide CD players)
- TENS pain-relief machine, if planning to use one
- toiletries: hairbrush, soap, toothbrush, deodorant, etc.
- water spray to cool you down
- newborn slcepsuits, vests and bootees.

Choices for childbirth

Choosing where to have the baby is an important decision. Every woman has the right to give birth in the place of her choosing. However, complications or problems with her pregnancy or labour may limit this choice. Most women in the UK have their babies in hospital and, unless there are complications, most babies are delivered by midwives.

The different types of NHS care available will depend on where you live. Options are likely to include:

1. Hospital birth
   - Consultant-led units: Larger maternity hospitals are led by consultant obstetricians – specialist doctors who have expertise in managing pregnancies and deliveries with complications.
   - GP- or midwife-led units: Smaller cottage hospital maternity units may be run by GPs working in partnership with midwives. (A few areas have birthing centres, which are led by midwives who care for women having normal births.)
2. Home birth: Birth takes place under the care of a midwife in the woman's own home. Water births are also available.
3. Domino scheme: When labour starts, the midwife comes into the hospital or GP unit to deliver the baby. Back-up care can be provided by the woman's GP or a hospital doctor. If both mother and baby are well, they can often go home within hours of the birth and the midwife continues to look after them at home.

Women also have the choice of paying for care in a private hospital or having the services of an independent midwife, who usually oversees the antenatal care and makes arrangements for home or hospital delivery.

Hospital birth

Every woman has the right to make an informed choice about where to give birth. However, there are some factors which prevent a woman from being able to choose a home or domino delivery.

The following factors mean that the woman will almost certainly be advised to have her baby in hospital:

babies likely to be born prematurely or requiring special care

women who live a long distance from the nearest hospital, in case of emergencies.

women with complications during pregnancy

those who had a difficult birth with a previous pregnancy

very young mothers (under 16 years)

women with placenta praevia

if the medical staff believe the baby should be induced

women expecting more than one baby

women with a very small pelvis, as they may require a Caesarean section

women who will need a Caesarean section

women with existing health problems, such as diabetes or obesity

those who will want an epidural for pain relief – this must be given by an anaesthetist

Some women opt for a hospital birth because they prefer to have technology nearby to monitor the progress of the labour and the activity of the baby.

Advantages of a hospital birth

- Hospitals have trained staff and all the equipment to hand if complications develop for either the mother or the baby.
- Assisted deliveries, such as forceps, ventouse and Caesarean section, must be carried out in a hospital.
- There are more options for pain relief – for example, an anaesthetist on call to provide an epidural.
- There are more opportunities for rest and relaxation, as the baby can be looked after in the nursery and visiting hours are limited.
- After the birth, midwives are available 24 hours a day. to assist with any concerns and to help get breastfeeding started.
- There are other mothers to share experiences and worries with.
- The mother is free from household responsibilities.

Home birth

A woman booked for a home birth must ensure the following are provided:

- a clean, well-ventilated room with adequate heating and lighting
- a comfortable bed for the mother and plastic sheets to protect the mattress and floor

- a table for the midwife's equipment: this includes a delivery pack containing sterilised instruments, sterile cotton wool and towels, an oxygen cylinder, Entonox cylinder (gas and air analgesia), baby resuscitation equipment, etc.
- two buckets or large bowls – one for waste and one for the placenta
- plenty of hot water
- a cot and bedding for the baby – with warm towels and clothes
- a packed overnight bag, including baby clothes, in case the woman needs to be transferred to hospital.

Advantages of a home birth

- The woman will feel more relaxed and in control.
- Medical intervention is less likely.
- If a birthing pool is hired, with a home birth you are guaranteed a water birth, providing there are no complications.
- The woman can have as many people present as she wishes, and can choose her own routine.
- Her partner can spend more time with her and their baby.
- Any other children are less disrupted, as their mother is not separated from them.
- The woman gets to know her midwife better and has more personalised care.
- The woman can still have pain relief: gas and air, pethidine and use of a TENS machine – these are all brought to the house by the midwife.

Domino scheme (home and hospital)

All antenatal care is provided by community midwives, exactly as it is for a home birth. The named midwife will visit the woman at home during her labour and accompany her to the hospital where she gives birth. She then comes home from hospital about six hours later. Postnatal care is provided as for a home birth. There must be someone at home with her 24 hours a day for the first seven days following the birth.

The advantages of the domino scheme

- The woman remains in the relaxed atmosphere of her own home for as long as possible.
- The midwife is present during labour and decides when to transfer the woman to hospital.
- Any specialist equipment or expertise is available during the birth itself.
- The woman can return home to her family, with support from a carer and regular visits from the midwife.

 DISCUSSION TOPIC

In groups, discuss the advantages and disadvantages of giving birth to a baby:

- in hospital
- at home.

The father's role during labour

It is almost always expected and taken for granted that the father will be present throughout his partner's labour, and this can be difficult for men who really do not feel up to coping with the situation, but who feel that a refusal would be letting their partner down. Some men are squeamish about the sight of blood; others do not think they could stand to see their loved one in pain and be unable to help.

In fact, 90 per cent of fathers in the UK *are* at their partner's side when they give birth, but fathers should not feel pressured into doing so. Some fathers – especially new ones – are not prepared for what they encounter in the delivery room and can be more of a hindrance than a help, both to their partner and to the staff.

Most women find it very reassuring to see a familiar face when they are giving birth – as it can be a frightening experience. Having a supportive birth companion can make a real difference to the experience and the outcome of labour and birth – but this companion does not have to be the father of the baby. Research has shown that having support from a loved one:

- reduces a woman's need for pain-killing drugs
- reduces the probability of medical interventions in labour
- increases a woman's general satisfaction with her birth experience
- increases the time a woman is likely to breastfeed her baby.

Some fathers like to cut the umbilical cord. If this is the case, they should ask the midwife in advance.

Giving practical support during labour

The father or birth partner can be a reassuring presence during labour and offer support by:

- helping the woman to express what she wants to the midwives and doctors
- suggesting and enabling different positions, to help the woman to stay comfortable
- offering drinks or snacks
- cooling down the woman's face and neck with a sponge or cloth
- helping with breathing or relaxation techniques already learnt
- massaging the woman's back, shoulders and legs
- timing the contractions, so she can see the progress being made
- being patient if the woman becomes cross and irritable – this often occurs during the transition stage.

The stages of labour

'Labour' is a good term to describe the process of giving birth. It is hard work because the woman needs to exert strong muscular effort to deliver her baby. Every woman's labour is different, and it is impossible to predict how long or how difficult it will be. Labour is divided into three stages and is triggered by the release of a hormone called oxytocin.

In the few days before labour begins, the woman may experience the following signs:

- a low, nagging backache, similar to period pain
- mild diarrhoea – because of the increased uterine activity
- Braxton Hicks contractions – sometimes called practice contractions, these are usually relatively painless contractions, similar to menstrual cramps; they often begin at around six months and occur when the uterus tightens and

then relaxes again; they are *irregular* (unlike the contractions during labour); towards the end of the pregnancy they might feel a bit more painful

- a sudden burst of energy – often called the 'nesting instinct' – when women often feel the urge to rush around making sure that everything is ready for the baby to arrive.

10 The birth

The stages of labour

Stage 1: the neck of the uterus opens

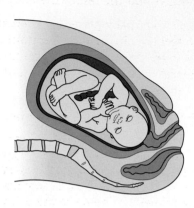

Figure 2.15 The first stage of labour

Towards the end of pregnancy, the baby moves down in the uterus and usually lies head downwards. A woman will recognise the onset of labour (the three-stage process of birth) by the following signs:

- A show – a discharge of blood-stained mucus from the vagina. (Not all women get a show in the early stages; the plug of mucus will come out naturally at some stage during the labour.)
- The breaking of the waters or rupture of membranes – when some amniotic fluid escapes via the vagina. Some women describe the release of fluid as a trickle, others as a gush.
- Regular muscular contractions – these may start slowly and irregularly, but become stronger and more frequent as labour progresses. They open up the cervix at the neck of the womb.

Stage 1 may last for up to 15 hours and is usually longer for the first-time mother. Once the membranes have ruptured, which may not occur until late in stage 1, the woman should contact the midwife or hospital, as there is a risk of infection entering the uterus if labour is prolonged.

> The transition stage links the first and second stages of labour. This stage occurs when the woman's cervix is 7–10 cm dilated. The body automatically releases more adrenaline at this time, to prepare for the pushing stage and increasing energy levels. The contractions become more frequent and very intense. Many women become tearful, saying that they really cannot take any more, but this is a certain sign that the pushing stage is very close.

Stage 2: the birth of the baby

This begins when the cervix is fully dilated (i.e. open) to 10 cm and the baby starts to move down the birth canal; it ends when the baby is born. During this stage:

- The contractions are very strong and the midwife encourages the mother to push with each contraction, until the baby's head is ready to be born.
- The contractions are more frequent: A typical pattern for early-phase contractions begins by lasting for about 40 seconds and coming every ten minutes. By the time the woman is ready to give birth, the contractions will last about a minute and come every two minutes.
- Crowning of the head: When the baby's head stays at the entrance to the vagina, it is said to be 'crowning' and the mother is asked to 'pant' as the head is born.
- Delivery of the head: Sometimes the vagina does not stretch enough to allow

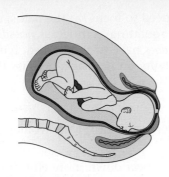

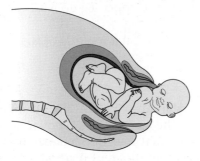

Figure 2.16 The second stage of labour

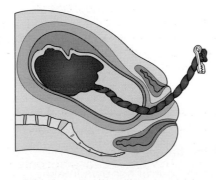

Figure 2.17 The third stage of labour

the baby's head to come out (especially if this is a first baby). The midwife may then ask for the mother's permission to perform an **episiotomy** – a small surgical cut in the **perineum**. The cut is later stitched, using a local anaesthetic (unless the woman has had an epidural).

- **Delivery of the body**: The baby will then rotate so that the shoulders are turned sideways and the rest of the body is born.

Many mothers prefer to have their baby placed on their abdomen immediately after birth, to feel the closeness and warmth. This is also thought to benefit the baby. The midwife will clamp and cut the umbilical cord and the baby is labelled with the mother's name on wrist and ankle bands.

Stage 3: the delivery of the placenta and membranes

Normally, the placenta separates from the lining of the uterus within 20 minutes of the birth and is pushed out through the vagina. The process is often speeded up by medical intervention – an injection of **Syntocinon®** (a synthetic form of oxytocin) – given to the mother by the midwife to help the uterus to expel the placenta and to prevent heavy blood loss.

Once the placenta is delivered, the midwife will feel the mother's abdomen to check that the uterus has started to contract now that the placenta has gone. The placenta will then be checked thoroughly to make sure that it is healthy and complete. Results of this check are recorded on the midwife's or doctor's notes.

The best positions for labour

Most women cope best if they are able to adopt different positions during labour. This can include lying or sitting on a bed, but could also mean:

- a supported standing squat (with her partner holding her from behind), which allows the pelvis to open wide
- leaning against the wall, bed or a beanbag, which also allows for massage
- rocking on all fours
- kneeling on a large cushion or pillow on the floor and leaning forwards onto the seat of a chair.

As contractions get stronger, the woman will need to focus on the pains, and work *with*, not *against*, gravity, by standing or squatting as much as possible, rather than lying flat on a bed. If the woman *does* have to stay in bed, lying on her left side is much better for the baby than lying on her back, because the baby gets more oxygen.

The best positions for pushing

When ready to push, the baby will find it easier to be born if the woman adopts one of the following positions:

- an upright squatting position, as it is easier to bear down more efficiently
- on her left side in bed, with her partner holding the upper leg up with each contraction
- kneeling on the mattress and leaning against a large pile of pillows placed at the top end.

Pain relief during labour

Labour is usually painful, but a thorough understanding of what is happening throughout the birth process can help to reduce the fear of the unknown. It is anxiety or fear that makes the body tense up and fight the contractions, instead of relaxing and working with them. There are various different methods of pain relief, including those using drugs and drug-free methods:

Pain relief using drugs

Gas and air (Entonox)

This is a mixture of oxygen and nitrous oxide ('laughing' gas). It is frequently offered to the mother towards the end of the first stage of labour, through a mask or plastic mouthpiece attached to the gas cylinder.

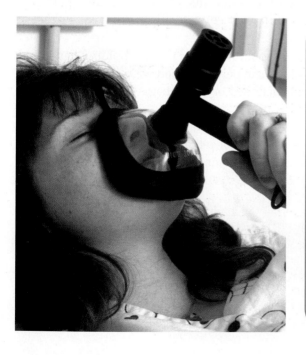

Advantages:

- It does not affect the baby.
- The mother is able to control her own intake.
- It works very quickly – after about 20 seconds.
- The drug does not stay in the system.
- It takes the edge off the pain of contractions.
- It contains oxygen, which is good for the baby.
- It can be used for a home birth and a water birth.
- It can also be used during procedures such as an episiotomy or when having an injection.

Disadvantages:

- It does not relieve all the pain.
- It may make the mother feel sick or light-headed.
- It gives the mother a very dry mouth.

Pethidine

This is a strong pain-killing drug given by injection; it relaxes the muscles and makes the mother very drowsy.

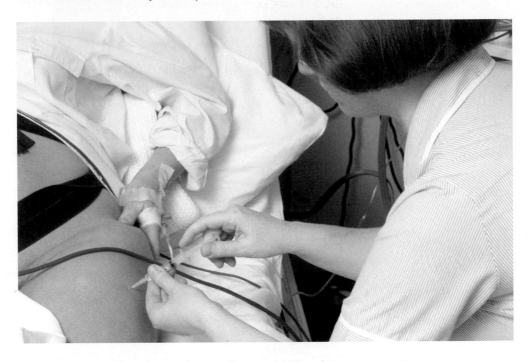

Advantages:

- It works quickly and is very useful for relieving pain in the early stages of labour.
- It is administered by a midwife – no need for a doctor.

Disadvantages:

- If given to the mother too close to the birth of the baby, it can cross the placenta and make the baby drowsy too.
- It can make the mother feel sick or disorientated.

Epidural anaesthetic

This is an anaesthetic drug injected into the space around the mother's spinal cord. It numbs the nerves and the pain of contractions, although the woman should still be able to feel a touch on her skin. An epidural will last for about two to four hours, but it can be 'topped up' through the catheter (a fine plastic tube), usually via a small pump that delivers the anaesthetic at regular intervals.

Many hospitals offer a mobile (or low-dose) epidural, which is designed to take away the pain of contractions without numbing the woman's legs completely. It may be combined with an initial spinal injection and enables the woman to move around more freely.

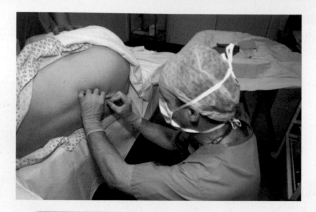

Advantages:

- It usually gives total pain relief from the waist down; more than 90 per cent of women get complete pain relief.
- It leaves the mother fully conscious – with a clear mind.
- It can help to control high blood pressure.
- It can put the woman back in control of her labour, and restore her confidence.
- It has little effect on the baby.
- An episiotomy can be stitched if the epidural is still effective after delivery.
- A Caesarean section may be given under an epidural.

Disadvantages:

- The woman has to stay in bed and must have a drip in her arm. (This is a safety precaution because epidurals make some women's blood pressure drop; in an emergency, the volume of her blood can be quickly boosted to bring her blood pressure back to normal again.)
- The woman will probably have a catheter into her bladder, as she cannot tell when she needs to pass urine.
- Labour often takes longer – especially the pushing stage – as the woman cannot feel her contractions.
- The baby's heartbeat will be monitored continuously; this makes it harder for the woman to move about freely.
- There is a greater incidence of a forceps or ventouse delivery because epidurals often prevent the baby moving into the best position to be born.
- If the epidural needle goes beyond the epidural space, there will be a leakage of cerebrospinal fluid after the tube is taken out. This fluid protects the brain and even a very small leak will give the woman a very severe headache.

Spinal anaesthetic

This is similar to an epidural and is also administered by an anaesthetist. The local anaesthetic numbs the nerves supplying the womb and cervix, so that the woman cannot feel contractions any more. Spinals are generally given during the pushing or second stage of labour if the woman needs a forceps or ventouse birth and there is no epidural in place already. They are also often used for pain relief in the first stage of labour, in conjunction with an epidural; this technique gives effective pain relief faster and is more popular with women than epidural alone.

Advantages:

- It provides very effective and rapid pain relief (works within five minutes).
- It can be very useful for emergencies – such as an emergency Caesarean.
- It is a single injection and, unlike an epidural, there is no tube left in the woman's back.

Disadvantages:

- It limits mobility because the mother will not be able to feel her legs.
- It lasts only one to two hours.
- It cannot be given more than once (unlike an epidural, a spinal cannot be 'topped up').
- The woman might feel very shivery and sick.
- She may have difficulty passing urine.

Pain relief without drugs

Water birth

The mother enters a special pool; this may be provided by the hospital or birthing centre, or hired privately. The pool is filled with warm water and kept at a constant temperature.

Advantages:

- It allows for freedom of movement and a feeling of weightlessness.
- It reduces the need for pain-relieving drugs as there is a natural release of endorphins (the body's natural pain-relieving hormone).
- It lowers the blood pressure.
- There is usually less need for medical interventions, and a gentler entry into the world for the baby.
- The partner can enter the birthing pool and help.

Disadvantages:

- There is a slight risk of infection.
- It is harder for the midwife to monitor the baby.
- It does not relieve all the pain.

Transcutaneous electrical nerve stimulation (TENS)

TENS is a method of pain relief consisting of a pack of electrode pads placed on the back. It discharges an electrical stimulus that interferes with the passage of pain signals to the brain and may help the body to produce endorphins, its own pain-killing hormones. The pack has a hand-held control which can be used to vary the strength of the stimulus.

Advantages:

- It has no side effects for either the mother or the baby.
- It can be used anywhere – at home or in hospital.
- The mother is able to control her own intake.
- The mother can move about freely.

Disadvantages:

- It may have little effect on severe pain.
- It cannot be used during a water birth.

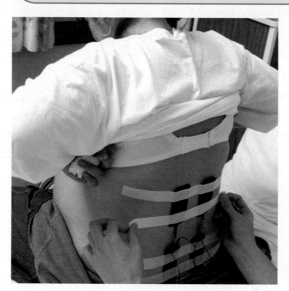

Breathing and relaxation techniques

Many women are frightened of the pain of labour. During labour, this fear can make a woman feel more tense and she will therefore feel the pain more acutely. Relaxation and breathing techniques are taught at antenatal or parentcraft classes to help women to control their labour naturally.

Breathing techniques

When we are tense and frightened, our breathing becomes shallow and the 'out' breath often gets stuck in our throat. We soon start to feel disorientated and out of control.

Most relaxation techniques focus on controlling your breathing; the key is to ensure that you *breathe out* properly. The following advice may be helpful:

- Try to keep breathing even during contractions.
- Breathe in through the nose and out through the mouth.
- As the woman breathes out, she should let her shoulders sink and try to release all the tension from her body.
- Think 'RE' with the 'in' breath and 'LAX' with the 'out' breath.
- Keep saying 'RE … LAX' over and over, to stay focused on the breathing.

It is important for the woman to remember that every contraction will come to an end and that there will be a break before the next one.

Relaxation techniques

Learning to relax will help to reduce any tension and will be good for both the woman and her baby.

Relaxation is good *for the woman* because:

- being relaxed conserves energy
- it ensures that blood is not diverted away from the womb – when we are tense and frightened, our body presumes that we need to escape from something dangerous and diverts blood to the muscles of our arms, legs and heart, so that we can run away
- staying calm enables the woman to communicate well with her midwife and her birth partner.

Relaxation is good *for the baby* because:

- if the woman is relaxed, her breathing will be calm and there will be plenty of oxygen for the baby
- the muscles of the womb will function more effectively, thus helping the baby to be born more quickly
- the woman will be alert rather than exhausted, and ready to give her baby her full attention when s/he is born.

Acupuncture, aromatherapy, reflexology and hypnosis are also used by some women to relieve the pain of labour, but these are not routinely offered within NHS units.

 REVISION QUESTIONS

1. Describe the signs and symptoms that indicate that labour is about to begin.

2. Labour is the name given to the process of giving birth. It is divided into three stages. Describe what happens during:

   a. the first stage of labour

   b. the second stage of labour

   c. the third stage of labour.

3. How can a birth partner assist the woman in labour?

4. List and describe four methods of pain relief in labour. Which methods of pain relief may be administered by the woman herself?

Medical interventions in the birth process

Induction

This means starting labour artificially; it involves rupturing the membranes and/or giving artificial hormones, via either a vaginal pessary or an intravenous infusion or drip. It is necessary if:

- the baby is very overdue
- the placenta is no longer working properly
- the mother is ill – for example, with heart disease, diabetes or pre-eclampsia.

Episiotomy

An episiotomy is a small cut made in the perineum (the area between the vagina and the rectum) and is used during the second stage of labour to:

- deliver the baby more quickly if there are signs of foetal distress
- prevent a large, ragged perineal tear that would be difficult to repair
- assist with a forceps delivery.

Forceps

Forceps are like tongs which fit around the baby's head to form a protective 'cage'; they are used during the second stage of labour to help deliver the head. They may be used:

- to protect the head during a breech delivery – that is, when the baby presents bottom-first
- if the mother has a condition such as heart disease or high blood pressure, and must not overexert herself
- if the labour is very prolonged and there are signs of foetal distress
- if the baby is very small or preterm (premature).

Vacuum delivery (ventouse)

This is an alternative to forceps, but can be used before the cervix is fully dilated; gentle suction is applied via a rubber cup placed on the baby's head.

Caesarean section

A Caesarean section is a surgical operation carried out while the mother is under either a general or an epidural anaesthetic; the baby is delivered through a cut in the abdominal wall. The need for a Caesarean section may be identified during

The face is examined for cleft palate – a gap in the roof of the mouth, and facial paralysis – temporary paralysis after compression of the facial nerve, usually after forceps delivery

Eyes are checked for cataract (a cloudiness of the lens)

Hands are checked for webbing (fingers joined together at the base) and creases – a single unbroken crease from one side of the palm to the other is a feature of Down's syndrome

The head is checked for size and shape: any marks from forceps delivery are noted

The heart and lungs are checked using a stethoscope; any abnormal findings will be investigated

The neck is examined for any obvious injury to the neck muscles after a difficult delivery

Feet are checked for webbing and talipes (club foot), which need early treatment

Genitalia and anus are checked for any malformation

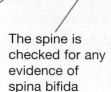

Skin – vernix and lanugo may still be present, milia may show on the baby's nose; black babies appear lighter in the first week of life as the pigment, melanin, is not yet at full concentration

The spine is checked for any evidence of spina bifida

Hips are tested for cogenital dislocation using Barlow's test

The abdomen is checked for any abnormality, e.g. pyloric stenosis, where there may be obstruction of the passage of food from the stomach; the umbilical cord is checked for infection

Figure 2.18 Doctor's examination of the newborn baby

pregnancy – an elective or planned operation – or as an emergency:

- when induction of labour has failed
- when there is severe bleeding
- when the baby is too large or in a position (such as breech) which makes vaginal delivery difficult
- in placenta praevia – when the placenta is covering the cervix
- in cases of severe foetal distress
- if the mother is too ill to withstand labour.

The newborn baby or neonate

Neonatal tests

The first question usually asked by parents is, 'Is the baby okay?' The doctor and midwife will observe the newborn baby closely and perform several routine tests and checks that will show whether the baby has any obvious physical problem (see figures 2.17 and 2.18).

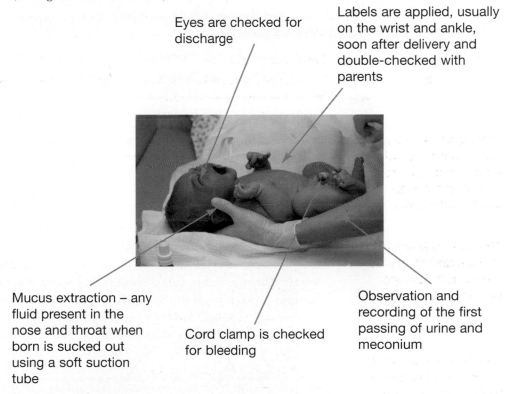

Eyes are checked for discharge

Labels are applied, usually on the wrist and ankle, soon after delivery and double-checked with parents

Mucus extraction – any fluid present in the nose and throat when born is sucked out using a soft suction tube

Cord clamp is checked for bleeding

Observation and recording of the first passing of urine and meconium

Figure 2.19 Midwife's examination of the newborn baby

The Apgar score

This is a standard method of evaluating the condition of a newborn baby by checking five vital signs (see table 2.3). The Apgar score is assessed at one minute and five minutes after birth; it may be repeated at five-minute intervals if there is cause for concern.

Most healthy babies have an Apgar score of 9, only losing one point for having blue extremities – this often persists for a few hours after birth. A low score at five minutes is more serious than a low score at one minute. In hospital, the paediatrician will be notified if the score is six or under at five minutes. Dark-skinned babies are assessed for oxygenation by checking for redness of the conjunctiva and inside the mouth.

The Apgar score is interpreted as follows:

Signs	0	1	2
Heartbeat	absent	slow – below 100	fast – over 100
Breathing	absent	slow – irregular	good; crying
Muscle tone	limp	some limb movement	active movement
Reflex response (to stimulation of foot or nostril)	absent	grimace	cry, cough, sneeze
Colour		body oxygenated, hands and feet blue	well oxygenated

Table 2.3 The Apgar score

10: The baby is in the best possible condition.

8–9: The baby is in good condition.

5–7: The baby has mild asphyxia (lack of oxygen in the blood) and may need treatment.

3–4: The baby has moderate asphyxia and will need treatment.

0–2: The baby has severe asphyxia and needs urgent resuscitation.

Neonatal screening tests

Three screening tests are carried out on the newborn baby to check for specific disorders that can be treated successfully if detected early enough.

- Barlow's test: This is a test for congenital dislocation of the hip and is carried out soon after birth, at six weeks and at all routine developmental testing opportunities until the baby is walking. There are varying degrees of severity of this disorder; treatment involves the use of splints to keep the baby's legs in a frog-like position.
- The newborn bloodspot test: All babies are screened for phenylketonuria and congenital hypothyroidism; in some areas babies are also screened for cystic fibrosis, sickle-cell disorders and some other conditions. A small blood sample is taken from the baby's heel and sent for analysis.
  a. Phenylketonuria is very rare, affecting 1 in 10,000 babies; it is a metabolic disorder which leads to brain damage and learning delay. Early diagnosis is vital, since treatment is very effective. This involves a special-formula protein diet which has to be followed throughout the person's life.
  b. Congenital hypothyroidism (CHT) affects 1 in 4000 babies in the UK. Babies born with this condition do not have enough thyroxin; untreated babies develop serious, permanent, physical and mental disability. Early treatment with thyroxin tablets prevents disability and should start by 21 days of age.

Multiple births

Multiple pregnancies – where there is more than one baby – always need special care and supervision. Twins are the most common multiple birth, occurring in about 1 in 87–100 pregnancies.

Diagnosing multiple pregnancies

A woman expecting more than one baby is likely to be larger than her dates would suggest and will put on more weight. Routine ultrasound scanning can usually diagnose the presence of more than one baby, unless one baby is 'hiding' behind the other.

Caring for twins and triplets

The main risk when there is more than one baby is that they will be born too early (be premature); this risk rises with the number of babies. Usually, women expecting twins or more babies are admitted to hospital for the birth. Twins may be delivered vaginally provided both babies are in the head-down position, but triplets and quadruplets are usually born by Caesarean section.

Support for parents with twins and more babies

The community midwife and health visitor will visit more frequently and will put the parents in touch with other parents in the same situation; extra help may be provided for a few weeks, and arrangements are made for routine tests and immunisations to be carried out in the home. The La Leche League, and the Twins and Multiple Births Association (TAMBA) can offer practical advice and a list of local support groups.

If one of the babies dies, either before birth or afterwards, the parents will require specialist bereavement counselling; the Child Bereavement Trust can offer invaluable advice and support.

Common neonatal problems and disorders

Jaundice

Jaundice is a common condition in newborn infants that usually shows up shortly after birth. In most cases, it goes away on its own; if not, it can be treated easily. A baby gets jaundice when bilirubin, which is produced naturally by the body, builds up faster than the newborn's liver can break it down (usually it would be excreted in the baby's stools). Too much bilirubin makes a jaundiced baby's skin look yellow. This yellow colour will appear first on the face, then on the chest and stomach, and finally on the legs. Older babies, children and adults get rid of this yellow blood product quickly, usually through bowel movements.

How is jaundice treated?

Mild to moderate levels of jaundice do not require any treatment. If high levels of jaundice do not clear up on their own, the baby may be treated with special light (phototherapy) or some other form of treatment. The special light helps to get rid of the bilirubin by altering it, to make it easier for the baby's liver to excrete. Another treatment is to give more frequent feeds of breast milk or formula, to help pass the bilirubin out in the stools. Increasing the amount of water given to a child is not sufficient to pass the bilirubin because it must be passed in the stools.

 REVISION QUESTIONS

1. What is induction of labour, and when is it necessary?
2. What is an episiotomy, and why is it used?
3. What does the Apgar score mean?
4. Give four reasons why a Caesarean section may be necessary to deliver a baby.
5. What is meant by:
   a. forceps delivery?
   b. ventouse extraction?

11 Preparing for the baby

Planning for the arrival of a new baby is an exciting time and it is easy to be tempted to overspend when visiting nursery shops. At first, the parents need only ensure the baby's safety and comfort, and stock up on the bare essentials. They need to:

- prepare a place in their home for the baby
- purchase essential nursery equipment.

Preparing a place for the baby

Safety

Before the baby comes home, parents should make sure that smoke alarms are fitted. Further safety measures must be taken before the baby is mobile – for example, stair gates, electric socket covers.

Baby's room or nursery

It is likely that the parents will want to have the baby sleeping in their room for the first few weeks or months following the birth. The baby's own room can be prepared for when s/he sleeps during the day, with the following:

- a dimmer switch for the main light (or a small lamp), for checking on the baby and giving night feeds
- adequate heating – the room needs to be kept at a temperature of 20° C (68° F)
- a comfortable chair to sit in while giving night feeds
- a nappy-changing area at worktop height
- a chest of drawers and/or shelves to store supplies such as clothes, nappies and toiletries
- well-lined curtains to keep out draughts and daylight when the baby needs to sleep.

If moving an older child out of the nursery in order to make room for a new brother or sister, parents should try to do so well before the baby's arrival, to avoid feelings of rejection and displacement.

Purchasing essential nursery equipment

Families are under a lot of pressure from friends, from advertising companies and from television programmes to provide the very best clothing and equipment for their new baby. Parents need to prioritise their needs by considering all factors relevant to their circumstances.

- **Cost:** How much can the parents afford to spend? What may be available on loan from friends who have children past the baby stage? Can some equipment, such as the pram, be bought second-hand or hired cheaply?
- **Lifestyle:** Is the family living in a flat where the lifts are often out of action, in bed-and-breakfast accommodation or in a house with a large garden? These factors will affect such decisions as pram versus travel system or buggy, or where the baby will sleep.
- **Single or multiple use:** Will the equipment be used for a subsequent baby (e.g. the priority may be to buy a large pram on which a toddler can also be seated)? It may be worth buying new, quality products if they are to be used again.
- **Safety and maintenance:** Does the item of equipment chosen meet all the British Safety Standards? What if it has been bought second-hand? How easy is it to replace worn-out parts?

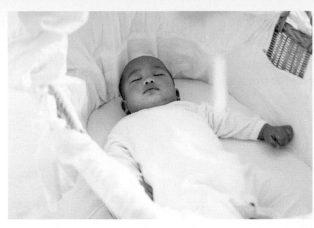

Figure 2.20 Moses basket

Figure 2.21 A traditional cot

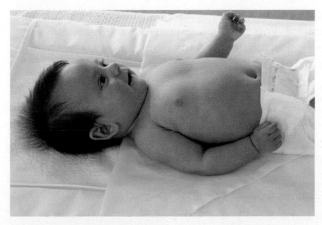

Figure 2.21 Changing mat

Parents will usually need to provide the following equipment:

- **Car seat**: The baby will only be allowed home from hospital by car if parents have a properly fitting baby car seat. This is a seat for newborns and usually fits in the rear of the car and is rear-facing. The modern car seats can also be used as a first seat in the home and can be bought separately or as part of a travel system.
- **Moses basket, carrycot** or **cot**: A Moses basket is fine for the first few months and is easy to carry from room to room. It is not suitable for transporting the baby outside or in a car. Carrycots can be bought separately or as part of a travel system.
- **Clothes**: Vests, stretch sleepsuits, socks or bootees, mittens, summer or winter hats and cardigans.
- **Nappies**: If using reusable nappies, sterilising solution and buckets are required.
- **Toiletries**: Nappy rash cream, cotton wool and baby lotion.
- **Hooded baby towels.**
- **Changing mat**: Ideally, this should have raised edges and a fabric cover that can be taken off and washed, as it is more comfortable for the baby.
- **Cot sheets and cot blankets**: These should be easy to wash and dry as they will need frequent laundering; the ideal fabric for sheets is brushed cotton. Blankets are often made from cellular acrylic fabric, which is lightweight, warm and easily washable.
- **Pram, buggy, pram/buggy combination** or **travel system** suitable for a newborn (see below).
- **Feeding equipment.**

Figure 2.22 Travel system

Equipment for feeding the baby

For breastfeeding

- Breast pads
- Easy-access tops and nighties (front-opening)
- Nursing bras (at least two)
- Bibs
- Muslin squares

For bottle feeding

- Sterilising system
- Four bottles, teats and caps
- Bottle brush
- Measuring jug
- Newborn formula feed

Other equipment

The following items are not absolutely essential, but parents often find them very useful:

- **Baby sling**: Baby slings, used on the front of the carer's body, enable close physical contact between carer and baby, but can cause back strain if used with heavy babies. They make using public transport easier, as the baby is carried close to the body, leaving the parent's hands free. Most parents also find that their baby loves being held close in a sling while they go about the daily chores.
- **Bouncing cradle**: This is a soft fabric seat, which can be used from birth to about six months. Babies and their carers generally appreciate it, as it is easily transported from room to room, encouraging the baby's full involvement in everyday activities. It should always be placed on the floor – never on a worktop or bed, as even young babies can 'bounce' themselves off.
- **Baby bath**: A large washing-up bowl can be used in the early weeks, but a sturdy bath on its own stand makes bath-time much easier and can be bought cheaply second-hand.
- **Toys**: Apart from a mobile, toys are not really necessary at first, and soft toys and rattles are often presented as gifts for the new baby.

Figure 2.23 A bouncing cradle

Guidelines for buying baby clothes and equipment

Many nursery items receive very little use and it is always worth looking for cheap second-hand items, as long as you check and clean the equipment carefully. Every parent enjoys dressing a baby up, but there is no need to spend a fortune, as babies do grow out of their clothes very quickly.

> ● **Important:** The one item of equipment that should never be bought second-hand is the baby's car seat. This is because the seat may have been weakened if the car was involved in an accident.

Choosing clothes for the new baby

The layette is the baby's first set of clothes. Some shops specialising in baby goods supply complete layettes.

Baby clothes should be:

- **loose and comfortable** to allow for ease of movement – as babies grow rapidly, care should be taken that all-in-one stretch suits do not cramp tiny feet (there should always be growing space at the feet to avoid pressure on the soft bones)
- **easy to wash and dry** – as babies need changing often; natural fibres (e.g. cotton and wool mixtures) are more comfortable
- **flame-resistant** – all garments for babies up to three months old must carry a permanent label showing that they have passed the low-flammability test for slow burning
- **easy to put on and take off** – avoid ribbons, bows and lacy-knit fabrics which can trap small fingers and toes
- **non-irritant** – clothes should be lightweight, soft and warm; some synthetic fibres can be too cold in winter as they do not retain body heat, and too hot in the summer as they do not absorb sweat or allow the skin pores to 'breathe'
- **appropriate for the weather** – for example, in cooler weather a hat is necessary to prevent the loss of heat from the baby's head; in hot weather, a hat with a wide brim will protect the baby's head from the sun.

> **Remember!**
> ● Several layers of clothing are warmer than one thick garment.
> ● Babies hate having their faces covered, so choose clothes with front fastenings or with wide 'envelope' necks.
> ● Clothing needs will vary according to the season, and the baby will need protective clothes such as pram suits, bonnet or sun hat, mittens and bootees.

Choosing a cot

Often a baby will move into a cot for sleeping when s/he has outgrown the carrycot, but they are also suitable for newborn babies. Cots usually have slatted sides, which allow the baby to see out, with one side able to be lowered and secured by safety catches. Safety requirements are:

- bars must be no more than 7 cm apart
- safety catches must be childproof
- the mattress should fit snugly with no gaps, and should carry a BS (British Standard) safety label
- cot bumpers (foam-padded screens tied at the head end of the cot) are not recommended, although they are on sale everywhere and can protect the baby from draughts – experts say that there is a danger of suffocation or strangulation if they loosen and the baby's head comes into contact with them; also, by restricting the flow of air in and out of the cot, they could

contribute to the baby overheating (if parents do use a bumper, they should ensure that the fabric ties that attach it are secured properly and out of the baby's reach, and also that the room temperature is well controlled; it should be removed altogether once a baby is sitting, as it may be used as a step to climb out)

- if the cot has been painted, check that lead-free, non-toxic paint has been used
- pillows should not be used until the child is at least two years old.

Choosing a buggy, pram or travel system

A newborn baby can be transported in a special buggy with a tilting seat that can be used for as long as the baby needs a pushchair. The buggy has the advantage of being easier to handle than a pram, easier to store at home and can be taken on public transport. However, it is not possible to carry heavy loads of shopping on a buggy or pushchair, and they should also not be used for long periods of sleeping.

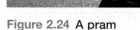

Figure 2.24 A pram

A pram is ideal for parents who do a lot of walking with their baby, but is not so good for families travelling mostly by car or on public transport.

The latest travel systems usually include either a carrycot, pushchair and car seat, or a pushchair and car seat, and are suitable for babies from birth. Some models have fully reversible seat units, so that the baby can face the person pushing the pushchair. Factors to consider when buying any baby travel equipment include:

- conforms to British Standards
- five anchor points for a safety harness
- easy to manoeuvre and to take apart for storing
- good stability, especially when carrying shopping
- effective brakes
- good suspension system
- easy to clean and maintain.

The role of the father

Some parents find the responsibility of looking after a young baby overwhelming; they may worry that they cannot cope or find that 'the baby' has completely taken over their life. A woman has the advantage of a *progressive* preparation for motherhood over the course of nine months. Once the baby is born, she benefits from a very close relationship. Both the new mother and the new father will experience changes in their relationship now that they are a family of three. Developing their own closeness and also a bond with their child is very important, both for them and for their growing child. The father–child relationship is harder to define. For example, a new father may:

- feel threatened, now that important decisions seem to be made in terms of their impact on the baby – that is, the baby now occupies a central part in their lives

- feel a strong burden of responsibility, as well as a stronger financial pressure to do well
- be frustrated to find that his partner appears to be completely 'wrapped up' in the baby and makes no time for him alone
- be nervous about handling the baby when s/he seems so tiny and vulnerable.

The foundations for a positive, caring relationship between the father and his baby can be strengthened in the following ways. The father should do the following:

- **Support his partner's feeding choices**: For some women, breastfeeding comes naturally; for others, it is a struggle from the first attempt. Whatever his partner chooses to do with regard to feeding, he should support her choice and back her up in front of others. If the baby is to be bottle-fed, the father will be able to take a more active role, making up feeds, sterilising bottles and giving feeds.
- **Help as much as possible around the house**: Doing the shopping, vacuuming the floor and preparing meals are important contributions when the baby is settling into a routine.

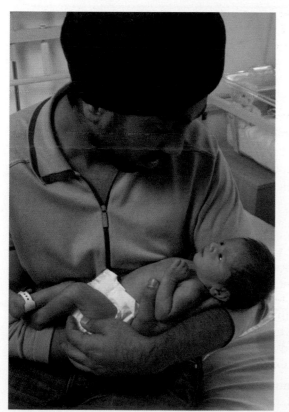

Figure 2.25 Father bonding with baby

- **Change nappies**: Changing a nappy provides an excellent opportunity for early interaction with the baby, as the baby's face is at a perfect distance for vision and communication. It also lessens the chores for his partner.
- **Check and screen visitors**: A new baby often seems to attract visitors at all times – and they can outstay their welcome. The mother needs rest and the baby needs to adjust to a routine. The father could tactfully suggest times when visitors would be most welcome and also discourage them from staying too long, until the baby is more settled at home.
- **Try to be home on time**: The work–life balance is particularly important in the early months, until a routine is established.
- **Bonding with the baby**: Babies change very quickly and are a constant source of joy and wonder. Cuddling, soothing and talking to the baby are easy ways to begin the bonding process. Fathers often learn to develop their own unique ways of soothing their baby.
- **Regularly have time alone with the baby**: This allows each parent to discover their own special set of parenting skills and to build the confidence that will allow them to be a 'complete' parent, even when their partner is around.
- **Think about claiming paternity leave**: Many fathers are able to obtain statutory paternity leave, which is time off work immediately following the birth of the baby.

 REVISION QUESTIONS

1. What safety points should be considered when buying:
   a. a cot?
   b. a pram or travel system?
2. When choosing clothes for a baby, what factors should be taken into account?

RESEARCH ACTIVITY

You have been asked to advise on the purchase of a layette for a newborn baby.

1. Make a list of the items you consider to be essential, excluding nappies and waterproof pants.
2. Visit several shops and find out the cost of all the items on your list.
3. Evaluate your selection, checking:
   - the ease of washing and drying
   - the design and colours used – are you reinforcing the stereotypes of pink for girls or blue for boys?
   - the safety aspects – no fancy bows, ties, etc.
   - the suitability of the fabrics used
   - the quantity of clothes needed
   - the final cost of the layette.

12 Post-natal care

The post-natal needs of the family

The pattern of postnatal care is determined by the needs of the woman and her family, and a midwife **must** be in attendance on a woman for at least 10 days following delivery. If the mother has had a complicated birth, the midwife can visit for 28 days after the birth. In these first weeks, families need:

- support from their own family and friends
- information, advice and support from the community health service – their GP, midwife and health visitor
- to register the birth of the baby up to six weeks after the birth (or up to three weeks in Scotland).

The puerperium

The period from birth to six weeks is called the puerperium. For the first ten days the mother will receive help and advice from a midwife, either in hospital or at home. The midwife will:

- feel if the uterus is getting back to its pre-pregnancy size
- check that any stitches have dissolved and that healing is complete
- take the mother's blood pressure
- give advice on minor problems, such as constipation
- help to establish feeding
- watch for signs of postnatal depression.

From ten days onwards, the health visitor visits mother and baby at home. The purpose of these visits is to:

- offer advice on health and safety issues, including advice on special exercises to strengthen the pelvic floor muscles, which will have been stretched after a vaginal delivery
- check that the baby is making expected progress
- offer support and advice on any emotional problems, including referral to a specialist if necessary
- advise the parents to attend a baby clinic
- discuss a timetable for immunisations
- put the parents in touch with other parents locally.

Giving birth is a momentous event; everyone reacts differently, and while many mothers feel an immediate rush of love and excitement, others can feel quite detached, needing time to adjust. Early contact with their newborn baby is equally important for fathers as for mothers, and learning how to care for a newborn baby can make couples feel closer.

The 'baby blues'

About half of new mothers will feel a bit weepy, flat and unsure of themselves on the third or fourth day after having a baby; this is called the 'baby blues'. It is a feeling of mild depression caused by hormonal changes, tiredness and reaction to the excitement of the birth, and it passes after a few days. It is more common in first-time mothers and in those who have experienced problems with premenstrual syndrome (PMS, or PMT – premenstrual tension). If these feelings persist for longer than a few days, the mother may develop a more serious condition, post-natal depression, and she will need medical help.

Post-natal depression

Post-natal depression (PND) usually develops within the first month following childbirth. Around one in ten mothers experiences PND. It may or may not develop out of the 'baby blues', and the mother will show similar symptoms to those seen in 'ordinary' depression:

- **Feeling low, miserable and tearful** for no apparent reason: These feelings persist for most of the time, though they may be worse at certain times of day, particularly the morning.
- **Feeling resentful and angry**: This may be particularly noticeable in first-time mothers, who feel that they are not enjoying having a new baby in the way they anticipated.
- **Feeling constantly tired**: Disturbed sleep patterns are a natural part of looking after a new baby; but mothers with post-natal depression find it hard to go to sleep even though they are tired, or they wake early in the morning.
- **Feeling tense and anxious**: The normal worries and anxieties which any mother feels for a new baby may become overwhelming. Also, some mothers experience panic attacks, which are episodes lasting several minutes when they feel as if something disastrous is about to happen – such as collapsing or having a heart attack.
- **Feeling unable to cope**: When people are depressed, they sometimes feel that there is no way out of their problems, and even the simplest of tasks seems too much.
- **Loss of appetite**: Mothers may not feel hungry and may forget to eat at a time when they need to have a good healthy diet.

Nobody knows why some mothers become depressed after childbirth, although it may occur partly because of the hormonal changes following childbirth.

Treatment for post-natal depression

PND is treated in much the same way as ordinary depression. The following measures are helpful:

- Talking about the problem with somebody, such as the health visitor or general practitioner.
- Getting extra support and help with looking after the baby, from a partner and close family members.
- Medication in the form of antidepressants may be necessary.

In severe cases of PND, the mother and her baby will be admitted to a psychiatric hospital for more intensive therapy. (Post-natal depression should not be confused with the much more serious condition of puerperal psychosis: this is a very rare mental illness – affecting fewer than 1 in 500 women – which always requires treatment in a psychiatric unit.)

Post-natal provision for the mother and baby

The post-natal check: six weeks after the birth

At the end of the puerperium, a post-natal check is carried out by a GP or hospital doctor. The mother has the following checks:

- **Weight**: Breastfeeding mothers tend to lose weight more quickly than those who are bottle-feeding, but most mothers are almost back to their pre-pregnancy weight.
- **Urine test**: To make sure the kidneys are working properly and that there is no infection.

- **Blood pressure** may be checked.
- **Perineal check**: The mother will be asked if she has any concerns about the healing of any tear, cut or stitches in her perineum (the area between the vagina and the rectum). If she is concerned, the midwife or doctor will offer to examine her.
- **Rubella immunity check**: If she is not immune to rubella (German measles) and was not given an immunisation before leaving hospital, the mother will be offered one now.
- **Discussion points**: The doctor will ask about the following:
  a. whether the mother has had a period yet or if there is any discharge
  b. any concerns about contraception or any aspect of sex
  c. how the mother is feeling – for example, if she is very tired, low or depressed.

The baby's six-week check is usually carried out at the same time as the mother's. This is a thorough examination of the baby's health and development – for example, the baby's heart is listened to, weight and length are measured and general behaviour is noted. The mother is asked about any problems, and the information is recorded on the **Personal Child Health Record** (PCHR).

6-8 WEEK REVIEW

This review is done by your health visitor or a doctor. Below are some things you may want to talk about when you see them. However, if you are worried about your child's health, growth or development you can contact your health visitor or doctor at any time.

Do you feel well yourself?	yes ☐	no ☐	not sure ☐
Do you have any worries about feeding your baby?	yes ☐	no ☐	not sure ☐
Do you have any concerns about your baby's weight gain?	yes ☐	no ☐	not sure ☐
Does your baby watch your face and follow with his/her eyes?	yes ☐	no ☐	not sure ☐
Does your baby turn towards the light?	yes ☐	no ☐	not sure ☐
Does your baby smile at you?	yes ☐	no ☐	not sure ☐
Do you think your baby can hear you?	yes ☐	no ☐	not sure ☐
Is your baby startled by loud noises?	yes ☐	no ☐	not sure ☐
Are there any problems in looking after your baby?	yes ☐	no ☐	not sure ☐
Do you have any worries about your baby?	yes ☐	no ☐	not sure ☐

Any other issues you would like to discuss? ....
....
....

Results of newborn bloodspot screening

Condition	Results received? yes / no / not done	Follow up required? no / yes & reason	If follow up, outcome of follow up
PKU			
Hypothyroidism			
Sickle Cell			
Cystic Fibrosis			
Other			

Figure 2.26 Personal Child Health Record

KEY TERMS

Perineum: The skin between the vagina and the rectum.

Post-natal: The first days and weeks after the birth of the baby (post = after, natal = birth).

Puerperium: The period of about six weeks which follows immediately after the birth of a child.

 REVISION QUESTIONS

1. What is the role of the health visitor during the post-natal period?
2. What is the difference between the baby blues and post-natal depression?
3. List four checks carried out on the mother at the post-natal check six weeks after the birth.

RESEARCH ACTIVITY

Find out about the training necessary to qualify as:

a. a midwife

b. a health visitor.

PHYSICAL DEVELOPMENT

1 The newborn baby

Characteristics of the newborn baby

Size

All newborn babies – or **neonates** – are weighed and their head circumference is measured soon after birth; these measurements provide vital information for professionals when charting any abnormality in development.

- **Length**: It is difficult to measure accurately the length of a neonate, and many hospitals have abandoned this as a routine; the average length of a full-term baby is 50 cm.
- **Weight**: The birthweight of full-term babies varies considerably because:
  a. first babies tend to weigh less than brothers and sisters born later
  b. boys are usually larger than girls
  c. large parents usually have larger babies and small parents usually have smaller babies.
  d. The average weight of a newborn baby is 3.5 kg.
- **Head circumference**: The average head circumference of a full-term baby is about 35 cm.

Appearance

The baby will be wet from the amniotic fluid and may also have some blood streaks on the head or body, picked up from a tear or an episiotomy.

- The head is large in proportion to the body, and may be oddly shaped at first, because of:
  a. **moulding** – the head may be long and pointed, as the skull bones overlap slightly to allow passage through the birth canal
  b. **caput succedaneum** – a swelling on the head, caused by pressure as the head presses on the cervix before birth; it is not dangerous and usually disappears within a few days
  c. **cephalhaematoma** – a localised, blood-filled swelling or bruise, caused by the rupture of small blood vessels during labour; it is not dangerous but may take several weeks to subside.
- **Vernix** (literally, varnish) – or protective grease – may be present, especially in the skin folds; it should be left to come off without any harsh rubbing of the skin.
- **Lanugo**, or fine downy hair, may be seen all over the body, especially on dark-skinned babies and those who are born preterm.
- **Head hair** – the baby may be born with a lot of hair or be quite bald; often the hair present at birth falls out within weeks and is replaced by hair of a different colour.
- **Skin colour** – this varies and depends on the ethnic origin of the baby. At least half of all babies develop jaundice on the second or third day after birth; this gives the skin a yellow tinge – usually no treatment is necessary.

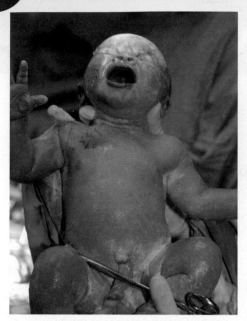

Figure 3.1 The newborn baby

- **Mongolian spot** – this is a smooth, bluish-black area of discoloration commonly found at the base of the spine on babies of African or Asian origin; it is caused by an excess of **melanocytes** – brown pigment cells – and is quite harmless.
- **Milia** – sometimes called milk spots, these are small, whitish-yellow spots which may be present on the face; they are caused by blocked oil ducts and disappear quite quickly.
- **Birthmarks** – the most common birthmark is a pinkish mark over the eyelids, often referred to as 'stork marks'; these usually disappear within a few months. Other birthmarks, such as strawberry naevus, persist for some years.

Movements of the newborn baby

Babies display a number of automatic – or **involuntary** – movements (known as **primitive reflexes**) which are reflex responses to specific stimuli. The presence of some of these reflexes is essential to survival. The most important of them is breathing, closely followed by the rooting and sucking reflexes which help them to search out the breast and to feed successfully. The reflexes are replaced by **voluntary** responses as the brain takes control of behaviour – for example, the grasp reflex has to fade before the baby learns to hold (and let go of) objects that are placed in his/her hand. Doctors check for some of these reflexes during the baby's first examination. If the reflexes persist beyond an expected time, it may indicate a delay in development.

- **Swallowing and sucking reflexes**: When something is put in the mouth, the baby at once sucks and swallows; some babies make their fingers sore by sucking them while still in the womb.
- **Rooting reflex**: If one side of the baby's cheek or mouth is gently touched, the baby's head turns towards the touch and the mouth purses as if in search of the nipple (see figure 3.2).
- **Grasp reflex**: When an object or finger touches the palm of the baby's hand, it is automatically grasped (see figure 3.3).
- **Stepping or walking reflex**: When held upright and tilting slightly forward, with feet placed on a firm surface, the baby will make forward-stepping movements (see figure 3.4).
- **Startle reflex**: When the baby is startled by a sudden noise or bright light, s/he will move his/her arms outwards, with elbows and hands clenched (see figure 3.5).
- **Asymmetric tonic neck reflex**: If the baby's head is turned to one side, s/he will straighten the arm and leg on that side and bend the arm and leg on the opposite side (see figure 3.6).

- **Falling reflex** (Moro reflex): Any sudden movement that affects the neck gives the baby the feeling that s/he may be dropped; s/he will fling out the arms and open the hands before bringing them back over the chest, as if to catch hold of something.

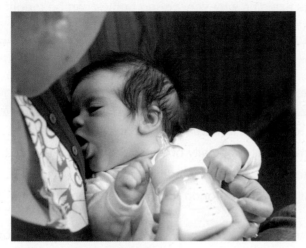

Figure 3.2 The rooting reflex

Figure 3.3 The grasp reflex

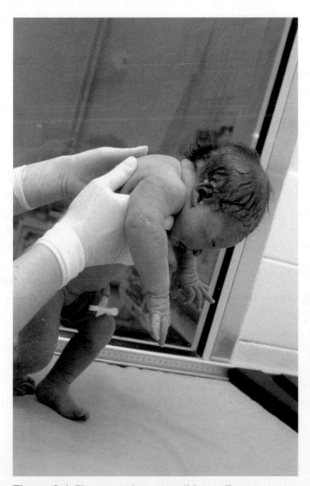

Figure 3.4 The stepping or walking reflex

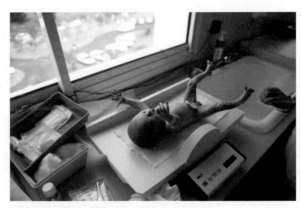

Figure 3.5 The startle reflex

Figure 3.6 The asymmetric tonic neck reflex

> **Did you know?**
>
> Babies have a diving reflex! If you were to submerge a baby in water, the valve at the top of the throat would instinctively close to prevent the baby from inhaling water. This reflex lasts until the age of 12–18 months. This explains why very young babies can be taught to swim underwater.

 KEY TERMS

Neonatal: Relating to the first few weeks of a baby's life.

Neonate: A newborn infant, especially one less than four weeks old.

Voluntary: Intentional or controlled by individual will.

Involuntary: Controlled by the autonomic nervous system, without conscious control.

Reflex: An involuntary action or response, such as a sneeze, blink or hiccup.

The senses of a newborn baby

Newborn babies are already actively using all their senses to explore their new environment. These senses are:

- sight
- hearing
- smell
- taste
- touch.

Vision or sight

Newborn babies are very near-sighted at first, and they can focus best on things that are within 25 cm of their faces. This means that they can see well enough to focus on their mother's face when being held to the breast. Their vision is quite blurry outside this range, but they can follow a light with their eyes and turn toward lights. Sometimes babies appear to have a squint, as their eyes may move independently of each other. This is normal and is because they are still gaining control of the eye muscles. Newborn babies prefer to look at:

- **people's faces and eyes**, especially those of their mothers
- **bright colours** – they will often reach for colourful objects
- **light and dark contrasts** and sharp outlines
- **patterns**, such as stripes or circles, rather than plain surfaces
- **things that are moving** – they will focus on and follow a moving ball with their eyes.

Hearing

Babies develop a very acute sense of hearing while in the womb. Ultrasound studies have shown that unborn babies as early as 25 weeks' gestation can startle in response to a sudden loud noise. Newborn babies can distinguish different voices and other sounds, and they can also determine from which direction a sound is coming. For example, if a small bell is rung above a newborn baby's head, s/he will turn the head in the direction of the sound and watch the object making the sound. Newborn babies prefer to listen to:

- **the human voice**, especially female voices – they usually recognise their own mother's voice from the start, since this is the voice they have heard, although muffled, throughout their time in the womb; newborn babies become quiet when they hear their mother's voice, and they turn the head towards the mother when she speaks; after about a week or so, most newborn babies will prefer their father's voice to that of other men
- **soft, melodic speech** – newborn babies can tell the difference between a calm, happy tone and an angry voice, and will respond with pleasure to a soft, lilting voice and may cry when they hear a loud, angry voice.

Hearing is an important part of speech development, so it is essential that babies are talked to. Parents and other adults automatically alter the pitch of their voices when talking to babies and use a lot of repetition. This is often called motherese, parentese or infant-directed talk.

Touch

Newborn babies are very sensitive to touch. They love to be held close, comforted, cuddled, stroked and rocked. Newborn babies prefer:

- **stroking of their skin** – this action helps newborn babies to sleep, and it helps to encourage closeness between baby and parent
- **the feel of soft fabrics**
- **skin-to-skin contact** with their parents
- **being cuddled.**

Babies who are fed, but not touched or held, often have problems with their physical and mental development. Gentle stroking is especially beneficial for **premature babies**. Research shows that it leads to increased weight gain, more alertness and activity, and an earlier discharge from hospital.

Taste

Newborn babies also have a well-developed sense of taste. They generally enjoy sweetness and dislike sour liquids. They can detect differences in the taste of their mother's milk, which can change depending on what the mother eats. Babies show that they find tastes unpleasant by screwing up their faces and trying to reject the taste from their mouth.

Smell

Newborn babies are sensitive to the smell of their mother, and they can tell it apart from that of other women. They are attracted not just to the smell of milk, but also to their mother's own unique body scent. Breastfed babies are more aware of their mother's smell than babies who are bottle-fed. This may be because breastfed babies spend more time in skin-to-skin contact with their mothers, compared with babies who are bottle-fed. Babies will turn away from a smell that they find unpleasant.

REVISION QUESTIONS

1. Make a list of all the things a newborn baby is able to do.

2. What is the name given to movements which are automatic and inborn? Describe six such movements and explain their importance in the study of child development.

2 The needs of the newborn baby

All babies depend completely on an adult to meet all their needs, but how these needs are met will vary considerably according to family circumstances, culture and the personalities of the baby and the caring adult. To achieve and maintain healthy growth and all-round (holistic) development, certain basic needs must be fulfilled. These basic needs are:

- food
- warmth
- sleep and rest
- love and security
- protection.

The need for food

Newborn babies need nourishment in the form of milk – either breast milk or special formula milk given by bottle. (See part four for more information.)

The need for warmth

From birth, babies have a heat-regulating mechanism in the brain that enables them to generate body warmth when they get cold. However, they can rapidly become very cold for the following reasons:

- they are unable to conserve body warmth if the surrounding air is at a lower temperature than normal
- they have a large surface area compared to body weight
- they lack body fat, which is a good insulator.

Maternity units are always kept at a high temperature (usually about 29° C) to allow for frequent undressing and bathing of newborn babies. At home, the room temperature for newborn babies should not fall below 20° C. This can be checked by using a nursery room thermometer. A preterm or smaller baby is at an even greater risk of **hypothermia** (see pages 193, 195 and 196).

Newborn babies cannot move to warm themselves up, so they must be dressed in clothing suitable for the weather. In winter, babies need to wear hats to protect them from losing heat through their heads.

Sleep and rest

Everyone needs sleep, but the amount that babies sleep varies enormously, and will depend on the maturity of the brain (the preterm baby may sleep for long periods) and on the need for food. At first, the pattern of sleep is irregular, but many newborn babies sleep for between 16 and 20 out of 24 hours. Gradually, a pattern is established where babies sleep longer at night and less during daylight hours. It is important not to wake babies during deep sleep, as it plays a vital part in restoring energy levels.

(For further information on rest and sleep in babies and children, see pages 123–126.)

The need for love and security

It is impossible to 'spoil' a newborn baby by giving too much love and affection. Babies need a lot of loving attention: being talked to, played with and cuddled are all good ways to show love, and they create strong bonds of affection within the family. A baby will feel safe and secure only if caring adults respond promptly when they are crying.

Handling a newborn baby

Newborn babies love to be cuddled close to the adult's body, but you need to make sure that the whole body is supported when you pick the baby up. A baby's head is very heavy compared to the rest of the body, and the neck muscles are not developed enough to hold up the head unaided.

- **Make eye contact** and tell the baby that you are going to hold him/her before you pick him/her up, so s/he is not startled. (Newborn babies sometimes cry when they are first picked up because they dislike the sensation of being in the air.)
- **When picking a baby up** from the prone (lying down) position, either:
  a. scoop him/her up with both arms, with one hand supporting the bottom, and the other against the head, or
  b. lift him/her up under the arms, gently resting your fingers on the back of the head, then turning the baby so s/he lies cradled in your arms, with the head in the crook of your elbow.
- **Try to keep your movements slow and gentle** – babies dislike any sudden, jerky movements.
- **Hold the baby confidently and securely** – the baby will then feel secure too.

> **Important:** You must **never** shake a baby. **Never** play swinging games with a young baby. Shaking moves the head back and forward very quickly and with great force. This can tear tiny blood vessels in the baby's brain, possibly leading to fits, brain damage or even death.

Crying babies

All babies use crying as a way of communicating their needs. These include physical needs, such as hunger, tiredness, a wet nappy, being too hot or too cold, or even discomfort from tight clothing. Babies also cry because of anxiety or an emotional need such as affection. Often visible tears are not produced until the baby is about one month old, but the crying is just as distressing to both the baby and the parents. Parents and carers have to work out why the baby is crying – for example, the baby may be:

- hungry (the most common reason in the early days)
- cold
- hot
- thirsty
- bored
- uncomfortable (in a dirty nappy, perhaps)
- wanting a cuddle
- insecure (a jerky movement or sudden noise can startle a baby; some babies get upset when being undressed and bathed).

Parents of earlier generations were led to believe that babies' cries are meaningless reflexes, and that crying is a good way 'to exercise the lungs'. Child experts in the 1950s warned that parents would spoil their babies if they responded to crying, and advised them to leave babies to cry alone. Current research in neuroscience shows that this advice was wrong. We should always respond to babies' crying.

How to help a crying baby

- First, try to find out why the baby is crying:
  a. Make sure the baby is not hungry or thirsty.
  b. Check that the baby is not too hot or too cold.
  c. Check that the baby is not physically ill.
  d. Check if the baby's nappy needs changing.
  e. Treat any condition that causes pain – e.g. colic or teething problems.
- Cuddle the baby and try rocking him/her gently in your arms.
- Talk and sing to the baby.
- Take the baby for a walk (or – if feasible – a car ride).
- Play soothing music.

The need for protection

Newborn babies are completely dependent on caring adults to protect them from harm. This means keeping them safe from accidents by removing any hazards, and ensuring that a responsible adult is always at hand. Later on, parents will decide whether to protect their child from infection by choosing immunisation.

 REVISION QUESTIONS

1. Explain why newborn babies must be handled carefully.
2. Why is it important never to shake a baby or swing them through the air?
3. List six reasons why a baby might cry.
4. Describe three ways in which parents can comfort a crying baby.

 CHILD STUDY ACTIVITY

1. Find out how often and why the child cries.
2. How do the child's parents comfort the child?

3 The specific needs of the preterm (premature) baby

The majority of babies admitted to a special care baby unit (SCBU) or neonatal intensive care unit are there because they were premature (born many weeks before their due date). However, some babies may be brought to the unit because they have an infection and need intravenous antibiotics; others need extra monitoring; and others need breathing support. The length of a baby's stay varies from days to months, and depends on each baby's individual special needs. Reasons for being admitted for special care include:

- preterm (or premature) babies – those babies born before 37 weeks of pregnancy
- light-for-dates babies – those babies below the expected weight for their gestational stage (length of pregnancy)
- infection
- breathing problems
- feeding problems
- difficult births.

Special care baby units (SCBUs)

SCBUs are usually located within the maternity departments of general district hospitals. They employ specially trained midwives and paediatric nurses, and are designed to care for the 5 babies out of every 100 who require extra care that cannot be provided within the normal post-natal environment.

The principles of care in an SCBU are to keep the newborn baby warm and free from infection. This is achieved by expert care of babies in incubators. Babies who are more seriously ill and who require more intensive care will be transferred to a neonatal intensive care unit.

Neonatal intensive care units are situated in large regional hospitals and care for the smallest and most ill babies, using the most sophisticated technology and specialist skills.

Equipment used in the special care baby unit

There is a lot of technical equipment – particularly in the neonatal intensive care section – and it can be frightening for parents to see their tiny baby hooked up to machines by wires and tubes.

Incubators

Sometimes premature and sick babies are unable to regulate their own body

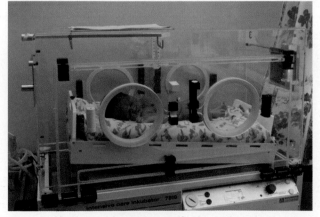

Figure 3.7 An incubator

temperature, which can drop quickly if they are left in normal air temperature. An incubator is a portable cot surrounded by a strong, clear, plastic covering. It incorporates an inbuilt alarm system, which monitors the baby's temperature to ensure that s/he does not become too cold or too hot.

Monitors

A monitor checks the baby's heartbeat, breathing and the amount of oxygen in the bloodstream. Small, soft sensor pads are placed on the baby's skin and are linked by cables to a monitor/display screen. These pick up the electrical signals given out by the baby's heart and constantly check that it is beating properly. The pads can also detect changes in breathing, and prolonged pauses in breathing may trigger an alarm.

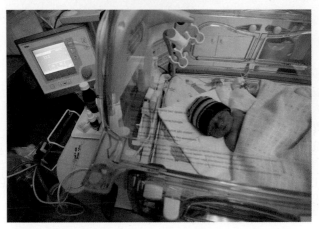

Figure 3.8 A monitor

Ventilators

A ventilator – or respirator – helps the baby to breathe. There are two types of ventilation. One helps the baby to breathe in a regular, mechanical way, and the other takes account of the baby's efforts and is called 'patient-triggered ventilation'.

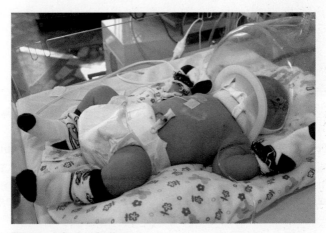

Figure 3.9 A ventilator

Nasogastric tube

Some premature or sick babies are unable to suck by themselves, so a small hollow tube is inserted into their mouth or nose to help carry either breast milk or formula directly into the baby's stomach. If the mother decides to breastfeed her baby, a midwife will show her how to express her milk from the day her baby is born. This breast milk will be fed to her baby through the feeding tube until the baby is strong enough to be fed naturally.

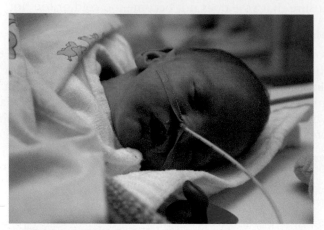

Figure 3.10 A nasogastric tube

Phototherapy units

Jaundice commonly occurs in premature infants, and treatment with the use of a phototherapy (light) unit can help to break down the yellow pigmentation caused by jaundice. These units are like mini sun lamps that shine light (often blue) on the baby while in the incubator. During the treatment, a soft mask will be used to cover the baby's eyes.

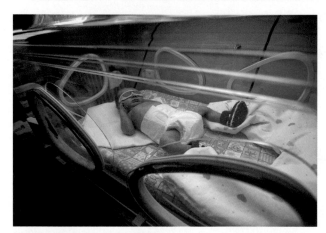

Figure 3.11 Phototherapy

The effects on the family when a baby is in a special care baby unit

Parents whose baby has had to be transferred to an SCBU or neonatal intensive care unit often feel very anxious and helpless. Such an environment can be very frightening for the parents, and staff will do everything they can to keep any separation to a minimum.

- **Feeling of helplessness:** The baby they had so eagerly anticipated now seems totally at the mercy of strangers and is surrounded by highly technical and often very noisy machinery. Parents frequently feel that there is nothing they can do to protect and care for their own child. Sometimes they feel guilty – that they did – or did not do – something which has caused their child to be ill.

- **Worry about the baby**: Low-birthweight babies usually sleep more and may seem less alert than full-term babies, and parents will welcome reassurance from the staff that this is normal behaviour. Premature babies also look very thin and frail and may have red, wrinkled skin. Parents will naturally worry whether their baby will survive and be healthy.
- **Bonding**: Some mothers may be too ill to visit their baby straightaway. Staff caring for neonates value the importance of early mother–baby bonding and encourage parents and close family to talk to and touch the baby, after observing the required hygiene precautions. If the baby is too ill or frail to leave the incubator, the hospital will take a photograph of the baby that the parents can have immediately.
- **Family members under strain**: Other children in the family will need caring for while the mother is with the new baby. Fathers may have to fit their visits around their normal working day.

 REVISION QUESTIONS

1. What are the basic needs of a newborn baby?
2. List three pieces of equipment in the special care baby unit (SCBU) and describe how they help in the care of premature or sick babies.

 RESEARCH ACTIVITY

Find out what advice and support are available for families with newborn babies in your area.

4 How the child develops physically from birth to five years

What are developmental norms?

Developmental norms are defined as **standards** by which the progress of a child's development can be measured. For example, the average age at which a child sits, learns to talk, walks or reaches puberty would be such a standard or norm, and would be used to judge whether the child is progressing normally.

Developmental norms are sometimes called **milestones** – they simply describe the recognised pattern of development that children are expected to follow. **Normative development** concerns the typical (normal) capabilities, as well as limitations, of most children of a given age within a given cultural group. It indicates a typical range of what children can and cannot be expected to do and learn at a given time.

It is important to keep in mind that each child will develop in a *unique* way. Using developmental norms helps in understanding these general patterns of development, while recognising the wide variation between individuals.

Holistic (or all-round) development

The various aspects of development are intricately linked – each affects and is affected by the others. For example, once children have reached the stage of emotional development when they feel secure being apart from their main carer, they will have access to a much wider range of relationships, experiences and opportunities for learning. Similarly, when children can use language effectively, they will have more opportunities for social interaction. If one aspect or area of development is hampered or neglected in some way, children will be challenged in terms of reaching their full potential.

Areas of development

Development is usually divided into four main areas:

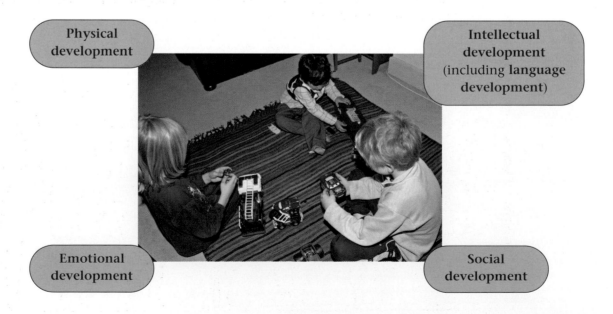

Physical development

Intellectual development (including **language** development)

Emotional development

Social development

These areas can be remembered by the acronym 'PIES'.

How the baby develops physically from birth to five years

Growth refers to an increase in physical size, and can be measured by height (or length in a baby), weight and head circumference. Growth is determined by:

- heredity
- hormones
- nutrition
- emotional influences.

Height

The most important factors controlling a child's growth in height are the genes and chromosomes inherited from the parents. Short parents will usually have short children, and tall parents will usually have tall children. As a child grows, the various parts of the body change in shape and proportion, as well as increasing in size. The different body parts also grow at a different rate – for example, the feet and hands of a teenager will reach their final adult size before the rest of the body.

From birth to adolescence there are two distinct phases of growth:

- **From birth to two years**: This period of very rapid growth lasts for about two years. The baby gains 25–30 cm in length and triples in body weight in the first year.
  Body proportions: The head of a newborn baby is a quarter of the length of the body.
- **From two years to adolescence**: This is a slower but steady period of growth that lasts from about two years of age through to puberty. The child gains 5–8 cm in height and about 3 kg in body weight per year until adolescence.
  Body proportions: A seven-year-old child's head is only about one-eighth of the length of the body.

This difference in body proportions explains why newborn babies appear to have such large eyes, and also why adolescents often appear to be clumsy or awkward in their physical movements.

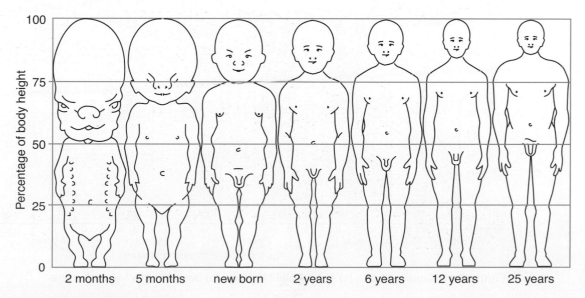

Figure 3.12 Body proportions

Weight-for-age GIRLS
Birth to 5 years (percentiles)

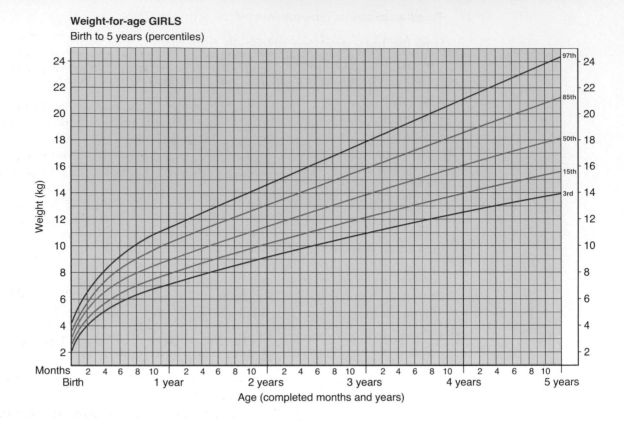

Length/height for age BOYS
Birth to 5 years (percentiles)

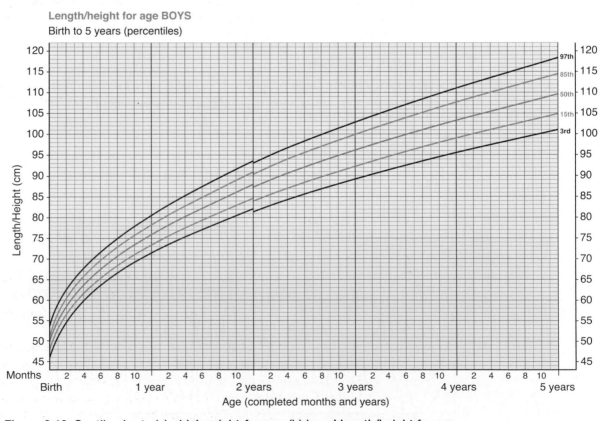

Figure 3.13 Centile charts (a) girls' weight-for-age (b) boys' length/height for age

Centile charts

These charts are used to compare the **growth pattern** of an individual child with the normal range of growth patterns that are typical of a large number of children of the same sex. The charts are used to plot height (or, in young babies, length) weight and head circumference. Note that:

- The 50th centile (or percentile) is the **median**. It represents the middle of the range of growth patterns. It means that in any typical group of 100 children, 50 would have a weight or height around this line.
- The 15th centile is close to the bottom of the range. If the height of a child is on the 15th centile, it means that in any typical group of 100 children, 85 would measure more and 15 would measure less.
- The 85th centile is close to the top of the range. If the weight of a child is on the 85th centile, then in any typical group of 100 children, 85 would weigh less and 15 would weigh more.

Physical development

Physical development involves the increasing skill and functioning of the body. The sequence of physical development involves gross motor skills first; these involve control of large muscles in the body, arms and legs. This is followed by development of fine manipulative skills, which depend on small muscle coordination.

1. **Gross motor skills**: These use the large muscles in the body, arms and legs, and include walking, running, climbing and so on.
2. **Fine motor skills**: These use the smaller muscles in the arms, hands and fingers, and involve precise use of the hands and fingers – for example, pointing, drawing, using a knife and fork or chopsticks, writing or doing up shoelaces.

Sensory development

Physical development also includes sensory development. **Sensation** is the process by which we receive information through the senses, which are:

- **sight**
- **hearing**
- **smell**
- **touch**
- **taste**.

Visual development

A newborn baby's eyes are barely half the size of an adult's, and although they are structurally similar, they differ in two ways:

- A baby's focus is fixed at about 20 cm, which is the distance from the baby to the mother's face when the baby is breastfeeding. Anything nearer or further away appears blurred. The baby remains short-sighted for about four months.
- The response to visual stimuli is slower in babies because the information received by the eye takes longer to reach the brain via the nervous pathway. A newborn baby is able only poorly to fix the eyes on objects and follow their movement. Head and eye movement is also poorly coordinated; in the first week or two, the eyes lag behind when the baby's head is turned to one side – a feature known by paediatricians as the 'doll's eye phenomenon'.

By around four months, a baby can focus on both near and distant objects, and the ability to recognise different objects is improving steadily. By six months, the baby will respond visually to movements across the room and will move the head to see what is happening. By one year, eye movements are smoother and the baby can follow rapidly moving objects with the eyes (a skill known as **tracking**). A squint is normal at this point.

The development of hearing

Newborn babies are able to hear almost as well as adults do.

* Certain rhythmic sounds – often called white noise – seem to have a special soothing effect on babies. The drone of a vacuum cleaner or a hairdryer is calming!
* The sound of a human voice evokes the greatest response, and the rhythms of lullabies have been used for centuries in all cultures to help babies to sleep, or to comfort them.
* Babies can recognise their own mother's voice from the first week, and can distinguish its tone and pitch from those of other people.
* Sudden changes in noise levels tend to disturb very young babies and make them jump.
* From about six months, a baby learns to recognise and distinguish between different sounds – for example, the sound of a spoon in a dish means that food is on its way.
* Babies can also discriminate between cheerful and angry voices, and will respond in kind.

The development of smell, taste and touch

The senses of smell and taste are closely linked. If our sense of smell is defective – for example, because of a cold – then our sense of taste is also reduced. Babies as young as one week old who are breastfed are able to tell the difference between their own mother's smell and other women's smells. From birth, babies are also able to distinguish the four basic tastes – sweet, sour, bitter and salty.

The sense of touch is also well developed in infancy, as can be demonstrated by the primitive reflexes (see pages 94–96). Babies seem to be particularly sensitive to touches on the mouth, the face, the hands, the soles of the feet and the abdomen. Research has shown that babies would rather be stroked than fed.

Proprioception is the sense that tells the baby the location of the mobile parts of his/her body (e.g. the legs) in relation to the rest of him/her – in other words, where his/her own body begins and ends.

Sensory deprivation

A congenitally blind baby (i.e. a baby who is born blind) will develop a more sophisticated sense of touch than a sighted baby, although they both start life with the same touch potential. As the sense of touch develops, so the area of the brain normally assigned to touch increases in size for the blind baby, and the area of the brain normally assigned to sight decreases.

Similarly, in a congenitally deaf baby, the part of the brain that normally receives auditory stimuli is taken over by the visual and movement input from sign language.

The pattern of development

Children's development follows a pattern:

* **From simple to complex**
  Development progresses from simple actions to more complex ones.

Example: Children stand before they can walk, and they can walk before they can skip or hop.

- **From head to toe**
  Development progresses downwards. Physical control and coordination begin with a child's head and develop down the body through the arms, hands and back, and finally to the legs and feet.
- **From inner to outer**
  Development progresses from actions nearer the body, to more complex ones further from the body.
  Example: Children can coordinate their arms, using gross motor skills to reach for an object, before they have learned the fine motor skills necessary to use their fingers to pick it up.
- **From generalised to specific**
  Development progresses from general responses to specific ones.
  Example: A young baby shows pleasure by a massive generalised response: the eyes widen, and the legs and arms move vigorously. An older child shows pleasure by smiling or using appropriate words or gestures.

The skills of locomotion and balance

- **Locomotion** is the ability to move around on your own. It is central to the pattern of developmental changes which occur at the end of the baby's first year, and begins with crawling or bottom-shuffling.
- **Balance** is the first of all the senses to develop. It is crucial to posture and movement.

The eight-month-old child who rolls backwards and forwards across the floor, with no particular goal in sight, is preparing his/her balance for:

- sitting
- standing
- walking.

Eye–hand coordination

The ability to reach and grasp objects in a coordinated way requires months of practice and close attention.

- In the first months after birth, eye–hand coordination takes effort.
- By around nine months of age, a baby can usually manage to guide his/her movements with a single glance to check for accuracy – for example, when feeding themselves with a spoon.

 KEY TERMS

Centile chart: Centile charts (also known as percentile charts or child growth charts) are used to monitor a child's growth regularly, and are usually contained in a child's Personal Child Health Record.

Holistic: Tending to see something as a whole – for example, seeing a child as a complete person, emotionally, intellectually, socially, physically, morally, culturally and spiritually.

Norm: An average or typical state or ability, used with others as a framework for assessing development. Norms are the result of observations by many professionals in the field of child development.

5 The development of fine and gross motor skills

As they develop from birth to the age of five years, most children will acquire the following skills. The age at which children acquire these skills varies greatly, but the average or normative development is shown below for gross and fine motor skills.

Gross motor skills

- Rolling over: 6 months
- Sitting: 9 months
- Crawling: 9–10 months
- Standing: 1 year
- Walking: 12–15 months
- Running: 2 years
- Pushing and pulling wheeled toys: 2 years
- Jumping: 2–3 years
- Climbing: 4 years
- Riding a trike: 4 years
- Bouncing a ball: 4 years
- Throwing and catching a beanbag or ball: 5 years

Fine motor skills

- Hand and finger play: 3 months
- Palmar grasp: 6 months
- Turning pages in book: 1 year
- Pointing to objects: 15 months
- Primitive tripod grasp: 18 months
- Fine pincer and tripod grasp: 2 years
- Threading large beads: 2.5 years
- Dynamic tripod grasp: 3 years
- Threading small beads: 4 years
- Dressing independently: 5 years

Physical development from birth to five years

It is important to know and understand the usual stages of development related to mobility, as well as being able to recognise differences between individual babies and children.

The following tables show the normative stages – or milestones – of children's physical development.

Age	Gross motor skills	Fine motor skills	Sensory development	How to promote development
Birth to 4 weeks	Lies **supine** (on the back), with head to one side. When placed on the front (the **prone** position), baby lies with head turned to one side, and by 1 month can lift the head. If pulled to sitting position, the head will lag, the back curves over and the head falls forward.	Turns head towards the light and stares at bright shiny objects. Is fascinated by human faces and gazes attentively at carer's face when fed or held. Hands are usually tightly closed and will grasp object placed in hand. Reacts to loud sounds, but by 1 month may be soothed by particular music.	Can focus on object 20–25 cm away. Startled by loud noises. Turns towards sounds.	Encourage the baby to lie on the floor to kick and experiment safely with movement. Provide an opportunity for the baby to feel the freedom of moving without a nappy or clothes on. Always support the head when playing with the baby, as the neck muscles are not strong enough to control movement. Provide a mobile over the cot and/or the nappy-changing area. Provide plenty of physical contact and maintain eye contact. Introduce the baby to different household noises. Provide contact with other adults and children. Encourage bonding with main carer by enjoying the relationship.
4 to 8 weeks	Can now turn from the side to the back. Can lift the head briefly from the prone position. Arm and leg movements are jerky and uncontrolled. There is head lag if the baby pulled to a sitting position.	Turns the head towards the light and stares at bright shiny objects. Will show interest and excitement by facial expression and will gaze attentively at carer's face while being fed. Will open the hand to grasp your finger.	Prefers female voices and high-pitched sounds. Eyes now work better together and can focus.	
2 to 3 months	When lying supine, the baby's head is in a central position. Can now lift the head and chest off the bed in a prone position, supported on forearms. There is almost no head lag in the sitting position. Legs can kick vigorously, both separately and together. Can wave the arms and bring the hands together over the body.	Moves the head to follow adult movements. Watches the hands and plays with the fingers. Holds a rattle for a brief time before dropping it.	Interest in faces and recognises mother. Prefers moving to still objects. Turns away from a foul smell.	Use a special supporting infant chair so that baby can see adult activity. Light rattles and toys strung over the pram or cot will encourage focusing and coordination. Sing while feeding or bathing the baby, allowing time for a response. Learn to distinguish the baby's cries and to respond to them differently. Tickling and teasing may induce laughter.

Table 3.1 The normative stages of physical development from birth to five years

Age	Gross motor skills	Fine motor skills	Sensory development	How to promote development
4 to 5 months	Has good head control.	Is beginning to use **palmar grasp.**	Explores objects with mouth.	Play rough-and-tumble games on the bed. Play bouncing games on the carer's knee to songs.
	Is beginning to sit with support and can roll over from the back to the side.	Can transfer objects from hand to hand.	Hands are open and the baby reaches out to touch and grasp.	Offer rattles and soft, squashy toys to give a variety of textures.
	Is beginning to reach for objects.	Is very interested in all activity.	Still prefers bright colours and contrasts.	Waterproof books in the bath give a lot of pleasure.
	When supine, the baby plays with the feet.	Everything is taken to the mouth (**mouthing**).		
	Holds the head up when pulled to a sitting position.	Moves the head around to follow people and objects.		
6 to 9 months	Can roll from front to back.	Is alert to people and objects.	Continues to explore objects with mouth.	Encourage confidence and balance by placing toys around the sitting baby. Ensure furniture is stable – no sharp corners when the baby is using it to stand.
	May attempt to crawl, but will often end up sliding backwards.	Is beginning to use **pincer grasp** with thumb and index finger.	Recognises voices and own name and tells tunes apart.	Encourage mobility by placing toys just out of the baby's reach.
	May grasp the feet and place them in the mouth.	Transfers toys from one hand to the other.	Looks towards sounds from above and below.	Small objects to encourage the pincer grasp (e.g. small pieces of biscuit), but **always** supervise.
	Can sit without support for longer periods of time.	Looks for fallen objects.		Provide simple 'musical instruments' (e.g. xylophone or wooden spoon and saucepan).
	May 'cruise' around furniture and may even stand or walk alone.	Everything is explored by putting it in the mouth.		
9 to 12 months	Is now mobile – may be crawling, bear-walking, bottom-shuffling or even walking.	**Pincer grasp** is now well developed and the baby can pick things up and pull them towards him/her.	Begins to look for things s/he has dropped.	Provide large-wheeled toys to push around – brick trucks serve the dual purpose of walking and stacking games.
	Can sit up on his/her own and lean forwards to pick things up.	Can poke with one finger and will point to desired objects.	Responds to simple commands.	Stacking and nesting toys.
	May crawl upstairs and onto low items of furniture.	Can clap hands and imitate adult actions.	Vision now almost as good as an adult's.	Cardboard boxes and saucepans to put things into and take things out of.
	May bounce in rhythm to music.	Throws toys deliberately.		Offer lots of play opportunities with adult interaction – sharing, taking turns, etc.
		Manages spoons and finger foods well.		Promote self-esteem by providing the baby's own equipment (e.g. flannel, toothbrush, cup and spoon).

Age	Gross motor skills	Fine motor skills	Sensory development	How to promote development
15 months	Probably walks alone, with feet wide apart and arms raised to maintain balance. Is likely to fall over and land suddenly on the bottom. Can probably manage stairs and steps, but will need supervision. Can stand without help from furniture or people. Kneels without support.	Can build with a few bricks and arrange toys on the floor. Holds crayon in **palmar grasp.** Turns several pages of a book at once. Can point to desired objects. Shows a preference for one hand, but uses either.	Stops using the mouth to explore as the hands become more skilled.	Provide stacking toys and bricks. Provide push-and-pull toys for children who are walking. Read picture books with simple rhymes. Big empty cardboard boxes are popular. Provide thick crayons or thick paintbrushes. Arrange a corner of the kitchen or garden for messy play involving the use of water or paint. **NB:** This is a high-risk age for accidents – be vigilant at all times.
18 months	Walks confidently and is able to stop without falling. Can kneel, squat, climb and carry things around. Can climb onto an adult chair forwards and then turn round to sit. Comes downstairs, usually by creeping backwards on the tummy.	Can thread large beads. Uses **pincer grasp** to pick up small objects. Builds a tower of three or more cubes. Scribbles to and fro on paper.	Hand–eye coordination is good. Recognises known people from a distance.	Push-and-pull toys are still popular. Teach the child how to manage stairs safely. Provide threading toys, and hammer and peg toys. Encourage and praise early attempts at drawing.
2 years	Is very mobile and can run safely. Can climb up onto the furniture. Walks up and down stairs, usually two feet to a step. Tries to kick a ball with some success, but cannot yet catch a ball.	Can draw circles, lines and dots, using preferred hand. Can pick up tiny objects using a **fine pincer grasp.** Can build a tower of six or seven bricks, with a longer concentration span. Enjoys picture books and turns pages singly.	At 2.5 years, begins to show a sense of colour.	Provide toys to ride and climb on, and space to run and play. Allow trips to parks, and opportunities for messy play with water and paints. Encourage use of safe climbing frames and sandpits, always supervised. Provide simple models to build (e.g. Duplo®), as well as jigsaw puzzles, crayons and paper, picture books and glove puppets.

Table 3.1 Contin.

Age	Gross motor skills	Fine motor skills	Sensory development	How to promote development
3 years	Can jump from a low step. Walks backwards and sideways. Can stand and walk on tiptoe and stand on one foot. Has good spatial awareness. Rides tricycle using pedals. Can climb stairs with one foot on each step – downwards with two feet per step.	Can build a tower of nine or ten bricks. Can control a pencil using thumb and first two fingers – the **dynamic tripod grasp.** Enjoys painting with a large brush. Can copy a circle.	Can name some colours – recognises red and yellow first. Enjoys listening to favourite stories.	Provide a wide variety of play things – dough for modelling, sand and safe household utensils. Encourage play with other children. Allow swimming and trips to park. May even enjoy long walks. Encourage art and craft activities. Promote independence by teaching the child how to look after and put away clothes and toys. Encourage visits to the library and story-times.
4 years	Sense of balance is developing; may be able to walk along a line. Can catch, kick, throw and bounce a ball. Can bend at the waist to pick up objects from the floor. Enjoys climbing trees and playing on climbing frames. Can run up and down stairs, one foot per step.	Can build a tower of ten or more bricks. Can draw a recognisable person on request, showing head, legs and trunk. Can thread small beads on a lace.	Names and matches four or five main colours. Blue and green usually follow red and yellow.	Provide plenty of opportunity for exercise. Play party games – musical statues, etc. Use rope swings and climbing frames. Obtain access to a bike with stabilisers. Provide small-piece construction toys, jigsaws and board games. Encourage gluing and sticking activities, also paint, sand, water and play dough. Prepare child for school by teaching how to dress and undress for games, and how to manage going to the toilet by him/herself.

Table 3.1 Contin.

Age	Gross motor skills	Fine motor skills	Sensory development	How to promote development
5 years	Can use a variety of play equipment – slides, swings, climbing frames. Can play ball games. Can hop and run lightly on toes, and move rhythmically to music. Sense of balance is well developed.	May be able to thread a large-eyed needle and sew large stitches. Can draw a person with head, trunk, legs, nose, mouth and eyes. Has good control over pencils and paintbrushes. Can copy a square and a triangle.	Names and matches ten or more colours. Can use knife and fork at mealtimes.	Provide plenty of outdoor activities. Encourage non-stereotypical activities (e.g. boys using skipping ropes, girls playing football). Team sports may be provided at clubs such as Beavers, Rainbows and Woodcraft Folk. Encourage the use of models, jigsaws, sewing kits and craft activities, as well as drawing and painting. Introduce tracing and image patterns.

Table 3.1 Contin.

6 Conditions for development

In order to ensure that children are able to grow and develop physically, certain conditions must be provided by their parents or carers. A warm home, nourishing food and safe, hygienic routines are all necessary to children's healthy development. (The routine care of children is covered on pages 123–141.)

There are very many factors which affect the healthy growth and development of children. These include:

- nutrition
- infection
- poverty and social disadvantage
- housing
- accidents
- environmental factors
- lifestyle factors
- emotional and social factors.

Many of the factors that adversely affect child health are closely interrelated, and make up a **cycle of deprivation**. For example, poorer families tend to live in poorer housing conditions and may also have an inadequate diet; lack of adequate minerals and vitamins as a result of poor diet leads to an increased susceptibility to infectious diseases and so on.

Nutrition

Milk – whether human or formula – is the fuel that makes babies grow more rapidly during the first year than at any other time. Both human and formula milk provide the right nutrients for the first months of life, with just the right balance of carbohydrates, proteins, fats, vitamins and minerals (see part four, pages 170–178).

Eating habits that are developed in childhood are likely to be continued in adult life. This means that children who eat mainly processed, convenience foods will tend to rely on these when they leave home. There are various conditions that may occur in childhood that are directly related to poor or unbalanced nutrition:

- **failure to thrive** (or faltering growth) – poor growth and physical development
- **dental caries** or tooth decay – associated with a high consumption of sugar in snacks and fizzy drinks
- **obesity** – children who are overweight are more likely to become obese adults
- **nutritional anaemia** – due to an insufficient intake of iron, folic acid and vitamin B12
- **increased susceptibility to infections** – particularly upper respiratory infections, such as colds and bronchitis.

Infection

During childhood there are many infectious illnesses that can affect children's health and development. Some of these infections can be controlled by childhood immunisations; these are diphtheria, tetanus, polio, whooping cough, measles, meningitis, mumps and rubella. Other infections can have long-lasting effects on children's health (see part four, pages 201–202).

Poverty and social disadvantage

Poverty is the single greatest threat to the healthy development of children in the UK. Growing up in poverty can affect every area of a child's development: physical, intellectual, emotional, social and spiritual.

- **Accident and illness:** Children living in poverty are four times more likely to die in an accident, and have nearly twice the rate of long-standing illness of those living in households with high incomes.
- **Quality of life:** A third of children in poverty go without the meals, toys or clothes that they need.
- **Poor nutrition:** Living on a low income means that children's diet and health can suffer.
- **Space to live and play:** Poorer children are more likely to live in substandard housing and in areas with few shops or amenities, where children have little or no space to play safely.
- **Growth:** They are also more likely to be smaller at birth and shorter in height.
- **Education:** Children who grow up in poverty are less likely to do well at school and have poorer school attendance records.
- **Long-term effects:** As adults, they are more likely to suffer ill health, be unemployed or homeless. They are more likely to become involved in offending, drug and alcohol abuse. They are more likely to become involved in abusive relationships.

Housing

Poor housing is another factor that puts people at a social disadvantage. Low-income families are more likely to live in:

- homes which are damp and/or unheated – this increases the risk of infection, particularly respiratory illnesses
- neighbourhoods that are unattractive and densely populated, with few communal areas and amenities – children without access to a safe garden or play area may suffer emotional and social problems
- overcrowded conditions – homeless families who are housed in 'hotels' or bed-and-breakfast accommodation frequently have poor access to cooking facilities, and have to share bathrooms with several other families; often children's education is badly disrupted when families are moved from one place to another.

Homelessness

It is estimated that about 180,000 children become homeless in England each year. Most of them will be living in temporary hostel accommodation or bed-and-breakfast housing. The vast majority of these children are in lone-parent families, with very little financial or extended family support. Most of these families become homeless to escape from violence from a partner or ex-partner, or from neighbours. The experience of homelessness causes many health problems for the children of such families:

- mental health problems, including delays in social or language development
- behavioural problems
- disruption of social relationships and difficulty in forming new friendships
- experience of marital conflict and domestic violence.

Accidents

Some childhood accidents have lasting effects on a child's healthy growth and development, and many are preventable (see pages 142–149).

Emotional and social factors

A child who is miserable and unhappy is not healthy, although s/he may *appear* physically healthy. All children need:

- **love and affection** – to receive unconditional love from their parents or primary carers
- **to feel secure**
- **stimulation** – healthy growth and development can be affected when a child receives too little (or too much) stimulation
- **opportunities to play**.

Child abuse, although not common, is bound to affect a child's health and well-being, and can have long-lasting health implications.

Environmental factors

Pollution of the environment can have a marked effect on children's health and development. The three main threats to health are **water pollution**, **air pollution** and **noise pollution**. Children are particularly vulnerable to air pollution. This is partly because they have a large lung surface area in relation to their small body size, which means that they absorb toxic substances quicker than adults do and they are slower to get rid of them. The effects of air pollution from factory chimneys, the use of chemical insecticides and car exhausts include the following:

- **Lead poisoning:** Children are particularly susceptible to lead poisoning, mostly caused by vehicle exhaust fumes. Even very low levels of lead in the blood can affect children's ability to learn.
- **Asthma:** Air pollution can act as a *trigger* for asthma and can make an existing condition worse. The incidence of asthma is much higher in traffic-polluted areas.
- **Cancer:** The use of insecticides and fertilisers by farmers has been linked with various childhood cancers. Radioactivity from nuclear power stations has also been found to cause cancer.

Lifestyle factors

Smoking

Children who live in a smoky atmosphere are more likely to develop:

- coughs and colds
- asthma
- chest infections (temperature with a bad cough)
- ear infections and glue ear.

Every year, 17,000 children are admitted to hospital with respiratory infections; research has found that many of these children are exposed daily to cigarette smoke. There is also an increased risk of children taking up the smoking habit themselves if one or both of their parents smoke.

Exercise

Some children take no regular physical exercise, apart from at school, and this is often because of the family's attitude and habits. Taking regular exercise allows children to develop their motor skills and to 'run off' any pent-up feelings of frustration and aggression.

- Coronary heart disease is the greatest single risk to health in the UK.
- Adults who are physically inactive have about double the chance of suffering from coronary heart disease.
- Children who do not take much exercise tend to become inactive adults.
- Obesity is more common in children who take little exercise.

7 The selection of clothing and footwear for babies and children

The same principles that apply to clothing for babies (see page 99) apply to the selection of clothes for children. Parents and carers should expect children to become dirty as they explore their surroundings, and they should not show disapproval when clothes become soiled.

Clothes for children should be:

- hard-wearing
- comfortable (i.e. soft fabrics which do not cause chaffing or friction)
- easy to put on and take off, especially when going to the toilet
- washable.

Types of clothes

- **Underwear** should be made of cotton, which is comfortable and sweat-absorbent.
- **Sleepsuits** – all-in-one pyjamas with hard-wearing socks – are useful for children who kick the bedcovers off at night. (These must be the correct size, to prevent damage to growing feet.)
- **Daytime clothes** should be adapted to the stage of mobility and independence of the child – for example, a dress will hinder a young girl trying to crawl; dungarees may prove difficult for a toddler to manage when being toilet-trained. Cotton jersey tracksuits, T-shirts and cotton jumpers are all useful garments which are easy to launder.
- **Outdoor clothes** must be warm and loose enough to fit over clothing while still allowing freedom of movement; a showerproof anorak with a hood is ideal, as it can be washed and dried easily.
- **Choose clothes which are appropriate for the weather** – for example, children need to be protected from the sun and should wear wide-brimmed hats with neck shields; they need warm gloves, scarves and woolly or fleece hats in cold, windy weather, and waterproof coats and footwear when out in the rain.

Footwear

Babies do not need shoes. The bones of the feet are not fully developed during the first year and can easily be damaged by shoes – and even socks – which restrict the natural movement of the toes and feet, especially if they are too small. The feet of babies and young children grow very quickly so that both socks and shoes can become too small in a matter of weeks. Although miniature versions of adult shoes are available in sizes to fit babies they should be discouraged; unfortunately, because of the availability of such products, there is a tendency to believe they are not harmful. Babies should be left barefoot as much as possible, especially once they become mobile, because their attempts to balance and efforts at walking strengthen and develop the supporting muscles of the foot, including the arch.

Once a child is walking, he or she will need shoes. Parents and carers should always go to a shoe shop where trained children's shoe-fitters can advise on a wide selection of shoes. Second-hand shoes should never be worn, as all shoes take on the shape of the wearer's foot.

Guidelines for choosing the correct footwear for children

- When shoes are fitted, there should be at least 1 cm between the longest toe and the inside of the shoe.
- Both feet should be measured for length, width and girth.
- Shoes must fit snugly around the heel and fasten across the instep, to prevent the foot sliding forward.
- The soles of the shoes should be flexible and hard-wearing; non-slip soles are safer.
- Leather is the ideal material for shoes that are to be worn every day, as it lets the feet 'breathe' – moisture can escape.
- Padders – soft corduroy shoes – keep a baby's feet warm when crawling or toddling, but should not be worn if the soles become slippery with wear.
- Shoes should never be bought a size too large, as they can cause friction and blistering.
- Wellington boots should not be worn routinely because they do not allow moisture to escape. However, they are very useful for outdoor play, with socks worn underneath.

8 The care needs of children

Children have certain basic needs:

- warmth
- rest and sleep
- cleanliness
- a healthy diet (see part four)
- fresh air and exercise
- routine
- a safe housing environment.

Warmth

Babies and young children need to be protected from cold and damp conditions. Newborn babies have not developed a way to keep themselves warm – for example, by shivering. They are totally dependent on the adults who care for them to keep them warm and protected from the effects of cold and damp weather. As their heads are relatively large in comparison with the rest of their body, they need to be dressed appropriately, in warm hats or bonnets.

Rest and sleep

Rest and sleep are important for our health and wellbeing. By the end of the first year, most babies are having two short sleeps during the day – before or after lunch and in the afternoon – and sleeping through the night, although there is much variation between individual children. It is important to have 'quiet periods', even if the baby does not want to sleep.

When we sleep, we rest and gain energy for a new day. But sleep does more than that. When we dream, we process all the events of our daily life. After a night without enough sleep, we often feel exhausted and irritable, but after a good night's sleep we feel rested, refreshed and full of energy. It is important to parents that their child sleeps through the night, as it influences the entire family's life and wellbeing. Children need more sleep than adults because the brain is developing and maturing and they are growing physically as well. Sleep is important to child health because:

- it rests and restores the body
- it enables the brain and the body's metabolic processes to recover (these processes are responsible for producing energy and growth)
- during sleep, growth hormone is released; this renews tissues and produces new bone and red blood cells
- dreaming is believed to help the brain sort out information stored in the memory during waking hours.

Children vary enormously in their need for sleep and rest. Some children seem able to rush around all day with very little rest; others will need to 'recharge their batteries' by having frequent periods of rest. You need to be able to recognise the signs that a child is tired; these may include:

- looking tired – dark rings under the eyes and yawning
- asking for their comfort object
- constant rubbing of the eyes
- twiddling their hair and fidgeting with objects
- showing no interest in activities or in their surroundings
- being particularly emotional – crying or being stubborn
- withdrawing into themselves – sucking thumb and appearing listless.

Guidelines: establishing a routine for rest and sleep

Children will sleep only if they are actually tired, so it is important that enough activity and exercise are provided. Some children do not have a nap during the day, but they should be encouraged to rest in a quiet area.

When preparing children for a daytime nap, rest or bedtime sleep, you need to:

- treat each child uniquely – every child will have their own needs for sleep and rest
- find out all you can about the individual child's sleep habits – for example, some children like to be patted to sleep, while others need to have their favourite **comfort object**
- be guided by the wishes of the child's parents or carers – for example, some parents prefer their child to have a morning nap but not an afternoon nap, as this fits in better with the family's routine
- reassure children that they will not be left alone and that you or someone else will be there when they wake up
- keep noise to a minimum and darken the room; make sure that children have been to the lavatory – children need to understand the signals which mean that it is time for everyone to have a rest or sleep
- provide quiet, relaxing activities for children who are unable or do not want to sleep – for example, jigsaw puzzles, a story tape or a book to read.

Different views about sleep and rest

There are cultural differences in how parents view bedtime and sleep routines. In some cultures it is normal for children to sleep with parents and to have a much later bedtime as a consequence. Some families who originate from hot countries, where having a sleep in the afternoon is normal, tend to let their children stay up in the evening. Such children are more likely to need a sleep while in day care – as long as the overall amount of sleep is sufficient for the child, it does not matter. As a carer, it is always worth discussing bedtime routines with parents when toddlers are struggling to behave well. Some areas have sleep clinics managed by the health visiting service, to help parents whose children have difficulty sleeping.

Even after they have established a good sleep routine, children's sleep patterns can become disrupted between the ages of one and three years. There are thought to be a number of factors for this, including developmental changes and behavioural issues.

Guidelines: establishing a bedtime routine for babies

Between three and five months, most babies are ready to settle into a bedtime routine:

- Give the baby a bath or wash and put on a clean nappy and night-wear.
- Take the baby to say goodnight to other members of the household.
- Carry the baby into his/her room, telling him/her in a gentle voice that it is time for bed.
- Give the last feed (breast or bottle) in the room where the baby sleeps.
- Sing a song or lullaby to help settle the baby, while gently rocking him/her in your arms.
- Wrap the baby securely and settle him/her into the cot or cradle, saying goodnight.
- If s/he likes it, gently 'pat' the baby to sleep.

The routine can be adapted as the baby grows. Advice from the Foundation for the Study of Infant Deaths (FSID) is that the safest place for a baby to sleep is in a cot in the parents' room for the first six months. After six months, the baby can be safely left in their own room.

When a baby dies suddenly and unexpectedly

Helpline
020 7233 2090
for families and professionals

Figure 3.14 A Foundation for the Study of Infant Deaths leaflet

Preventing sudden infant death syndrome

Sudden infant death syndrome (SIDS) is often called cot death. It is the term applied to the sudden, unexplained and unexpected death of an infant. The reasons for cot deaths are complicated and the cause is still unknown. Although cot death is the commonest cause of death in babies up to one year old, it is still very rare, occurring in approximately 2 out of every 1000 babies.

'Side' sleeping is not as safe as sleeping on the back, but it *is* much safer than sleeping on the front. Healthy babies placed on their backs are *not* more likely to choke. To prevent a baby wriggling down under the covers, place the baby's feet at the foot of the cot and make the bed up so that the covers reach no higher than the shoulders. Covers should be tucked in securely so that they cannot slip over the baby's head. Duvets or quilts, baby nests and pillows have the potential to trap air and may increase the risk of overheating.

How to put babies down to sleep

- Place babies on their back to sleep, with the feet near to the end of the cot to prevent the baby slipping under the covers ('feet to foot').
- Make sure the room is not too hot or too cold (it should be about 18–20° C). If the room is warm enough for you to be comfortable wearing light clothing, then it is the right temperature for babies.
- Do not overdress the baby – keep the head uncovered.
- Do not place the baby's cot in direct sunlight or near a radiator.
- Do not use duvets or quilts until the baby is over one year old.
- Do not smoke or let anyone else smoke near the baby.

How to help children to sleep

When preparing children for the night-time sleep, you need to follow the guidelines above and also to warn the child that bedtime is approaching (e.g. after the bath and story), and then follow a set **routine**. The following routine is just an example:

- Have a family meal about one and a half hours before bedtime. This should be a relaxing, sociable occasion.
- After the meal, the child could play with other members of the family.
- Make bath-time a relaxing time to unwind and play with the child – this often helps the child to feel drowsy.
- Give a final bedtime drink, followed by teeth cleaning. (Never withhold a drink at bedtime when potty-training – see pages 133–134.)
- Read or tell a story – looking at books together develops a feeling of closeness between the child and their carer.
- Settle the child in bed, with curtains drawn and nightlight on – if wanted – and then say goodnight and leave.

 REVISION QUESTIONS

1. When should a baby start to wear shoes?
2. Give four reasons why children need to sleep.
3. List five signs that a child is tired and needing to sleep.
4. What is the recommended position when putting babies down to sleep?
5. What other factors – apart from the sleeping position – could increase the baby's risk of cot death (sudden infant death syndrome)?
6. Describe a suitable bedtime routine for a toddler.

 CHILD STUDY ACTIVITY

Find out about the child's sleeping patterns – for example:

- Do they like to have a night-light on?
- Do they find it easy to settle on their own?
- Once asleep, do they wake up during the night?

Cleanliness: promoting and maintaining good hygiene and care routines

Caring for babies' skin and hair

A baby's skin is soft and delicate, yet it is also tough and supple. Young babies do not have to be bathed every day because only their bottom, face and neck, and skin creases get dirty, and because the skin may tend towards dryness. If a bath is not given daily, the baby should have the important body parts cleansed thoroughly – a process known as 'topping and tailing'; this limits the amount of undressing and helps to maintain good skin condition.

Whatever routine is followed, the newborn baby needs to be handled gently but firmly, and with confidence. Most babies learn to enjoy the sensation of water and are greatly affected by the attitude of their carer. The more relaxed and unhurried you are, the more enjoyable the whole experience will be.

Guidelines: topping and tailing for babies

- Babies do not like having their skin exposed to the air, so should be undressed for the shortest possible time. Always ensure the room is warm – no less than 20° C – and that there are no draughts.
- Collect all the equipment you will need before you start:
  a. a changing mat
  b. a small bowl of water that has been boiled and allowed to cool
  c. cotton-wool swabs
  d. lidded buckets, for soiled nappies and used swabs, and for clothes
  e. a large bowl of warm water
  f. protective cream (e.g. Vaseline®)
  g. clean clothes and a nappy.
- Warm a large, soft towel on a not-too-hot radiator and have it ready to wrap the baby in afterwards.
- Wash your hands. Remove the baby's outer clothes, leaving on the vest and nappy. Wrap the baby in the towel, keeping the arms inside.
- Using two separate pieces of cotton wool (one for each eye – this will prevent any infection passing from one eye to the other), squeezed in the boiled water, gently wipe the baby's eyes in one movement, from the inner corner outwards.
- Gently wipe all round the face and behind the ears. Lift the chin and wipe gently under the folds of skin. Dry each area thoroughly by patting with a soft towel or dry cotton wool.
- Unwrap the towel and take the baby's vest off, raise each arm separately and wipe the armpit carefully. The folds of skin rub together here and can become quite sore. Again, dry thoroughly and dust with baby powder, if used.
- Wipe and dry the baby's hands.
- Take the nappy off and place in a lidded bucket.

- Clean the baby's bottom with moist swabs, then wash with soap and water; rinse well with a flannel or sponge, pat dry and apply protective cream.
- Put on clean nappy and clothes.

Bathing the baby

When the bath is given will depend on family routines, but it is best not to bath the baby immediately after a feed, as s/he may be sick. Some babies love being bathed; others dislike even being undressed. Bath-time has several benefits for babies.

Benefits of bath-time

Bath-time provides:

- the opportunity to kick and exercise
- the opportunity to clean and refresh the skin and hair
- the opportunity for the carer to observe any skin problems, such as rashes or bruises
- a valuable time for communication between the baby and the carer
- a time for relaxation and enjoyment.

Before you start, ensure the room is warm and draught-free, and collect all the necessary equipment:

- small bowl of boiled water and cotton swabs (as for topping and tailing procedure)
- baby bath filled with warm water – test temperature with your elbow, not with hands, as these are insensitive to high temperatures; the water should feel warm but not hot
- changing mat
- lidded buckets
- two warmed towels
- clean nappy and clothes
- brush and comb
- toiletries and nail scissors.

Guidelines for a bathing routine

1. Undress the baby, except for the nappy, and wrap him/her in a towel while you clean the face, as for topping and tailing.
2. Wash the baby's hair before putting him/her in the bath: support the head and neck with one hand, hold the baby over the bath and wash the head with baby shampoo or soap; rinse the head thoroughly and dry with the second towel.
3. Unwrap the first towel from round the body, remove the nappy and place it in bucket.

4. Remove any soiling from the baby's bottom with cotton wool; remember to clean baby girls from front to back, to avoid germs from faeces entering the urethra or vagina.

5. Lay the baby in the crook of one arm and gently soap the body front and back with baby soap. (If preferred, use baby bath liquid added to the bath beforehand.)

6. Lift the baby off the towel and gently lower him/her into the water, holding one arm round the back of the neck and shoulders, and holding the far arm to stop the baby from slipping.

7. Talk to the baby and gently swish the water to rinse off the soap, paying particular attention to all skin creases – under arms, between legs and behind knees. Allow time for the baby to splash and kick, but avoid chilling.

8. Lift the baby out and wrap him/her in a warm towel; dry the baby thoroughly by patting, not rubbing.

9. Baby oil or moisturiser may now be applied to the skin; do not use talcum powder with oils, as it will form lumps and cause irritation.

10. Check if fingernails and toenails need cutting. Always use blunt-ended nail scissors and avoid cutting nails too short.

11. Dress the baby in clean nappy and clothes.

Additional advice: keeping babies clean

- Cultural preferences in skin care should be observed; cocoa butter or special moisturisers are usually applied to babies with black skin, and their bodies may be massaged with oil after bathing.

- Always put cold water in the bath before adding hot – many babies have been severely scalded by contact with the hot surface of the bath.

- Do not wear dangling earrings or sharp brooches, and keep your own nails short and clean.

- Do not top up with hot water while the baby is in the bath; make sure that taps are turned off tightly, as even small drops of hot water can cause scalds.

- From a few months old, babies may be bathed in the big bath, keeping the water shallow and following the same guidelines regarding temperature and safety. A non-slip mat placed in the bottom of the bath will prevent slipping.

- Avoid talcum powder because of the risk of inhalation or allergy; if it is used, place on your hands first and then gently smooth it on to completely dry skin.

- Do not use cotton-wool buds – they are not necessary and can be dangerous when poked inside a baby's ears or nose, which are self-cleansing anyway.

- Nail care should be included in the bathing routine. A young baby's nails should be cut when necessary. Do this after a bath when they are soft. Some parents use their own teeth to bite them off gently.

- Hair should be washed daily in the first few months, but shampoo is not necessary every day. A little bath lotion added to the bath water could be gradually worked into the baby's scalp until a lather forms; it may then be rinsed off using a wrung-out flannel.

- If the baby dislikes having his/her hair washed, try to keep hair washing separate from bath-time, so that the two are not associated as unpleasant events.

Important: Never leave a baby or young child alone in the bath – *even for a few seconds*.

Caring for children's skin and hair

As children grow and become involved in more vigorous exercise, especially outside, a daily bath or shower becomes necessary. Most young children love bath-time, and adding bubble bath to the water adds to the fun of getting clean.

Guidelines: caring for children's skin and hair

- Wash face and hands in the morning. (**NB:** Muslims always wash under running water.)

- Always wash hands after using the toilet and before meals; dry hands thoroughly – young children will need supervision.

- After using the toilet, girls should be taught to wipe their bottom from front to back to prevent germs from the anus entering the vagina and urethra.

- Wash hands after playing outside, or after handling animals.

- Nails should be scrubbed with a soft nailbrush, and trimmed regularly by cutting straight across; never cut into the sides of the nails, as this can cause sores and infections.

- Find out about any special skin conditions, such as eczema or dry skin, and be guided by the parents' advice concerning the use of soap and creams.

- Children should have their own flannel, comb and brush, which should be cleaned regularly.

- Skin should always be dried thoroughly, taking special care of such areas as between the toes and under the armpits; black skin tends towards dryness and may need massaging with special oils or moisturisers.

- Babies' and young children's hair should ideally be washed during bath-time, using a specially formulated mild baby soap or shampoo.

(Adult shampoos contain many extra ingredients, such as perfumes and chemicals – all of which can lead to irritation of children's delicate skin.)

- Hair usually only needs washing twice a week; children with long or curly hair benefit from the use of a conditioning shampoo, which helps to reduce tangles. Hair should always be rinsed thoroughly in clean water and not brushed until it is dry – brushing wet hair damages the hair shafts. A wide-toothed comb is useful for combing wet hair.

- Afro-Caribbean hair tends towards dryness and may need special oil or moisturisers; if the hair is braided (with or without beads), it may be washed with the braids left intact, unless otherwise advised.

- Rastafarian children with hair styled in dreadlocks may not use either combs or shampoo, preferring to brush the dreadlocks gently and secure them with braid.

- Regular combing and brushing will also help to prevent the occurrence of head lice.

Important: Children under the age of ten should NEVER be left alone in the bath or shower, because of the risk of drowning and scalding.

Care for a baby's bottom

Excretion

The first stool a newborn baby passes is **meconium** – a greenish-black, treacle-like substance which is present in the baby's bowels before birth and is usually passed within 48 hours of birth. Once the baby starts to feed on milk, the stools change:

- A breastfed baby has fluid, yellow mustard-coloured stools, which do not smell unpleasant.
- A bottle-fed baby has more formed stools which may smell slightly.

Babies pass urine very frequently. Bottle-fed babies tend to pass stools less often than breastfed babies. Constipation can occur in bottle-fed babies, but can be relieved by giving extra boiled and cooled water to drink.

Nappies

The choice of nappies will depend on several factors: convenience, cost, personal preference and concern for the environment. There are two main types of nappy:

- **Fabric nappies:** These are made from cotton terry towelling and come in different qualities and thicknesses. Two dozen are required for everyday use. Fabric nappies may be squares or shaped to fit. The latest style is similar in shape to the disposable nappy and has popper fastenings. If using fabric squares, you will also need special nappy safety pins and six pairs of plastic pants. Disposable one-way liners may be used with towelling nappies to keep wetness away from the baby's skin and to make solid matter easier to dispose of, by flushing down the toilet.
- **Disposable nappies:** These are nappy, liner and plastic pants all in one and are available in a wide range of designs. Some have more padding at the front for

boys and there are different absorbencies for day- and night-time use. Some makes have resealable tapes so that you can check if the nappy is clean.

Changing a nappy

Young babies will need several changes of nappy each day – whenever the nappy is wet or soiled. As with any regular routine, you should have everything ready before you begin:

- a plastic-covered, padded changing mat
- a bowl of warm water (or baby wipes)
- baby lotion
- barrier cream (e.g. zinc and castor oil cream)
- nappy sacks for dirty nappies
- cotton wool
- baby bath liquid
- new, clean nappy.

If you are using a special changing table or bed, make sure the baby cannot fall off. Never leave the baby unattended on a high surface. As long as there are no draughts and the room is warm, the changing mat can be placed on the floor.

A nappy routine

Guidelines for cleaning a girl:

1. First, wash your hands and put the baby girl on the changing mat.

2. Undo her clothing and open out the nappy.

3. Clean off as much faeces as possible with the soiled nappy.

4. Use wet cotton wool or baby wipes to clean inside all the skin creases at the top of the baby's legs. Wipe down towards her bottom.

5. Lift her legs using one hand (finger between her ankles) and clean her buttocks and thighs with fresh cotton wool, working inwards towards the anus. Keep clear of her vagina and never clean inside the lips of the vulva.

6. Dry the skin creases and the rest of the nappy area thoroughly. Let her kick freely and then apply barrier cream.

Guidelines for cleaning a boy:

1. First, wash your hands and place the baby boy on the changing mat. It is quite common for baby boys to urinate just as you remove the nappy, so pause for a few seconds with the nappy held over the penis.

2. Moisten cotton wool with water or lotion and begin by wiping his tummy across, starting at his navel.

3. Using fresh cotton wool or a wet wipe, clean the creases at the top of his legs, working down towards his anus and back.

4. Wipe all over the testicles, holding his penis out of the way. Clean under the penis. Never try to pull back the foreskin.

5. Lift his legs using one hand (finger between his ankles) and wipe away from his anus, to the buttocks and the back of the thighs.

6. Dry the skin creases and the rest of the nappy area thoroughly. Let him kick freely and then apply barrier cream.

Nappy rash

Almost all babies have occasional bouts of redness and soreness in the nappy area. This may be caused by leaving wet and dirty nappies on too long, poor washing techniques, infections, skin disorders such as eczema or seborrhoeic dermatitis, or reaction to creams or detergents.

The most common types of nappy rash are as follows:

1. **Candidiasis** or **thrush dermatitis** – this is caused by an organism called candida albicans, a yeast fungus which lives naturally in many parts of the body. The rash is pink and pimply and is seen in the folds of the groin, around the anus and in the genital area; it is sometimes caused in breastfed babies whose mothers have taken a course of antibiotics, or in bottle-fed babies where the teats have been inadequately cleaned and sterilised.

   Treatment:
   - Use a special antifungal cream at each nappy change. This is prescribed by the doctor.
   - Do not use zinc and castor oil cream until the infection has cleared, as the thrush organism thrives on it.
   - If oral thrush is also present, a prescribed ointment may be used.

2. **Ammonia dermatitis** – this produces the most severe type of nappy rash. It is caused when the ammonia present in the baby's urine and stools reacts with the baby's skin; it is more common in bottle-fed babies because their stools are more alkaline, providing a better medium for the organisms to thrive. The rash is bright red, may be ulcerated and covers the genital area; the ammonia smells very strongly and causes the baby a lot of burning pain.

   Treatment:
   - Wash with mild soap and water, and dry gently.
   - Expose the baby's bottom to fresh air as much as possible.
   - Only use creams if advised and leave plastic pants off.
   - If using towelling nappies, a solution of 30 ml vinegar to 2.5 litres of warm water should be used as a final rinsing solution to neutralise the ammonia.

Toilet training: learning bladder and bowel control

Children will not achieve control over their bowel or bladder function until the nerve pathways that send signals to the brain are mature enough to indicate fullness. This usually happens between two and three years of age, with most children achieving control by four years. Gaining control over these basic functions is a major milestone that relies on both psychological and physical readiness.

Guidelines: toilet-training

- Carers must discuss toilet-training with the parents and agree on when to start.
- Parents should not feel pressured into toilet-training their child; however, children do exhibit certain signs and behaviours that will indicate that they are developmentally ready to consider training – that is, they are likely to achieve control successfully and without too much difficulty, and parents may find this information helpful.

- You need to be able to recognise the signs that children are ready to be toilet-trained; these include:
  a. ability to pull down pants
  b. has bowel movements at regular times (e.g. after breakfast)
  c. is willing to sit on the toilet/potty without crying or fuss
  d. shows an interest in using it and will usually pass urine if placed on toilet/potty
  e. has a word or gesture to indicate a wet or soiled nappy.
- Anticipate when the child is likely to need the toilet – such as after meals, before sleep and on waking – and sit the child on the potty or toilet.
- Give children praise on 'going' and have a no-nonsense and sympathetic attitude to 'accidents'.
- Demonstrate that using the toilet is a normal activity that everyone does when they are old enough to manage it.

There are different opinions on using a potty or placing the child straight on the toilet. Privacy must be considered within the nursery setting and the potty placed in a cubicle if the child is used to a potty; however, if the toilet is child-sized, then they can be encouraged to use it. Aids such as clip-on seats and steps can be used to enable children to use an adult-sized toilet and still feel safe – some children are anxious about falling down the toilet.

Oral hygiene – caring for children's teeth

During the first year of life, babies eat their first solid food with the help of their primary teeth (or milk teeth). These 20 teeth start to appear at around the age of six months. There are three types of primary teeth:

- **incisors** – tough, chisel-shaped teeth, with a sharp edge to help in biting food
- **canines** – pointed teeth which help to tear food into manageable chunks
- **molars** – large, strong teeth which grind against each other to crush food.

Teething

The first tooth – usually in the middle of the lower jaw – appears at around six months of age. The complete set of 20 primary teeth (baby teeth) is usually present by the age of two-and-a-half years. Some teeth come through with no trouble at all. In other cases, the gum may become sore and red where the tooth is pushing its way out. A child may dribble and chew a lot or just appear fretful; it is often difficult to tell if this is really due to teething. To help a child with teething problems, you can:

- give the child something hard to chew on
- use teething rings that can be cooled in the fridge to soothe the sore gums
- use a special teething gel – available from chemist shops. These contain a local anaesthetic to provide some pain relief from sore gums.

Care of the first milk teeth is as important as for permanent teeth, since it promotes good habits and encourages permanent teeth to appear in the proper place. Every time the child eats sweet things, acid is produced which attacks the enamel of the tooth. Saliva protects the teeth from this and more saliva is produced during meals.

The protective effect lasts for about half an hour, so the more frequently the child eats sweets or sugary drinks, the more exposure to acid the teeth have. After the child's first birthday, children can be taught to brush their own teeth; but they will need careful supervision. You can help by following these guidelines.

Guidelines: caring for children's teeth

- Babies under one year should have their teeth brushed with a soft brush once or twice a day, using gentle toothpaste.

- Drinks should be given after meals – with water between meals. Bottles and cups should not contain fizzy or sweetened drinks, and fruit juice should be limited to mealtimes.

- Babies should not be allowed to have constant access to a bottle or cup.

- Babies should be encouraged to drink from a cup between 12 and 15 months.

- Teach children to brush their teeth after meals: show them how to brush up and away from the gum when cleaning the lower teeth and down and away from the gum when cleaning the upper teeth. (Younger children will need help in brushing the back teeth.)

- Crusty bread, crunchy fruit and raw vegetables such as carrot or celery help to keep teeth healthy and free of plaque – a substance that builds up on the teeth, attracting bacteria and causing tooth decay.

- Sweets may be given after meals, if at all.

- Take children to the dentist regularly so that they get used to the idea of having their mouth looked at.

The use of dummies

Parents often have strong views about the use of soothers and dummies. These are only likely to be harmful to tooth development if they are used constantly and habitually, or if they are sweetened, which is likely to cause decay. Dummies should be sterilised regularly and changed if they have been dropped on the floor. Dummies should *never* be sucked by adults before giving to babies, as this merely transfers bacteria from adult to child and can cause stomach upsets.

 REVISION QUESTIONS

1. Which areas must be washed when topping and tailing a baby?
2. Why should you always put cold water in the bath before adding hot water?
3. List five benefits of bath-time for young children.
4. What is meconium?
5. When do children begin to learn control over their bladder and bowel functions? Describe how an adult can help them to become toilet-trained.
6. What is plaque and how can it be prevented?

CHILD STUDY ACTIVITY

Observe the child during bath-time. Record your observation, noting, for example:

- the child's behaviour and enjoyment
- which toys are provided and played with
- the language used by the child
- the interaction between adult and child.

Physical activity and exercise

Exercise is essential for children's growth and development, because it:

- reduces their risk of developing heart disease in later life
- strengthens muscles
- helps to strengthen joints and promotes good posture
- improves balance, coordination and flexibility
- increases bone density, so bones are less likely to fracture.

Apart from these obvious physical benefits, regular exercise develops a child's **self-esteem**, by creating a strong sense of purpose and self-fulfilment; children learn how to interact and cooperate with other children by taking part in team sports and other activities.

Promoting exercise in children

Children need to learn that exercise is fun; the best way to convince them is to show by example. Bear in mind that some team games do not provide all children with the same opportunity for exercise, as they often involve several children standing around for long periods. Some children dislike competitive sports and prefer other activities – for example, dancing. Parents should try to find an activity that the individual child will enjoy, such as swimming or roller-skating. Older children could be encouraged to join a local sports or gym club; some areas provide 'gym and movement' or yoga classes for toddlers. It is often easier to persuade a child to take up a new activity if they know they will meet new friends. Family outings could be arranged to include physical activity, such as swimming, walking or boating.

The importance of physical play

Through opportunities for physical play, children steadily become better at those skills requiring coordination of different parts of the body, such as:

- hands and eyes for throwing and catching
- legs and arms for skipping with a rope.

Physical play helps children to:

- **express ideas and feelings** – children become aware that they can use their bodies to express themselves by moving in different ways, as they respond to their moods and feelings, to music or to imaginative ideas
- **explore what their bodies can do** and become aware of their increasing abilities, agility and skill; children's awareness of the space around them and what their bodies are capable of can be extended by climbing and balancing on large-scale apparatus, such as a climbing frame, wooden logs and a balancing bar, and by using small tricycles, bicycles and carts

- **cooperate with others** in physical play and games; children become aware of physical play as both an individual and a social activity – in playing alone or alongside others, in playing throwing and catching with a partner, in using a seesaw or pushcart, or in joining a game with a larger group
- **develop increasing control of fine movements** of the fingers and hands (fine motor skills) – for example, playing musical instruments and making sounds with the body, such as clapping or tapping, help develop fine motor skills in the hands and fingers, while also reinforcing the link between sound and physical movement; helping with household tasks – washing up, pouring drinks, carrying bags – also develops fine motor skills
- **develop balance and coordination**, as well as an appreciation of distance and speed; energetic play that involves running, jumping and skipping helps children to develop these skills
- **develop spatial awareness** – for example, dancing and moving around to music develop spatial awareness while also practising coordination and muscle control.

The benefits of playing outdoors

Opportunities for physical activity should be provided both inside and out. Regular sessions of indoor physical play or visits to local sports and leisure centres are particularly important when the weather limits opportunities for outdoor play. The outdoors environment can provide a scale and freedom for a type of play that is difficult to replicate indoors. For example, outdoors there are opportunities for children to:

- ride a bicycle or tricycle
- dig a garden
- explore woodland

Figure 3.15 Children playing outdoors

- play hide-and-seek or a chasing game
- run on the grass and roll down a grassy slope
- play with bats and balls.

Visits to swimming pools, where these can be arranged, can help children to enjoy and gain confidence in the water at an early stage.

Children benefit from playing in the fresh air, as long as they are suitably dressed for the weather. All places in which children play should be checked regularly to make sure a safe and hygienic environment is being provided.

Guidelines for ensuring a hygienic outdoor environment

- Check the outdoor play area daily for litter, dog excrement and hazards such as broken glass, syringes or rusty cans.
- Follow the sun safety code; provide floppy hats and use sun cream (SPF 15) to prevent sunburn (if parents give their permission).
- Check all play equipment for splinters, jagged edges, protruding nails and other hazards.
- Supervise children at all times.
- Keep sand covered and check regularly for insects, litter and other contamination.
- Keep gates locked and check that hinges are secure.

Routines

The importance of routines

One aspect of children's need for love and security is the need for **routine** (i.e. the usual way that tasks or activities are arranged) and predictability. This is why having daily routines is so important in all aspects of childcare. By meeting children's need for routine, parents and carers are helping the child to:

- feel acknowledged
- feel independent
- have increased self-esteem.

Routines – for example, around mealtimes and bedtimes – can be very useful in helping babies and toddlers to adapt both physically and emotionally to a daily pattern; this will suit both them and those caring for them. It will prove especially helpful during times of **transition** and change in their lives, such as starting nursery or moving house. If certain parts of the day remain familiar, children can cope better with new experiences. Having routines for everyday activities also ensures that care is consistent and of a high quality.

All settings that provide care and education for children have **routines** for daily activities. This does not mean that every day is the same; rather, it means that there is a recognised structure to the child's day – one that will help children to feel secure and safe. Such routines include:

- hygiene – changing nappies and toileting older children; ensuring there is a hand-washing routine after messy activities and before eating and drinking
- health and safety – tidying away toys and activity equipment; making regular checks on equipment for hazards
- safety at home-time and during trips away from the setting – ensuring there is a correct ratio of adults to children, permission from parents, contact numbers and so on

- mealtimes and snack-times – serving of meals and drinks under close supervision
- sleep and rest
- outdoor play.

Supporting hygiene routines

All children benefit from regular routines in daily care. You need to encourage children to become independent by helping them to learn how to take care of themselves. Ways of helping children to become independent include:

- teaching children how to wash and dry their hands before eating or drinking
- making sure that children always wash and dry their hands after going to the toilet and after playing outdoors
- providing children with their own combs and brushes, and encouraging them to use them every day
- providing a soft toothbrush and teaching children how and when to brush their teeth
- ensuring that you are a good role model for children – for example, always covering your mouth when you cough or sneeze
- making sure that children are provided with a healthy diet, and that there are opportunities for activity, rest and sleep throughout their day.

Planning routines to meet individual needs

Anyone looking after children should be able to adapt to their individual needs, which will change from day to day. You therefore need to be flexible in your approach and allow, whenever feasible, the individual child to set the pattern for the day – as long as all the child's needs are met. Obviously, parents and carers have their own routines and hygiene practices, and these should always be respected. (For example, Muslims prefer to wash under running water, and Rastafarians wear their hair braided and so may not use a comb or brush.)

Whenever you are caring for children, you should always treat each child as an individual. This means that you should be aware of their individual needs at all times.

- Sometimes a child may have special or additional needs.
- Children may need specialist equipment or extra help with play activities.
- Routines may need to be adapted to take into account individual needs and preferences.

Guidelines: everyday routines for babies and young children

- Be patient – even when pressed for time, try to show children that you are relaxed and unhurried.
- Allow time for children to experiment with different ways of doing things.
- If you work directly with parents, encourage them to make a little extra time in the morning and evening for children to dress and undress themselves. Children could be encouraged to choose their clothes the night before from a limited choice; the choosing of clothes to wear is often a fertile ground for disagreements and battles of will.
- Resist the urge to take over if children are struggling, since this

deprives them of the sense of achievement and the satisfaction of success.

- Show children how to do something and then let them get on with it. If they ask for help, they should be shown again. If adults keep doing things for children that they could do for themselves, they are in danger of creating 'learned helplessness' – the child knows that if they give up on a task, someone else will do it.

- Offer praise and encouragement when children are trying hard, not just when they succeed in a task.

 REVISION QUESTIONS

1. Why are physical play and exercise important for children?
2. How do children benefit from having routines for sleeping, mealtimes, bathing and so on?

 RESEARCH ACTIVITY

Visit a nursery or crèche and find out what routines they have for:

- sleep and rest
- feeding or mealtimes and snack-times
- hygiene – washing hands
- play
- story-time or quiet period.

The importance of the housing environment

The environment in which children grow and develop has a profound influence on all aspects of their lives, including their physical, cultural, emotional, social and spiritual development. In addition, the surroundings in which we all live have an effect on our lifestyle and behaviour.

Difficult environments

In recent years, the UK's inner cities have become less pleasant places to live because of the increase in:

- **air pollution** (e.g. from car exhausts and industrial effluents)
- **poverty** and **unemployment**
- **poor living conditions**, often with no access to outdoor play space
- **social isolation** – there are increasing numbers of one-parent families who have no access to an extended family network
- **discrimination** on the basis of ethnicity or disability – this is often reinforced by planning decisions (e.g. lack of access or mobility for people with physical disabilities).

The rural environment also poses problems for families where there is high unemployment or subsistence on low incomes; public transport may be limited and housing may be difficult to obtain.

There is far more to creating a positive environment for children than just meeting their basic needs. Children and families need an integrated environment – that is, one that provides:

- safety and hygiene
- adequate housing
- education and stimulation
- freedom from discrimination
- a caring ethos – everyone who works with young children should have a caring attitude
- access to health and social care services
- equality of opportunity
- a nourishing diet
- opportunities for play – with peers, indoors and outdoors in gardens.

If any of these needs are not met, the family (and the children) will experience stress.

9 Safety and prevention of common childhood accidents

Understanding why accidents happen and how to prevent them

Accidents are the main cause of death and serious injury in children. Every child is likely to go to hospital three times before the age of 15 as a result of an accident. Accidents happen to children every day – some of them serious – but that does not mean they simply have to be a part of growing up. Many serious and fatal accidents can be prevented, and injuries caused by accidents can be reduced.

Children need to explore and to learn about the things around them – they are naturally inquisitive. The safer you make the child's home and nursery, the less likely it is that their exploration will end in an accident. There are dangers outside the home – on the roads, in the car and just being outdoors. The pattern of accidents tends to vary with age, depending on the child's developmental progress and exposure to new hazards.

 QUICK FACTS

In the UK:
- most accidents involving children occur in the family home
- the commonest cause of accidental death in babies under one year old is **choking** – followed by **suffocation**
- three children are killed in accidents every day
- 10,000 children are permanently disabled each year
- each year, one in six children attends an accident and emergency department.

Why do accidents happen?

- **Babies** are vulnerable to accidents because they have no awareness of danger and cannot control their environment; they are *totally* dependent on their parents or carers to make their world safe.
- **Children** are naturally curious and need to investigate their surroundings. As children get older and their memory develops, they start to realise that certain actions have particular consequences (e.g. touching a hot oven door hurts), so they begin to learn a measure of self-protection.

Parents need to have a good understanding of child development in order to anticipate when an accident is likely to happen. Not all childhood accidents are preventable, but parents have a duty to make their home a safe place for children.

Situations when accidents are more likely to happen

Lack of awareness: Parents tend to react to an existing threat of danger, rather than anticipating things that may happen. For example, parents may report that they had not even realised their child could climb onto a stool, so had not thought to remove the dangerous object.

Over-protection: A child whose parents are overprotective may become timid and will be less aware of dangers when unsupervised.

Stress: When adults and children are worried or anxious, they are less alert and less aware of possible dangers.

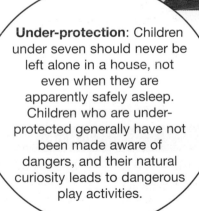

Under-protection: Children under seven should never be left alone in a house, not even when they are apparently safely asleep. Children who are under-protected generally have not been made aware of dangers, and their natural curiosity leads to dangerous play activities.

Poor role models: Adults who are always in a hurry may dash across the road instead of crossing in a safe place. Children will imitate their actions, and are less able to judge the speed of traffic than adults.

Common childhood accidents

The likelihood of different types of accidents occurring depends on the following:

- **The age and developmental capabilities** of the child – for example, bicycle accidents are more likely in older children; accidents involving poisoning are commoner in younger children.
- **The environment**: indoor or outdoor, child-aware or not – for example, toddlers visiting childless relatives are more likely to find hazards, such as trailing electrical flexes, loose rugs or unsecured cupboards containing potentially dangerous cleaning products, than they would in a household with children.

- **The degree of supervision** available – for example, inquisitive toddlers with little appreciation of danger need more supervision in an environment that is not child-aware. At the same time, the adult may be less aware of potential dangers due to the distractions – for example, holding an adult conversation with a friend, talking on the phone (especially mobile phones) or in a busy shopping centre where there is a lot of visual stimulation.

Common childhood accidents include:

- choking and suffocation
- falls
- burns and scalds
- poisoning.

Table 3.2 shows the injuries most common to children and the age group that is most likely to experience them

Choking and suffocation	High-risk age	Burns and scalds	High-risk age
Use of pillows Unsupervised feeding Play with small parts of toys Plastic bags Peanuts Cords and ribbons on clothes	Under 1 year	Matches, lighters, cigarettes Open fires and gas fires Baths Kettles and irons Cookers Bonfires and fireworks	From 9 months on, when children are newly mobile
Falls	**High-risk age**	**Poisoning**	**High-risk age**
Stairs Unlocked windows Bouncing cradles left on worktops, etc. Pushchairs and high chairs Climbing frames	Under 3 years	Household chemicals, e.g. bleach and disinfectant Medicines Berries and fungi Waste bins Vitamins	1 to 3 years
Electric shocks	**High-risk age**	**Road accidents**	**High-risk age**
Uncovered electric sockets Faulty wiring	Under 5 years	Running into the road Not wearing child restraints in cars Playing in the road	All ages up to 14 years
Drowning	**High-risk age**	**Cuts**	**High-risk age**
Unsupervised in the bath Ponds and water butts Swimming pools, rivers and ditches	Under 4 years	Knives, scissors and razor blades Sharp edges on doors and furniture Glass doors	1 to 8 years

Table 3.2 Risks of accidental injury to children

The prevention of accidents

Children need a safe environment, so that they can explore, learn and grow. As they develop, older children need to learn how to tackle everyday dangers so that they can become safe adults. Children learn some realities of safety the hard way – by banging their heads or grazing their knees. You cannot prevent them from hurting themselves altogether, but you can alert them and keep reminding them. Parents and child carers can reduce the risks of childhood accidents by following these guidelines.

> - Be a good role model – set a safe example.
> - Make the home, garden and nursery as accident-proof as possible.
> - Teach children about safety – make them aware of dangers in their environment.
> - Never leave children alone in the house.
> - Always try to buy goods displaying the appropriate safety symbol (see section on 'Safety issues' on pages 152–155).

Guidelines for preventing choking and suffocation

Choking (followed by suffocation) is the largest cause of accidental death in babies under one year. Older children are also at risk when playing on their own or eating unsupervised.

> **DO NOT:**
> - leave rattles, teething rings or squeeze-toys in the baby's cot – they can become wedged in the baby's mouth and cause suffocation
> - use a pillow for babies under one year old; baby nests must have a flat head and should only be used for carrying a baby – not for leaving a sleeping baby unattended
> - let a baby or young child get hold of tiny items like coins, marbles, dried peas, buttons or Lego® – small children explore with their mouths and can easily choke on small objects
> - leave babies alone with finger foods such as bananas, carrots, cheese; always supervise eating and drinking
> - give peanuts to children under four years because they can easily choke on them or inhale them into their lungs, causing infection and lung damage
> - leave a baby alone propped up with a bottle – always hold the baby while feeding
> - leave a baby alone who is playing with paper, as s/he may bite off small pieces and choke on them.
>
> **DO:**
> - use a firm mattress – for children over one year old, use a pillow that allows air to pass through freely, whatever position the child is in
> - check that there are no hanging cords – for example, from a window

blind – which could catch around a child's neck and strangle them if they fell

- keep all plastic bags away from babies and children, and teach older children never to put plastic bags on their heads
- be aware that dummies on long ribbons, and cardigans with ribbons around the neck, can pull tight around a baby's neck if caught on a hook or knob; a dummy must meet safety standards, with holes in the flange, in case it is drawn into the back of the throat; older children have been strangled by tie-cords on anoraks
- check that any toys given to babies and young children are safe, with no small loose parts or jagged edges.

Guidelines for preventing burns and scalds

As children learn to crawl, climb and walk, the risk of scalds or burns increases.

DO NOT:

- leave burning cigarettes in ashtrays
- use tablecloths that young children can pull down on top of themselves
- use gas or paraffin heaters in children's bedrooms
- leave a hose lying in the sun – water in it can get hot enough to scald a baby
- leave a hot iron unattended
- iron where children are likely to run past (and you should try to use a coiled flex).

DO:

- keep the water temperature for the house set at about 60° C (140° F), to prevent scalds and burns
- protect fires with a fixed fine-mesh fireguard (NB: It is illegal to leave a child under 12 in a room with an open fire)
- keep matches and lighters well out of reach
- choose nightclothes and dressing gowns that are flame-resistant
- install automatic smoke alarms
- use fire doors in nurseries and schools, and check you know the location of fire extinguishers and fire blankets
- keep children away from bonfires and fireworks; attend only safe, public displays
- keep a young child away from your area while you are cooking; always turn pan handles inwards; cooker guards are not a good idea as they can get very hot
- keep kettles and hot drinks well out of reach; use a coiled kettle flex, and never pass hot drinks over the heads of children
- test bath water before putting a child in; always put cold water in first and then add the hot water; a special plastic-strip thermometer can be stuck to the side of the bath to check the temperature
- teach children about the dangers of fire.

Guidelines for preventing falls

All children fall, but there are ways of ensuring that they do not fall too far or too hard.

DO NOT:

- use baby-walkers – child-safety experts agree that these are dangerous and cause many accidents, as babies steer themselves into dangerous situations
- place furniture under windows where children may be tempted to climb
- leave babies unattended on a table, work surface, bed or sofa; lie them on the floor instead.

DO:

- use stair-gates at the top and bottom of stairs, and at doors that might be left open
- fit vertical bars to dangerous windows (NB: Horizontal bars encourage climbing)
- fit childproof window safety catches on all windows
- use a safety harness in the highchair, pram, pushchair or supermarket trolley
- teach children how to use the stairs safely – teach them to come downstairs backwards on all fours.

Guidelines for preventing poisoning

The peak age for accidents with poisons is one to three years old, when children are highly mobile and inquisitive.

DO NOT:

- store dangerous household chemicals (bleach, disinfectant, white spirit) in the cupboard under the sink – use a safer, locked cupboard instead
- transfer chemicals (e.g. weed killer) into other containers, such as a lemonade bottle, as a child will not know the difference until it is too late.

DO:

- keep all medicines in a locked cupboard
- use childproof containers and ensure that they are closed properly
- teach children not to eat berries or fungi in the garden or in the park
- keep rubbish and kitchen waste in a tightly covered container or, better still, behind a securely locked door
- make sure that if surma is used on a child's eyes it is a lead-free brand (surma or kohl is a preparation used as eyeshadow in some Asian cultures) – check with a pharmacist
- store children's vitamins in a safe place – poisoning by an overdose of vitamins is very common.

Guidelines for preventing cuts

Glass presents the biggest safety hazard to young children; every year, about 7000 children end up in hospital after being cut by glass.

DO:

- use special safety glass in doors – this is relatively harmless if it does break, whereas ordinary glass breaks into sharp, jagged pieces
- mark large picture windows with coloured strips to make it obvious when they are closed
- use plastic drinking cups and bottles
- keep all knives, scissors and razors out of reach
- teach children never to run with a pencil or lolly stick in their mouth
- use safety scissors when cutting paper and card
- teach children never to play with doors; if possible, fit a device to the top of doors to prevent them from slamming and pinching fingers.

Guidelines for preventing drowning

A baby or toddler can drown in a very shallow amount of water – even a bucket with a few inches of water in it presents a risk. If a small child's face goes underwater, they will automatically breathe in so that they can scream. This action will fill their lungs with water.

DO NOT:

- ever leave a child alone in the bath
- leave an older child looking after a baby or toddler in the bath.

DO:

- use a non-slip mat in the bath
- always supervise water play
- guard ponds, water butts and ditches
- keep the toilet lid down at all times or fit a locking device – toddlers are fascinated by the swirling water action, and can fall in and drown.

Guidelines for preventing electric shocks

Children may suffer electric shock from poking small objects into sockets or from playing with electric plugs.

DO:

- fit safety dummy plugs or socket covers to all electric sockets
- check that plugs are correctly wired and safe; when buying Christmas tree lights, check for the Kitemark
- prevent children from pulling at electric cords by installing a cord holder which will make the cord too short to reach over the edge of the table or work surface.

Guidelines for sun safety

> **DO NOT:**
> - let children run around in only a swimsuit or without any clothes on
> - let children play in the sun between 11 a.m. and 3 p.m. when the sun is at its highest and most dangerous.
>
> **DO:**
> - keep babies under the age of nine months out of the sun altogether
> - cover children in loose baggy cotton clothes, such as an oversized T-shirt with sleeves; some special fabrics have a sun protection factor
> - protect a child's shoulders and back of neck when playing, as these are the most common areas for sunburn – let a child wear a legionnaire's hat, or a floppy hat with a wide brim that shades the face and neck
> - cover exposed parts of the child's skin with a sunscreen, even on cloudy or overcast days – use one with a minimum sun protection factor (SPF) of 15 and reapply often
> - use waterproof sunblock if the child is swimming.

❓ REVISION QUESTIONS

1. What are the most important factors in preventing childhood accidents?
2. What is the commonest cause of accidental death in babies under one year old?
3. List four possible ways of preventing each of the following childhood accidents:
   a. poisoning
   b. scalds and burns
   c. choking
   d. falls
   e. cuts.

CHILD STUDY ACTIVITY

Identify the risks of accident in the child's home by checking for hazards.

10 The importance of road and car safety

Road safety

Educating children about safety on the roads should begin at a very early age, the best method being by example.

Children need to learn about road safety in the same way as they learn any new skill: the message needs to be repeated over and over again until the child really has learned it.

> When walking on the pavement, parents and carers should:
>
> - set a good example, as young children will copy adults
> - hold their child's hand and put reins on a younger child if they are not strapped in a pushchair
> - not allow their child to run ahead
> - look out for and encourage their child to be aware of hidden entrances or driveways crossing the pavement
> - make sure their child walks on the side of the pavement away from the traffic
> - not let their child out alone or even with an older child
> - always use a zebra or light-controlled crossing, or a school crossing patrol, if there is one.
>
> 'Walking bus' schemes, which allow children to walk to and from school in supervised groups safely, can also help children to learn how to negotiate roads safely.

The Green Cross Code

The Green Cross Code is a very good method of teaching road safety to young children.

The Green Cross Code

1. Think first. Find the safest place to cross then stop.

2. Stop. Stand on the pavement near the kerb.

3. Use your eyes and ears. Look all around for traffic and listen.

4. Wait till it is safe to cross. If traffic is coming let it pass.

5. Look and listen. When it is safe, walk straight across the road.

6. Arrive alive. Keep looking and listening for traffic while you cross.

Figure 3.16 The Green Cross Code

QUICK FACTS

- Every year in the UK, more than 400 children under the age of 15 years are killed on the roads, and many more are seriously injured.
- If hit by a car travelling at 40 mph, four out of five child pedestrians will die. If hit by a car travelling at 30 mph, four out of five will survive. Children's survival rates increase even more as the speed of the car decreases.
- The peak time for child casualties is weekdays, 3 p.m. to 5 p.m., coinciding with the end of the school day. Friday is the peak day for child casualties.
- Children under five cannot judge how fast vehicles are going or how far away they are.

Safety when travelling in cars

Children travelling in a car who are not strapped in with a seatbelt, or who are not placed in a child seat, are at risk of serious injury or death in the event of a car accident. The relatively large weight of a child's head makes them particularly vulnerable if they are thrown forward.

The law states that children of all ages must be fastened in a car, using a safety restraint. This applies to a newborn baby as well as a teenager. The driver of the car is responsible for making sure that everyone is wearing their seat belts. If the car does not have enough seat belts for everyone, children who are younger than three years old must be fastened first. Child seats are designed for various weights of child and must – since 2006 – have been approved by one of the two standards for child seats: *ECE Regulation R44.03* or later *Standard R44.04.*

- **Baby seats – group 0 or 0+ (from birth to about 9 months):** These are for babies weighing up to 13 kg. They face backwards and are fitted with a seat belt. They should never be used in the front, where the front seat is protected with a frontal airbag. (This is because airbags are designed to protect adults weighing about 75 kg; a child placed in front of an airbag may suffocate or be severely injured by the impact of a rapidly inflating airbag.) Baby seats can also be used to carry the baby outside the car. A baby may also be placed on the rear seat in a **carrycot** with hard sides. The carrycot must be fastened with a special belt that is fitted in the car, or with the car's three-point seat belts.
- **Child car seats – group 1 (from 9 months to about 4 years):** These are for children weighing 9–18 kg and have their own straps. They face forwards and are usually fitted in the back seat of a car with a seat belt.
- **Booster seats and cushions – groups 2 & 3 (from about 4 to 11 years):** These are for children weighing 15–25 kg and measuring up to 135 cm in height. They are designed to raise them so they can use an adult seat belt safely across their chest and their hips.

As well as using approved, correctly fitted safety restraints, parents and drivers should observe the following safety guidelines:

- A child must never be left unattended in a child seat. They may hurt themselves or accidentally put their head under the seat belt and be suffocated.
- All harnesses and straps should be checked and adjusted before each journey.
- If the child opens his or her seat belt, pull over to a safe place and stay there until the child is safely fastened again.
- If the child repeatedly undoes their seat belt, fit a new buckle so they cannot undo it.
- Child locks must be fitted to the rear doors and switched on for the duration of the journey.

Figure 3.17 (a) A child safety seat (b) A baby seat

Safety issues

Some parents – and many more grandparents – of today's under-fives look back to their childhood and remember a time when children were cared for by their family at home until the time came for them to go to school. Grandparents remember being allowed to play outdoors in their neighbourhoods. Today's way of living, or lifestyle, presents a number of safety issues, as explored below.

Children being cared for by people other than their family

During the 1980s and 1990s, there was a significant growth in the proportion of women returning to work after childbirth in Britain. This growth was due to the introduction of maternity rights and family-friendly policies, as well as changes in attitudes towards work. Now it is estimated that approximately half of mothers with children under five years old have jobs outside the home. Although the majority of mothers work part-time, increasing numbers are now working full-time. This means that many parents leave their children with carers (including grandparents or other family members), and this is known as **informal care** – even when the carers are being paid for their services. Parents often have to combine a number of arrangements to meet their childcare needs. **Formal care** of children under five includes:

- childminder
- day nursery
- nursery school, nursery class or special nursery

- playgroup
- nanny, au pair or babysitter

There are strict **safety regulations** in the first four types of childcare. All establishments providing care for young children must be registered and inspected regularly, to ensure that the care they are providing is up to standard. Childcare within a parent's own home, however, does not have to be registered. Nannies are child carers who are employed *directly* by parents, and they provide care within the parent's own home. There is no central governing body which registers and inspects nannies, au pairs or babysitters, although most childcare agencies do carry our reference and police checks on job applicants. Parents are advised to do their own checks too, and to ask about and follow up details of previous employment and qualifications. (For more information on childcare outside the home, see part six, pages 266–269.)

Road safety

The car is very important for many families. There are a lot more cars being driven on the road and parked on residential roads. Young children are especially vulnerable as pedestrians because:

- they are unable to judge distances and speeds of cars
- they are impulsive and quite likely to run out into the road
- they are less likely than adults to be noticed by a driver if they try to cross the road between parked cars.

Safety of toys and clothing

More than 30,000 children go to hospital every year in the UK following an accident involving a toy. Most of these accidents happen to toddlers between one and three years old. As well as accidents associated with the toys themselves, injuries also happen when children – and adults – trip on toys. The most serious of these accidents occur when toys are left on stairs or steps.

A warning symbol telling you that a toy is not suitable for children under 36 months is important, because it means that the toy may contain parts that could choke a very young child. All toys and children's clothes sold in the UK must bear a label to show that the product meets specific safety standards. Toys and playthings display the following labels:

- The **Kitemark** (see figure 3.18a): This confirms that the British Standards Institution (BSI) has tested a product and found that it meets a particular standard.
- The **BSI Safety Mark** (see figure 3.18b): Toy regulations in the UK are governed by a Europe-wide regulation, *EN71* (or *BS EN71*), which governs the safety of all toys sold in the UK and within the European Union. The Safety Mark means that a product has been checked to ensure that it meets the requirements of the BSI for safety only.
- The **Lion Mark** (see figure 3.18c): This symbol is only found on British-made toys and means that they have met the safety standards required.

Figure 3.18 (a) Kitemark (b) BSI Safety Mark (c) Lion Mark (d) age advice symbol (e) CE symbol

- The **age advice safety symbol** (see figure 3.18d): This means that the toy is unsuitable for children under three years old – for instance, because it might contain small parts. It is very important to choose the right toy for the age of child. (Most toys also have a suggested age range on the packaging. These are mostly for guidance only and reflect what age groups the manufacturer believes will find the toy most appealing.)
- The **CE mark** (see figure 3.18e): This is the toy manufacturer's self-declaration that their product meets basic EU legal requirements. This is not, in fact, a safety symbol.

NB: Toys and games bought from market stalls, and cheap foreign imports, may be copies of well-known brand-name toys but may not meet the UK safety standards.

Safety of children's nightwear

There are also safety laws that govern the sale of nightwear for children. Children's nightwear, except pyjamas, babies' garments and cotton terry-towelling bathrobes, must be made of fabrics which (after having been washed) comply with the 'flammability test'.

- Pyjamas and cotton terry-towelling bathrobes, which (after washing) *do not* comply with the flammability test, must bear a label stating, in red letters: KEEP AWAY FROM FIRE.
- Pyjamas and cotton terry-towelling bathrobes which *do* comply with the flammability test, must bear a label stating, in black letters: LOW FLAMMABILITY TO BS5722.
- Advertisements for pyjamas, babies' garments, cotton terry-towelling bathrobes (being children's nightwear) and adults' nightwear, which do not satisfy the flammability test, must include the KEEP AWAY FROM FIRE symbol.
- Advertisements for garments which satisfy the flammability test must include the LOW FLAM symbol.

Terry towelling can be very flammable, and fabric bought by parents making their children's clothes at home must also be chosen with care.

 KEY TERM

Flammable: Capable of burning; easily set on fire; able to burn easily (inflammable also has the same meaning).

Personal safety

Many parents worry that their child might be abducted or murdered by a stranger. In fact, this is rare, compared with, for example, the risk of a traffic accident. However, it makes sense to teach children the following rules:

- Never go with anyone (even someone they know well) without telling the grown-up who is looking after them.
- If someone they do not know tries to take them away, it is okay to scream and kick.
- Make sure children know always to tell you if they have been approached by someone they do not know.
- Make sure that children know what to do if they become separated from you or are lost.
- If they are in a crowded place, they should stand still and wait to be found.
- They can tell a police officer that they are lost.
- They can go into a shop and tell someone behind the counter.
- They can tell someone who has other children with them.
- As soon as they are old enough, teach a child his or her address and phone number, or the phone number of another responsible person.

 REVISION QUESTIONS

1. Why are children under the age of five particularly vulnerable when crossing a road?
2. What is the Green Cross Code?
3. When should a rear-facing baby car seat not be fitted in the front passenger seat? Why not?
4. Whose responsibility is it that any children travelling in the car are wearing an appropriate child restraint?
5. What is the flammability test and which items of children's clothing must pass it?

NUTRITION AND HEALTH

1 Nutrition and feeding

Good nutrition, or healthy eating, is one of the most important ways we can help ourselves to feel well and be well. We need food:

- to provide **energy** for physical activity and to maintain body temperature
- to provide material for the **growth** of body cells
- for the **repair and replacement** of damaged body tissues.

The substances in food that fulfil these functions are called **nutrients** (see page 170).

Food and energy requirements

Food requirements vary according to age, gender, size, occupation or lifestyle, and climate. Food energy is traditionally measured in calories (kcal) or kilojoules (kJ).

> 1 kcal = 4.2 kJ
>
> 1000 kJ = 1 MJ (megajoule) = 239 kcal

Different foods contain different amounts of energy per unit of weight; foods that contain a lot of fat and sugar have high energy values. An excess of calories will result in weight gain, as the surplus 'energy' is stored as fat; an insufficient intake of calories will result in weight loss, as the body has to draw on fat reserves to meet energy requirements. Babies and young children have relatively high energy requirements in relation to their size.

2 Breastfeeding and bottle-feeding

The way babies and children are fed involves more than simply providing enough food to meet nutritional requirements; for the newborn baby, sucking milk is a great source of pleasure, and it is also rewarding and enjoyable for the mother. The *ideal* food for babies to start life with is breast milk, and **breastfeeding** should always be encouraged as the first choice in infant feeding; however, mothers should not be made to feel guilty or inadequate if they choose not to breastfeed their babies or are unable to do so.

Breastfeeding

How breast milk is produced

The breast is made up of 15–20 segments or lobes, each of which contains alveoli or cells which produce milk (see figure 4.1). Milk ducts drain milk from these cells to reservoirs in the area of the **areola** (the pigmented ring around the nipple). The nipple has several openings through which the baby can obtain milk. During pregnancy the breasts produce **colostrum**, a creamy yellowish fluid, low in fat and sugar, which is uniquely designed to feed the newborn baby. Colostrum also has higher levels of antibodies than mature milk and plays an important part in protecting the baby from infection. Mature milk is present in the breasts from around the third day after birth. Hormonal changes in the mother's bloodstream cause the milk to be produced, and the sucking of the baby stimulates a steady supply. (Unfortunately, this mechanism also operates in the event of stillbirth or miscarriage and can cause the mother severe distress, especially if she has had no warning that this may happen.)

Management of breastfeeding

The most difficult part of breastfeeding is usually the beginning and it may take two to three weeks to establish a supply and to settle into some sort of pattern. Even if the mother does not intend to breastfeed her baby, she should be encouraged to try for the first few days so that the baby can benefit from the unique properties of colostrum. Many of the problems which cause women to give up breastfeeding can be overcome with the right advice and support.

Breast milk may be expressed by hand or by breast pump, for use when the mother is unavailable; expressed breast milk (EBM) can be stored in a sterilised container in a freezer for up to three months.

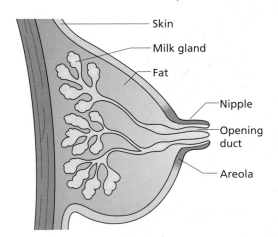

Skin
Milk gland
Fat
Nipple
Opening duct
Areola

Figure 4.1 The structure of the breast

Guidelines for the successful management of breastfeeding

- The mother should consume a well-balanced diet; her diet will affect the composition of the breast milk and some foods may cause colic. (Vegetarian mothers who drink cow's milk, eat a varied vegetarian diet and take vitamin supplements produce breast milk that is similar in nutrient value to that of non-vegetarian mothers; vegan mothers may need to take calcium and vitamin B12 supplements while breastfeeding.)

- Put the baby to the breast straight after the birth; this has been shown to be a key factor in successful breastfeeding.

- Feed on demand – that is, when the baby is hungry – rather than routinely every four hours.

- Arrange extra help in the home if possible, at least until breastfeeding is established.

- Find the most comfortable position for feeding; if the mother has a sore perineum or Caesarean scar, the midwife or health advisor will be able to advise.

- Try not to give extra (complementary) milk feeds by bottle.

- Let the baby decide when s/he has had enough milk and allow the baby to finish sucking at one breast before offering the other.

Figure 4.2 A baby being breastfed

 KEY TERMS

Areola: The dark area on the breast surrounding the nipple, which may spread or darken further during pregnancy.

Colostrum: The first 'milk' the breasts produce as a precursor to breast milk. It is rich in fats, protein and antibodies, which protect the baby against infection and kick-start the immune system.

Lactation: Production of milk by the breasts.

Advantages of breastfeeding

- Human breast milk provides food constituents in the correct balance for human growth. It also changes its composition to meet the baby's needs as s/he grows.
- The milk is sterile and at the correct temperature; there is no need for bottles and sterilising equipment.
- Breast milk initially provides the infant with maternal **antibodies** and helps protect the child from infection – for example, against illnesses such as diarrhoea, vomiting, chest, ear and urine infections, eczema and nappy rash.
- The child is less likely to become overweight, as overfeeding by concentrating the formula is not possible, and the infant has more freedom of choice as to how much milk to suckle.
- Generally, breast milk is considered cheaper, despite the extra calorific requirement of the mother.
- Sometimes it is easier to promote mother–infant bonding by breastfeeding, although this is certainly not always the case.
- Some babies have an intolerance to the protein in cow's milk (which is the basis of formula milk).
- The mother's uterus returns to its pre-pregnancy state more quickly, as a result of the action of oxytocin released when the baby suckles.
- It will help the mother to lose weight, by getting rid of any excess fat stored while she was pregnant.

Disadvantages of breastfeeding

- In rare cases (about 2 per cent), the mother may not be able to produce enough breast milk to feed her baby.
- She may feel uncomfortable about breastfeeding her baby in public.
- If employed, and breastfeeding her baby, the mother may need to arrange to breastfeed the baby during working hours, or may need to extend her maternity leave, which could have financial implications.
- The mother can become very tired, as breastfeeding tends to be more frequent than bottle-feeding.
- The mother may suffer from sore or cracked nipples, which makes breastfeeding painful.

Bottle-feeding

Commercially modified baby milks (formula milks) *must* be used for bottle-feeding. Any other type of milk, such as cow's milk or goat's milk, will not satisfy a baby's nutritional needs and should not be given to babies under one year of age. A young baby's digestive system is unable to cope with the high protein and salt content of cow's milk, and it is likely to cause an adverse reaction. Soya-based milks can be used if the baby develops an intolerance to modified cow's milks. (This happens very rarely.) For the first 4–6 months the baby will be given infant formula milk as a substitute for breast milk; s/he may then progress to **follow-on milk**, which should be offered until the age of 12 months.

Advantages of bottle-feeding

- The mother knows exactly how much milk the baby has taken.
- The milk is in no way affected by the mother's state of health, whereas anxiety, tiredness, illness or menstruation may reduce the quantity of breast milk.

- The infant is unaffected by such factors as maternal medication. Laxatives, antibiotics, alcohol and drugs affecting the central nervous system can affect the quality of breast milk.
- Other members of the family can feed the infant. In this way, the father can feel equally involved with the child's care, and during the night could take over one of the feeds so that the mother can get more sleep.
- There is no fear of embarrassment while feeding.
- The mother is physically unaffected by feeding the infant, avoiding such problems as sore nipples.
- It is useful for mothers who want to return to work before the baby is weaned.

Disadvantages of bottle-feeding

- Babies who are bottle-fed using formula milk do not have the same protection against allergies and infections as breastfed babies.
- When making formula milk, it is possible to get the mixture wrong and make it too strong, too weak or too hot.
- Babies tend to swallow more air when bottle-fed and need to be 'winded' more often.
- Babies may bring up feeds more often; this is known as **possetting**.

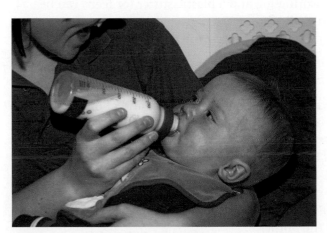

- Babies who are bottle-fed tend to suffer more from constipation.
- There is a lot of work involved in thoroughly washing and sterilising all the equipment that is needed for bottle-feeding.
- Studies indicate that bottle-fed babies are found to have an increased risk of obesity at least until six years of age.
- Using formula milk can be expensive. It has been estimated that it costs at least £450 a year to feed a baby using formula milk.
- There is a greater risk of the baby developing **gastroenteritis** – usually when equipment is not sterilised properly, or the milk is incorrectly stored or becomes contaminated.

Figure 4.3 A baby being bottle-fed

Making the choice between breastfeeding and bottle-feeding

A range of factors influences the mother's decision on how to feed her newborn baby:

- Breastfeeding is harder for some mothers than for others – for example, if a new mother does not receive the support she needs to establish breastfeeding, the 'let-down' reflex (when milk flows from the ducts towards the nipple) is more difficult to stimulate.

- Some babies can have medical conditions that make breastfeeding difficult – for example, they may have tongue-tie or may have been born prematurely.
- The mother may have to return to work and may find that bottle-feeding is more convenient when leaving her baby in the care of others.
- Many new mothers feel that there is a bottle-feeding culture in the UK. Breastfeeding is often seen as an embarrassing activity when carried out in front of others.

The important thing is that a mother makes her own choice and is happy that her baby is feeding properly.

Preparation of feeds

A day's supply of bottles may be made and stored in the fridge for up to 24 hours. A rough guide to quantities is: 150 ml of milk per kilogram of body weight per day – thus a baby weighing 4 kg will require approximately 600 ml in 24 hours. This could be given as 6 x 100 ml bottles.

The following equipment will be needed:

- a container for sterilising bottles, large enough to submerge everything completely; steam sterilisers are very effective but costly
- eight wide-necked feeding bottles and teats designed for newborn babies
- a large plastic or Pyrex® measuring jug and a plastic stirrer (or feeds can be made directly in bottles and shaken to mix)
- sterilising liquid or tablets – check the manufacturer's instructions for length of time and correct dilution.

How to make up a feed

1. Wash hands and nails thoroughly; boil some fresh water and allow it to cool – for no more than half an hour. Take a bottle from the steriliser; shake, but do not rinse, as this would de-sterilise it.
2. Pour the correct amount of boiled water into the bottle (check quantity at eye level on a firm surface).
3. Measure the exact amount of formula milk powder, using the scoop provided, following the manufacturer's instructions. Level with a plastic knife but do not pack down; add powder to the bottle.
4. Take a teat from the steriliser, taking care to handle it by the edges, and fit into the bottle; put cap, ring and top on.
5. Shake the bottle vigorously until any lumps have dissolved.
6. Test the temperature of the formula milk on the inside of your wrist. If it feels too hot, put the cap over the teat and hold the bottle under cold running water.

NB: You should make up formula milk freshly for each feed and use it immediately. Do not store made-up formula. If there is any formula milk left after a feed, throw it away.

The following methods are generally preferred for sterilising bottles:

- **Steam steriliser:** This sterilises bottles, rings and teats by heating a small amount of water into steam, which works quickly to kill off bacteria. Make sure the openings of the bottles and teats are facing down in the steriliser and follow the manufacturer's instructions.
- **Microwave steriliser:** This works in a similar way to the steam steriliser. It can take up less space in your kitchen if you already own a microwave, and it is quicker than a steam or cold-water steriliser.

Guidelines for bottle-feeding

- Always wash hands thoroughly before preparing feeds for babies.
- Never add sugar or salt to the milk, and never make the feed stronger than the instructions state – this could result in too high a salt intake, which can lead to severe illness.
- Always check the temperature of the milk before giving it to a baby.
- Do not use a microwave oven to warm the bottle, as it may produce isolated hot spots.
- Always check that the teat has a hole of the right size and that it is not blocked.
- Never prop up a baby with a bottle – choking is a real danger.
- Always supervise siblings when feeding small babies.

Sterilising feeding equipment

It is very important that all bottles and equipment are thoroughly sterilised.

- After use, scrub all the bottles, caps and covers, using hot soapy water and a special bottle brush. Rinse thoroughly in clean, running water.
- Teats may be cleaned using a special teat cleaner; turn teat inside out to ensure all milk deposits are removed and wash as the bottles.
- Submerge bottles, teats and all other equipment needed for bottle-feeding in the sterilising solution, checking that no bubbles are trapped inside bottles and that teats are completely immersed.

Guidelines: how to bottle-feed a baby

Collect all the necessary equipment before picking up the baby. The bottle may be warmed in a jug of hot water. Have a muslin square or bib and tissues to hand.

1. Check the temperature and flow of the milk by dripping it onto the inside of your wrist (it should feel warm – not hot or cold).
2. Make yourself comfortable with the baby. Do not rush the feed – babies always sense if you are not relaxed and it can make them edgy too.
3. Try to hold the baby in a similar position to that for breastfeeding and maintain eye contact; this is a time for cuddling and talking to the baby.
4. Stimulate the rooting reflex (see pages 94 and 95) by placing the teat at the corner of the baby's mouth; then put the teat fully into the mouth and feed by tilting the bottle so that the hole in the teat is always covered with milk.
5. After about ten minutes, the baby may need to be helped to bring up wind; this can be done by leaning the baby forwards on your lap and gently rubbing the back, or by holding the baby against your shoulder. Unless the baby is showing discomfort, do not insist on trying to produce a burp – the baby may pass the wind out in the nappy.

The National Children's Bureau states that:

'Babies who are bottle-fed should be held and have warm physical contact with an attentive adult whilst being fed. It is strongly recommended that a baby [in a childcare setting] is fed by the same staff member at each feed. Babies should never be left propped up with bottles, as it is dangerous and inappropriate to babies' emotional needs.'

 KEY TERM

Gastroenteritis: Inflammation of the stomach and intestines, often causing sudden and violent upsets – diarrhoea, cramps, nausea and vomiting are common symptoms. Babies can become seriously ill and dehydrated if infected and will need urgent medical attention.

 REVISION QUESTIONS

1. What is colostrum and why is it important?
2. Why must babies who are being bottle-fed have formula milk rather than ordinary cow's milk?
3. List four advantages of breastfeeding a baby.
4. List four advantages of bottle-feeding a baby.
5. What factors influence the mother's decision on how to feed her newborn baby?

 CHILD STUDY ACTIVITY

Find out if the child is or was breastfed or bottle-fed. What were the parents' reasons for making their decision?

3 Weaning

Weaning is the gradual introduction of solid food to the baby's diet. The reasons for weaning are to:

- meet the baby's nutritional needs – from about six months of age, milk alone will not satisfy the baby's increased nutritional requirements, especially for iron
- satisfy increasing appetite
- develop new skills – for example, use of feeding beaker, cup and cutlery
- develop the chewing mechanism; the muscular movement of the mouth and jaw also aids the development of speech
- introduce new tastes and textures; this enables the baby to join in family meals, thus promoting cognitive and social development.

When to start weaning

Solid foods should be introduced when a baby:

- is putting objects in their mouth or sucking on their fist
- appears still to be hungry, even though milk feeds have been increased for a few days
- begins waking because s/he is hungry, after a period of sleeping through the night.

Babies ready to take solids will also use their tongue to push back food placed in their mouth. Babies who are born prematurely should not be introduced to solid foods just because they have reached a certain age or weight. They will need individual assessment before weaning.

Giving solids too early – often in the mistaken belief that the baby might sleep through the night – places a strain on the baby's immature digestive system; it may also make the baby fat and increases the likelihood of allergy.

The Department of Health recommends introducing solid foods at six months (26 weeks). If a mother *does* choose to introduce solid foods before 26 weeks, she should consult her health visitor or GP first. There are also some foods that should be avoided. These include:

- foods containing gluten, which is in wheat, rye, barley, oats
- eggs
- fish and shellfish
- liver
- citrus fruit juices
- nuts and seeds.

Note on honey: Babies under one year old should not be given honey because it is not pasteurised and can cause infant botulism, a rare – but very serious – illness, which occurs when clostridium botulinum or related bacteria produce toxins in the intestines of babies under one year old.

Stages of weaning

- **Stage 1 (from around 6 months)** – Give puréed vegetables, puréed fruit, baby rice, finely puréed dhal or lentils. Milk continues to be the most important food.
- **Stage 2 (about 7–9 months)** – Increase variety; introduce puréed or minced meat, chicken, liver, fish, lentils, beans. Raw eggs should not be used (see table 4.1), but cooked egg yolk can be introduced; wheat-based foods (e.g. mashed Weetabix®, pieces of bread). Milk feeds decrease as more solids rich in protein are offered.

- **Stage 3 (about 9–12 months)** – Cow's milk can safely be used at about 12 months; introduce lumpier foods such as pasta, pieces of cooked meat, soft cooked beans, pieces of cheese, a variety of breads; additional fluids such as diluted unsweetened fruit juice or water can also be given. Three regular meals should be taken, as well as drinks.

Methods of weaning

Some babies take very quickly to solid food; others appear not to be interested at all. The baby's demands are a good guide for weaning; mealtimes should never become a battleground. Even babies as young as four months have definite food preferences and should never be forced to eat a particular food, however much thought and effort have gone into the preparation. Table 4.1 provides guidelines on introducing new solids to babies. The best foods to start with are puréed cooked vegetables, fruit, and ground cereals such as rice. Chewing usually starts at around the age of six months, whether the baby has teeth or not, and coarser textures can then be offered. The baby should be in a bouncing cradle or high chair – not in the usual feeding position in the carer's arms.

Food can be puréed by:

- rubbing through a sieve, using a large spoon
- mashing with a fork (for soft foods such as banana or cooked potato)
- using a Mouli® sieve or hand blender
- using an electric blender (useful for larger amounts).

	6 months	**6–8 months**	**9–12 months**
You can give or add	Puréed fruit Puréed vegetables Thin porridge made from oat or rice flakes or cornmeal Finely puréed dhal or lentils	A wider range of puréed fruits and vegetables Purées which include chicken, fish and liver Wheat-based foods, e.g. mashed Weetabix® Egg yolk, well cooked Small-sized beans such as aduki beans, cooked soft Pieces of ripe banana Cooked rice Citrus fruits Soft summer fruits Pieces of bread	An increasingly wide range of foods with a variety of textures and flavours Cow's milk Pieces of cheese Fromage frais or yoghurt Pieces of fish Soft cooked beans Pasta A variety of breads Pieces of meat from a casserole Well-cooked egg white Almost anything that is wholesome and that the child can swallow
How	Offer the food on the tip of a clean finger or on the tip of a clean (plastic or horn) teaspoon	On a teaspoon	On a spoon or as finger food
When	A very tiny amount at first, during or after a milk feed	At the end of a milk feed	At established mealtimes
Why	The start of transition from milk to solids	To introduce other foods when the child is hungry	To encourage full independence

Table 4.1 Introducing new solids to babies

	6 months	6–8 months	9–12 months
Not yet	Cow's milk – or any except breast or formula milk Citrus fruit Soft summer fruits Wheat (cereals, flour, bread, etc.) Spices Spinach, swede, turnip, beetroot Eggs Nuts Salt Sugar Fatty food	Cow's milk, except in small quantities mixed with other food Chillies or chilli powder Egg whites Nuts Salt Sugar Fatty food	Whole nuts Salt Sugar Fatty food

Table 4.1 Contin.

Guidelines for weaning

- Try to encourage a liking for savoury foods.
- Only introduce one new food at a time.
- Be patient if the baby does not take the food – feed at the baby's pace, not yours.
- Do not add salt or sugar to feeds.
- Make sure that food is the right temperature.
- Avoid giving sweet foods or drinks between meals.
- Never leave a baby alone when s/he is eating.

 REVISION QUESTIONS

1. What is weaning? Describe the three stages of weaning.
2. How does a baby show that s/he is ready for weaning?
3. At what age does the Department of Health recommend that babies should be started on solid food?
4. Which foods should be avoided during the weaning process?
5. Which non-milk drinks may be offered to babies being weaned?

 RESEARCH ACTIVITY

Visit a pharmacy or supermarket to find out about the wide variety of foods for weaning babies.

- Draw up a week's menu for a baby of nine months, using a variety of commercially prepared foods in jars and packets.
- Work out how much it would cost to provide your menu for one week.

4 Promoting healthy attitudes to food and eating patterns in childhood

During childhood we develop food habits that will affect us for life. By the time we are adults, most of us will suffer from some disorder that is related to our diet – for example, tooth decay, heart disease or cancer. Establishing healthy eating patterns in children will help to promote normal growth and development, and will protect against later disease.

A **healthy diet** consists of a wide variety of foods to help the body to grow and to provide energy. It must include enough of the following **nutrients** – proteins, fats, carbohydrates, vitamins, minerals and fibre – as well as **water**, to fuel and maintain the body's vital functions. Children need a varied, **energy-rich** diet for good health and growth. For balance and variety, choose from the five main food groups (see pages 170–171).

Respecting the individual

Every child and young person is unique; they gradually develop a whole catalogue of likes, strong dislikes and mild preferences regarding food and mealtimes.

- Some like their food covered in sauces, while others prefer it dry.
- Some like every food kept separate from the others on the plate.
- Many do not like 'tough' meat or foods that are difficult to chew.

It is important to respect a child's likes and dislikes and offer alternative foods from the same food group where necessary. With time, tastes often change, so it is important to keep offering young children different foods.

Guidelines for making mealtimes healthy and fun

- Offer a wide variety of different foods – give babies and toddlers a chance to try a new food more than once; any refusal on first tasting may be due to dislike of the new rather than of the food itself.

- Set an example – children will imitate both what you eat and how you eat it. It will be easier to encourage a child to eat a stick of raw celery if you eat one too! If you show disgust at certain foods, young children will notice and copy you.

- Be prepared for messy mealtimes! Present the food in a form that is fairly easy for children to manage by themselves (e.g. not difficult to chew).

- Do not use food as a punishment, reward, bribe or threat – for example, do not give sweets or chocolates as a reward for finishing savoury foods. To a child, this is like saying, 'Here's something nice after eating those nasty greens.' Give healthy foods as treats – for example, raisins and raw carrots – rather than sweets or cakes.

- Encourage children to feed themselves – either using a spoon or by offering suitable finger foods.

- Introduce new foods in stages – for example, if switching to wholemeal bread, try a softgrain white bread first. And always involve the children in making choices as far as possible.

- Teach children to eat mainly at mealtimes and avoid giving them high-calorie snacks – for example, biscuits and sugary drinks – which might take the edge off their appetite for more nutritious food. Most young children need three small meals and three snacks a day.

- Presentation is important – food manufacturers use a variety of techniques to make their children's food products exciting – colours, shapes, themes and characters. Using these tactics can make mealtimes more fun.

- Avoid adding salt to any food – too much salt can cause dehydration in babies and may predispose certain people to hypertension (high blood pressure) if taken over a lifetime.

- Allow children to follow their own individual appetites when deciding how much they want to eat. If a child rejects food, do not ever force-feed him/her. Simply remove the food without comment. Give smaller portions next time and praise the child for eating even a little.

- **Never** give a young child whole nuts to eat – particularly peanuts. Children can very easily choke on a small piece of the nut or even inhale it, which can cause a severe type of pneumonia. More rarely, a child may have a serious allergic reaction to nuts.

5 A healthy diet

Food groups

Types of food can be arranged into five groups, based on the **nutrients** they provide. To ensure a balanced, healthy diet, some foods from each group should be included in a child's diet every day (see table 4.2). The easiest way to monitor our nutrition is to keep in mind the **five food groups**; eating a variety of foods from each of these food groups every day automatically balances our diet. The *proportions* of the **balance of good health** (see figure 4.4) do not apply *directly* to children under five years; however, their eating patterns should involve a combination of foods from all five groups to ensure that all nutrient requirements are met.

Figure 4.4 The balance of good health

🔑 **KEY TERMS**

Nutrients: Nutrients are the essential components of food which provide the individual with the necessary requirements for bodily functions.

Nutrition: The study of the food process in terms of the way that it is received and utilised by the body to promote healthy growth and development.

Food groups	Main nutrients	Types to choose	Portions per day	Suggestions for meals and snacks
1. Bread, other cereals and potatoes All types of bread, rice, breakfast cereals, pasta, noodles, and potatoes (beans and lentils can be eaten as part of this group)	Carbohydrates (starch), fibre, some calcium and iron, B-group vitamins	Wholemeal, brown wholegrain or high-fibre versions of bread; avoid fried foods too often (e.g. chips). Use butter and other spreads sparingly	FIVE All meals of the day should include foods from this group	One portion = • 1 bowl of breakfast cereal • 2 tabsp pasta or rice • 1 small potato Snack meals include bread or pizza base

Table 4.2 Food groups

Food groups	Main nutrients	Types to choose	Portions per day	Suggestions for meals and snacks
2. Fruit and vegetables Fresh, frozen and canned fruit and vegetables, dried fruit, fruit juice (beans and lentils can be eaten as part of this group)	Vitamin C, carotenes, iron, calcium folate, fibre and some carbohydrate	Eat a wide variety of fruit and vegetables; avoid adding rich sauces to vegetables, and sugar to fruit	FOUR/FIVE Include 1 fruit or vegetable daily high in vitamin C, e.g. tomato, sweet pepper, orange or kiwi fruit	One portion = • 1 glass of pure fruit juice • 1 piece of fruit • 1 sliced tomato • 2 tabsp of cooked vegetables • 1 tabsp of dried fruit – e.g. raisins
3. Milk and dairy foods Milk, cheese, yoghurt and fromage frais (this group does not contain butter, eggs and cream)	Calcium, protein, B-group vitamins (particularly B12), vitamins A and D	Milk is a very good source of calcium, but calcium can also be obtained from cheese, flavoured or plain yogurts and fromage frais	THREE Children require the equivalent of one pint of milk each day to ensure an adequate intake of calcium	One portion = • 1 glass of milk • 1 pot of yogurt or fromage frais • 1 tabsp of grated cheese, e.g. on a pizza Under 2s – do not give reduced-fat milks, e.g. semi-skimmed – they do not supply enough energy
4. Meat, fish and alternatives Lean meat, poultry, fish, eggs, tofu, quorn, pulses – peas, beans, lentils, nuts and seeds	Iron, protein, B-group vitamins (particularly B12), zinc and magnesium	Lower-fat versions – meat with fat cut off, chicken without skin etc. Beans and lentils are good alternatives, being low in fat and high in fibre	TWO Vegetarians will need to have grains, pulses and seeds; vegans avoid all food associated with animals	One portion = • 2 fish fingers (for a 3-year-old) • 4 fish fingers (for a 7-year-old) • baked beans • a small piece of chicken
5. Fatty and sugary foods Margarine, low-fat spread, butter, ghee, cream, chocolate, crisps, biscuits, sweets and sugar, fizzy soft drinks, puddings	Vitamins and essential fatty acids, but also a lot of fat, sugar and salt	Only offer small amounts of sugary and fatty foods. Fats and oils are found in all the other food groups	NONE Only eat fatty and sugary foods sparingly, e.g. crisps, sweets and chocolate	Children may be offered foods with extra fat of sugar – biscuits, cakes or chocolate – as long as they are not replacing food from the four main food groups

Table 4.2 Contin.

Group 1: bread, other cereals and potatoes

We need the foods in group 1 to provide energy. They also contain **vitamins** and **minerals** (see pages 175–177). Foods in this group include:

- rice
- bread
- breakfast cereals
- potato
- pasta
- chapatti
- couscous
- yam and green banana.

Wholemeal bread, wholegrain cereals and potatoes in their skins all increase the **fibre** content of the diet. Bran should *not* be given to children as an extra source of fibre as it can interfere with the absorption of **calcium** and **iron**, and may also cause stomach cramps. All meals throughout the day should include foods from group 1.

NB: For children *between one and four years*, a mixture of some white and some wholegrain varieties of bread should be offered; this is because the fibre content from only wholegrain cereals would be too high for toddlers. Excess fibre can fill up the stomach and reduce their food intake; this would lead to a restriction of their energy and nutrient intake.

Group 2: fruit and vegetables

Fruit and vegetables are full of **vitamins**, **minerals** (see table 4.3) and **fibre**, all of which are needed to maintain good health; they are also very low in fat. A fruit or vegetable that is **high in vitamin C** should be included in children's diets every day – for example:

- tomatoes
- citrus fruits, such as oranges and grapefruit
- kiwi fruit
- sweet peppers.

Many children will eat slices of raw vegetables or salad in place of cooked vegetables – for example, carrots, cucumber, tomato or peppers. Children who are reluctant to eat vegetables should be given fruit or fruit juice instead. Fruit and vegetables are best eaten raw, as their vitamin content is easily destroyed by cooking and processing.

Group 3: milk and dairy foods

Foods in this group are needed to provide energy, and also to store energy in the body and insulate it against the cold. This group includes:

- milk
- yoghurt and fromage frais
- cheese.

Children require about 500 ml (1 pt) of milk each day to ensure an adequate intake of **calcium**. Goat's milk or calcium-enriched soya milk and their products can be substituted directly for cow's milk. If a child cannot achieve this milk intake, equivalent amounts of calcium can be taken from yoghurt, cheese, fromage frais and so on. Reduced-fat milks should not generally be given to children under five years because of their lower energy and fat-soluble vitamin content; however, semi-skimmed milk may be introduced from two years of age, provided that the child's overall diet is adequate.

Milk from baby bottles should have been discontinued by around the age of one year. Milk and other drinks should be given in cups or beakers, as continued bottle sucking can become a comforting habit that is difficult to break.

NB: Toddlers need less milk than they did in their first year of life; drinking too much milk may reduce their appetite and also decrease their intake of other foods, especially those higher in iron.

Group 4: meat, fish and alternatives

This group provides the richest sources of **iron** in the diet. Foods include:

- lean meat
- fish
- tofu and Quorn®
- poultry
- eggs
- pulses: peas, beans (baked beans, kidney beans), lentils, ground nuts and seeds.

The amount of group 4 food that makes up one portion varies according to the age of the individual child – for example, a three-year-old may have two fish fingers, while a seven-year-old may have three or four. When eggs, pulses and nuts are served, a food or drink high in vitamin C should also be included in the meal to ensure good absorption of iron.

Nuts: Children under five years should not be offered whole nuts as they may cause choking. Nut butters and ground or chopped nuts in recipes are fine.

Group 5: fatty and sugary foods

Fats and oils are found in the foods from the four groups – for instance, meat and cheese contain fat and some vegetables contain oil. Sweets, cakes, chocolate and crisps are all *high-energy* foods, but they have little other nutritional value. If children eat a lot of these foods, they run the risk of putting on a lot of weight and suffering from tooth decay.

However, children may be offered *limited* amounts of foods with extra fat or sugar – biscuits, cakes, chocolate, crisps and sweet drinks – as long as these items are not *replacing* food from the other four food groups.

They provide toddlers with energy and vitamins A, E and D. Olive, walnut, rapeseed and soya oils give a good balance of omega fats. Sweetened drinks should be well diluted and offered with food at a meal or snack, to lessen their tendency to cause dental decay. Salty snacks such as crisps should be offered only rarely.

The dangers of too much salt

Salt (sodium chloride) should be avoided as far as possible in the diets of young children, as their kidneys are not mature enough to cope with large amounts. Be aware that many common foods, such as cheese, manufactured soup, packet meals and bread, are already quite high in added salt. Children will receive sufficient salt for their dietary needs from a normal balanced diet, without adding any to food – either as it is cooked or at the table.

QUICK FACTS

- On average, children today are eating twice the recommended amount of salt. The recommended nutrient intake (RNI) for infants aged between one and three years is no more than 1.25 g of salt each day; children aged four to six years should consume no more than 1.75 g. Many manufactured foods are marketed at children, and some of these can top their daily salt requirement in just one serving – for example, a bag of crisps. A small can (200 g) of pasta shapes in tomato sauce contains *twice* the daily RNI of salt for a child aged one to three years, and a third more than the daily RNI for a child aged four to six years.

Guidelines for reducing salt in children's diets

- Cut down gradually on the amount of salt used in cooking, so that children become used to less salty foods.
- If preparing baby food at home do not add salt, even if it tastes bland. Manufactured baby food is tightly regulated to limit the salt content to a trace.
- Try using a low-salt substitute, such as LoSalt®, Solo® or a super-market's own brand low-sodium salt, in cooking or at the table. These products substitute up to 70 per cent of the sodium chloride with potassium chloride.

Dietary fibre

Dietary fibre – or roughage – is found in cereals, fruits and vegetables. Fibre is made up of the indigestible parts or compounds of plants, which pass relatively unchanged through our stomach and intestines. Fibre is needed to provide roughage to help keep the food moving through the gut. A small amount of fibre is important for health in preschool children, but too much can cause problems as their digestive system is still immature. It could also reduce energy intakes by 'bulking up' the diet. Providing a mixture of white bread and refined cereals, white rice and pasta, as well as a few wholegrain varieties occasionally, helps to maintain a healthy balance between fibre and nutrient intakes.

Providing drinks for children

An adequate fluid intake will prevent dehydration and reduce the risk of constipation. You should offer children something to drink several times during the day. Milk and water are the best drinks to give young children between meals and snacks, as they do not harm teeth when taken from a cup or beaker.

- **Water** is a very underrated drink for the whole family. It quenches thirst without spoiling the appetite. If bottled water is preferred it should be still, not carbonated (fizzy), as this is acidic. More water should be given in hot weather in order to prevent **dehydration**.
- Research into how the brain develops has found that water is beneficial; many early years settings now make water available for children to help themselves.
- **Milk** is an excellent, nourishing drink which provides valuable **nutrients**.

Other drinks

All drinks that contain sugar can be harmful to teeth and can also take the edge off children's appetites. For example:

- flavoured milks
- fruit squashes
- flavoured fizzy drinks
- fruit juices (containing natural sugar).

Unsweetened *diluted* fruit juice is a reasonable option – but not as good as water or milk – for children, but ideally should only be offered at mealtimes. Low-sugar and diet fruit drinks contain artificial sweeteners and are best avoided. Tea and coffee should *not* be given to children under five years, as they prevent the absorption of iron from foods. They also tend to fill children up without providing any nourishment.

For children aged 1 to 5:

- Offer around six to eight drinks per day from a beaker or cup (although more may be needed in very hot weather or when they are very active). One drink for this age group will be about 100–150 ml.
- Sweetened drinks, including diluted fruit juice, should only be consumed *with*, rather than between, meals, to lessen the risk of dental decay. Consumption of sugar-free fizzy or fruit-based drinks, although not recommended, should also be confined to mealtimes, because the high acidity level of these drinks can cause dental decay.

How much food should children be given?

Children's appetites vary enormously, so common sense is a good guide on how big a portion should be. Always be guided by the individual child:

- Do not force them to eat when they no longer wish to.
- Do not refuse to give more if they really are hungry.

Some children always feel hungry at one particular mealtime; others require food little and often. You should always offer food that is nourishing, as well as satisfying their hunger.

Meals and snacks

Some children really do need to eat between meals. Their stomachs are relatively small, so they fill up and empty faster than adult stomachs. Sugary foods should not be given as a snack, because sugar is an appetite depressant and may spoil the child's appetite for the main meal to follow. Healthy snack foods include:

- pieces of fruit – banana, orange, pear, kiwi fruit, apple or satsuma
- fruit-bread or wholemeal bread with a slice of cheese
- milk or home-made milkshakes
- sticks of carrot, celeriac, parsnip, red pepper, cauliflower
- dried fruit and diluted fruit juices
- wholegrain biscuits, oatcakes or sesame seed crackers.

Minerals and vitamins

Iron

Iron is an important dietary mineral that is involved in various bodily functions, including the transport of oxygen in the blood. This is essential in providing energy for daily life. Lack of iron often leads to **anaemia** – which can hold back

Breakfast	Orange juice Weetabix® + milk 1 slice of buttered toast	Milk Cereal, e.g. corn or wheat flakes Toast and jam	Apple juice 1 slice of toast with butter or jam	Milk Cereal with slice of banana, or scrambled egg on toast	Yoghurt Porridge Slices of apple
Morning snack	Diluted apple juice 1 packet raisins	Blackcurrant and apple drink Cheese straws	1 glass fruit squash 1 biscuit	Peeled apple slices Wholemeal toast fingers with cheese spread	Diluted apple juice Chapatti or pitta bread fingers
Lunch	Chicken or macaroni cheese Broccoli Fruit yoghurt Water	Thick bean soup or chicken salad sandwich Green beans Fresh fruit salad Water	Vegetable soup or fish fingers/cakes Sticks of raw carrot Kiwi fruit Water	Sweet potato casserole Sweetcorn Spinach leaves Chocolate mousse Water	Bean casserole (or chicken drumstick) with noodles Peas or broad beans Fruit yoghurt Water
Afternoon snack	Diluted fruit juice Cubes of cheese with savoury biscuit	Milk shake Fruit cake or chocolate biscuit	Diluted fruit juice Thin-cut sandwiches cut into small pieces	Hot or cold chocolate drink 1 small packed dried fruit mix, e.g. apricots, sultanas	Lassi (yoghurt drink) 1 banana 1 small biscuit

Table 4.3 Providing a balanced diet

both physical and mental development. Children most at risk are those who are poor eaters or are on restricted diets.

Iron comes in two forms:

- in foods from **animal sources** (especially meat), which is easily absorbed by the body
- in **plant foods**, which is not quite so easy for the body to absorb.

If possible, children should be given a portion of meat or fish every day, and kidney or liver once a week. Even a small portion of meat or fish is useful, because it also helps the body to absorb iron from other food sources.

If children do not eat meat or fish, they must be offered plenty of iron-rich alternatives, such as egg yolks, dried fruit, beans and lentils, and green leafy vegetables. It is also a good idea to give foods or drinks that are high in vitamin C at mealtimes, as this helps the absorption of iron from non-meat sources.

Calcium and vitamin D

Children need calcium for maintaining and repairing growing bones and teeth, and for the correct functioning of muscles and blood clotting. Calcium is:

- found in milk, cheese, yoghurt and other dairy products
- only absorbed by the body if it is taken with vitamin D.

The skin can make all the vitamin D that a body needs when it is exposed to gentle sunlight. People with darker skin are at greater risk of vitamin D deficiencies – such as **rickets** – because increased pigmentation reduces the capacity of the skin to manufacture the vitamin from sunlight.

Sources of vitamin D include:

- milk
- fortified breakfast cereals
- oily fish
- meat
- fortified margarine
- soya mince, soya drink
- tahini paste (**NB**: Made from sesame seeds, which may cause an allergic reaction in a small number of children)
- tofu.

The UK health departments recommend that children under the age of five be given vitamin drops which contain vitamins A, C and D.

Children on vegetarian diets

Children who are on a vegetarian diet do not eat meat or fish, so they need an alternative to meat, fish and chicken as the main sources of **protein**. These could include:

- milk, cheese, eggs and pulses (lentils and beans).

They also need enough **iron**. As iron is more difficult to absorb from vegetable sources than from meat, a young child needs to obtain iron from sources such as:

- leafy green vegetables (e.g. spinach and watercress)
- pulses (beans, lentils and chickpeas)
- dried fruit (such as apricots, raisins and sultanas)
- some breakfast cereals.

It is easier to absorb iron from our food if it is eaten *with* foods containing vitamin C – foods such as fruit and vegetables or diluted fruit juices at mealtimes; these make it easier to absorb the iron.

The vegan diet

A vegan diet completely excludes **all** foods of animal origin – that is, animal flesh, milk and milk products, eggs, honey and all additives which may be of animal origin. A vegan diet is based on cereals and cereal products, pulses, fruits, vegetables, nuts and seeds. Human breast milk is acceptable for vegan babies.

The 'five-a-day' scheme

The government recently launched the five-a-day scheme to encourage people to eat at least five portions of fruit and vegetables every day. The portions do not have to be fresh – frozen or canned fruit and vegetables can provide the same nutrients – vitamins and minerals – and dietary fibre that are all essential for good health.

1 medium apple

2 broccoli florets

2 halves of canned peaches

1 handful of grapes

1 medium banana

3 heaped tablespoons of peas

1 medium glass of orange juice

7 strawberries

3 whole dried apricots

5 A DAY

Just Eat More
(fruit & veg)

3 heaped tablespoons of cooked kidney beans

16 okra

NHS

www.doh.gov.uk/fiveaday

© Crown copyright 2003

Figure 4.5 Just Eat More portion poster for the NHS 5 A Day programme (NHS, Crown Copyright 2003)

 REVISION QUESTIONS

1. List the five main food groups which provide nutrients in the diet.
2. Which food group provides children with energy? Give four examples of foods in this group.
3. Why is it important for children to have calcium in their daily diet?
4. What is the difference between a vegan and a vegetarian diet?

CHILD STUDY ACTIVITY

Find out what sort of diet the child eats. What are the child's food preferences and dislikes?

6 The importance of healthy eating and its relationship to diet-related illnesses

Some children can be choosy about the food they eat, and this can be a source of anxiety for parents and for those who work with children. However, as long as children eat *some* food from each of the **five food groups** – even if they are the same old favourites – there is no cause for worry. Poor eating habits and lack of physical activity in childhood may increase the risk of health problems later in life.

In recent years there has been increasing public concern about the quality of children's diets, rapidly increasing rates of **child obesity**, diet-related diseases, and low consumption of fruit and vegetables by children. The quality of our diet during childhood is a factor in the development of a number of disorders, either in childhood itself or during adult life. There are various conditions that may occur in childhood that are directly related to a poor or unbalanced diet; these include:

- **failure to thrive** (or faltering growth) – poor growth and physical development
- **dental caries** or tooth decay – associated with a high consumption of sugar in snacks and fizzy drinks
- **obesity** – children who are overweight are more likely to become obese adults
- **nutritional anaemia** – due to an insufficient intake of iron, folic acid and vitamin B12
- **increased susceptibility to infections** – particularly upper respiratory infections, such as colds and bronchitis.

Childhood obesity

Obesity (fatness) results from taking in more energy from the diet than is used up by the body. Some children appear to inherit a tendency to put on weight very easily, and some parents and carers offer more high-calorie food than children need. Some associated dietary problems are:

- **Changing lifestyles:** Fast food is overtaking traditionally prepared meals. Many convenience meals involve coating the food with fatty sauces or batters.
- **Foods high in sugar and fat:** Children eat more sweets and crisps and drink more fizzy drinks – this is partly because of advertising, but also because such foods are more widely available.
- **Poor fruit and vegetable consumption:** Despite fresh fruit and vegetables being more readily available, many children do not eat enough of these, preferring processed varieties that often contain added sugar and fat.

Obesity can lead to emotional problems as well as to the physical problem of

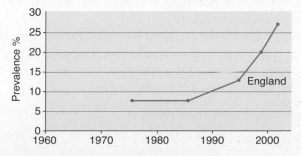

Figure 4.6 Overweight children

being more prone to infections: an obese child may be taunted by others, and will be unable to participate in the same vigorous play as their peers.

A child who is diagnosed as being overweight will usually be prescribed a diet low in fat and sugar; high-fibre carbohydrates are encouraged – for example, wholemeal bread and other cereals. The child who has to go without crisps, chips and snacks between meals will need a lot of support and encouragement from parents and carers.

Other diet-related issues

Food refusal

Many children go through phases of refusing to eat certain foods or not wanting to eat anything much at all. This is particularly common in children up to the age of five and is a normal part of growing up and asserting their independence. Eating can quickly become a focus for conflict and tension at home, with parents feeling anxious and out of control. Food refusal often starts because it is one of the few ways in which children can exert influence over their parents. Reasons for food refusal in young children include the following:

- **Slower growth and small appetites**: Growth slows down in the second year. This means that toddlers often have small appetites and need less food. Children eat according to their appetite, and this can vary from day to day. Some children eat in spurts – they may eat a lot one day and very little the next. It also depends on how active they have been during the day.
- **Distraction**: Young children have no concept of time. Their world has become an exciting place to explore and food can seem less important when there are so many other things to do.
- **Grazing and snacking**: Toddlers rarely follow a traditional meal pattern. They tend to need small and regular snacks. Parents may offer sweets or crisps throughout the day so that children 'won't go hungry'. Children then become even less inclined to eat their meals when they know that they can fill up on their favourite snacks. Large quantities of milk or other drinks throughout the day also take the edge off a child's appetite.
- **Fussy eating and food fads**: Showing independence is part of normal child development and this often includes refusing to eat foods 'to see what will happen'. It is quite normal for children to have certain times when their food choices become very limited – for example, they will only eat food prepared and presented in a certain way. Some decide they do not like mixed-up food or different foods touching each other on the plate, and they develop strong likes and dislikes that change frequently.
- **New textures and tastes**: Children are experimenting with, or being asked to try, new textures and tastes. Rejecting a food does not always mean the child does not like it. They may well eat it when offered it the very next day. Many adults reject certain foods that are eaten widely in other cultures – for example, sheep's eyeballs or dog.
- **Seeking attention**: Children are testing their parents' reactions and learning what effect their uncooperative behaviour has. They have learnt to say 'no' and may welcome all the attention they are getting by refusing to eat – or taking ages to eat – a lovingly prepared meal.

How to cope with food refusal

Research shows that one-third of all parents worry that their child is not eating enough; however, unless they are ill, a young child will never voluntarily starve themselves. If a child seems to be healthy and energetic, they are almost certainly eating enough. There is plenty of advice for parents from health experts and child dieticians on how to cope with their child's refusal of food. Parents should:

- never force-feed a child – either by pushing food into his/her mouth or by threatening punishment or withdrawal of a treat
- keep calm and try not to make a fuss of whether the child is eating or not; instead, try to make mealtimes pleasant, social occasions, because if children associate mealtimes with an enjoyable event, they will want to repeat it
- encourage self-feeding and exploration of food from an early age, without worrying about the mess
- offer alternative foods from every food group – for example, if a child dislikes cheese, they may eat yoghurt
- provide healthy, nutritious snacks between meals, as these play an important part in the energy intake of young children; ideas include fresh and dried fruits, crackers with cheese or peanut butter, yoghurt, plain biscuits, scones or buns
- avoid giving sweets and crisps between meals to children who refuse food at mealtimes.

Food intolerances and allergies

Food intolerance is an adverse reaction to some sort of food or ingredient that occurs *every time* the food is eaten, but particularly if larger quantities are consumed. Food intolerance:

- is not the same as a **food allergy**, because the **immune system** is not activated
- is not the same as **food poisoning**, which is caused by toxic substances that would cause symptoms in anyone who ate the food.

Food intolerance does not include *psychological* reactions to food; it is much more common than food allergy.

A **food allergy** is an abnormal response (an allergic reaction) of the **immune system** to otherwise harmless foods. Up to 5 per cent of children have food allergies. Most children outgrow their allergy, although an allergy to peanuts and some other tree nuts is considered lifelong.

There are eight foods that cause 90 per cent of all food allergic reactions:

- peanuts
- soya and soya products
- tree nuts (e.g. almonds, walnuts, pecans)
- wheat and gluten
- cow's milk and cow's milk products
- shellfish
- eggs
- fish.

Milk is the most common cause of food allergies in children, but peanuts, other nuts, fish and shellfish commonly cause the most severe reactions.

What are the symptoms of an allergic reaction?

Symptoms of an allergic response can include:

- vomiting
- hives (or urticaria) – an itchy, raised rash, usually found on the trunk or limbs
- itching or tightness in the throat
- diarrhoea
- eczema

- difficulty breathing
- cramps
- itching or swelling of the lips, tongue or mouth
- wheezing.

Allergic symptoms can begin within minutes or up to one hour after ingesting the food.

Anaphylaxis

In rare cases of food allergy, just one bite of food can bring on **anaphylaxis**. This is a severe reaction that involves various areas of the body simultaneously. In extreme cases, it can cause death.

Anaphylaxis is a sudden and severe, potentially life-threatening allergic reaction. It can be caused by insect stings or medications, as well as by a food allergy. Although, potentially, any food can cause anaphylaxis, **peanuts**, **nuts**, **shellfish**, **fish** and **eggs** are foods that most commonly cause this reaction.

Symptoms of anaphylaxis may include all those listed above for food allergies. In addition, the child's breathing is seriously impaired and the pulse rate becomes rapid.

Anaphylaxis is fortunately very rare, but it is also very dangerous:

- Symptoms can occur in as little as 5 to 15 minutes.
- Just half a peanut can cause a fatal reaction in severely allergic individuals.
- Some severely allergic children can have a reaction if milk is splashed on their skin.
- Being kissed by somebody who has eaten peanuts, for example, can cause a reaction in severely allergic individuals.

Emergency treatment of anaphylaxis:

1. **Summon medical help immediately.** The child will need oxygen and a life-saving injection of adrenaline.

2. **Place the child in a sitting position** to help relieve any breathing difficulty.

3. **Be prepared to resuscitate** if necessary.

 (In some settings attended by a child or children known to be at risk from anaphylaxis, the staff may be trained to give the adrenaline injection.)

How can food allergies be managed?

The only way to manage food allergies is strictly to avoid the foods to which the child is allergic. It is important to learn how to interpret ingredients on **food labels** and how to spot high-risk foods. Many children outgrow earlier food-allergic symptoms as they get older – usually by the time they are five – but parents will need professional support and advice to ensure that their child is receiving a safe, balanced diet.

Food additives

A food additive is any substance intentionally added to food for a specific function – for example, to preserve or colour it – that is not normally eaten as a food or used as a characteristic ingredient in food. When additives are used in food, they must be declared in the list of ingredients, either by name or by **E number**. All food additives must comply with European Union (EU) legislation. They can only be used if experts decide that they are necessary and safe. However, some people can react to certain additives, just as some people react to certain foods that most people can eat without any reaction. People who react to additives generally have asthma or other allergies already. Reactions to additives may bring on an asthma attack or cause nettle rash (urticaria).

Food additives and behaviour

Research commissioned by the Food Standards Agency in 2007 has found that a combination of additives can cause **hyperactivity** in children. The additives include several food colours and a preservative, all of which are often found in children's soft drinks, sweets and ice cream.

The following additives were found to increase the levels of hyperactivity in children:

- **Sunset yellow (E110)** – found in orange jelly, apricot jam, packet soup, canned fish, hot chocolate mixes and infant medicines.
- **Tartrazine (E102)** – found in fizzy drinks, ice creams, sweets, chewing gum, jam, yoghurt and infant medicines.
- **Ponceau 4R (E124)** – found in dessert toppings, jelly, canned strawberries and fruit pie fillings, salami, seafood dressings and infant medicines.
- **Quinoline yellow (E104)** – found in ice creams, ice lollies and smoked haddock.
- **Carmoisine (E122)** – found in jams, sweets, sauces, yoghurts, jellies, cheesecake mixes and infant medicines.
- **Allura red (E129)** – found in sweets, drinks and medicines.
- **Sodium benzoate (E211)** – found in soft drinks (fizzy drinks, squashes and fruit juices), cakes, jellies, sweets, crisps and infant medicines.

 KEY TERMS

Allergy: Abnormal sensitivity reaction of the body to substances that are usually harmless.

Anaphylaxis: An immediate and severe allergic response; a shock reaction to a substance.

Vegan: A person who avoids using or consuming animal products. While vegetarians avoid flesh foods, vegans also avoid dairy and eggs, as well as fur, leather, wool and cosmetics or chemical products tested on animals.

Vegetarian: There are two types of vegetarianism: **lacto-ovo vegetarians**, who exclude red meat, poultry and fish, and **lacto-vegetarians**, who exclude red meat, poultry, fish and eggs.

 REVISION QUESTIONS

1. Why has there been an increase in childhood obesity? Give four possible reasons.
2. What is food intolerance?
3. What is anaphylaxis?
4. Name six foods that commonly cause allergic reactions.
5. What is an E number? What effects may foods with E numbers have on children?

RESEARCH ACTIVITY

1. Visit a supermarket and look at the food labels on branded products.

   a. What information is provided relating to the products' nutritional content (e.g. fats – saturated and polyunsaturated – energy values, protein, vitamins)?

   b. How would the information provided help in planning a balanced diet for young children?

2. Find out about the dietary requirements and restrictions in *one* cultural or religious group that is not your own. Choose from:

   a. Jewish

   b. Muslim (Islamic)

   c. Hindu

   d. Rastafarian.

7 Food hygiene

Young children are particularly vulnerable to the bacteria which can cause food poisoning, or **gastroenteritis**. Bacteria multiply rapidly in warm, moist foods and can enter food without causing the food to look, smell or even taste bad. So it is very important to store, prepare and cook food safely, and to keep the kitchen clean.

Food hygiene is important to everyone. The food we eat is one of the key factors in good health. If you are caring for children you need to know the principles of food hygiene.

What is food poisoning?

Any infectious disease that results from consuming food or drink is known as food poisoning. The term is most often used to describe the illness – usually diarrhoea and/or vomiting caused by bacteria, viruses or parasites.

What causes food poisoning?

Most cases of food poisoning result from eating large numbers of **pathogenic** (or harmful) **bacteria** which are living on the food. Most food poisoning is preventable, although it is not possible to completely eliminate the risk.

At risk: babies and young children

Babies and very young children are at particular risk from food poisoning, partly because they have immature immune systems. Also, in young children infection can spread very quickly if there is a lack of supervised, thorough hand washing after using the toilet and before eating, and from touching contaminated toilet seats and tap handles. Many young children also put their hands, fingers and thumbs in their mouths frequently, so hands should be kept clean.

How bacteria from food sources make you ill

Bacteria – or germs – found in food can lead to food poisoning, which can be dangerous and can kill – though this is rare. They are very hard to detect since they do not usually affect the taste, appearance or smell of food.

Bacteria can either be present in food, or can come from other people, surfaces or equipment, or other food by **cross-contamination**. The main causes of bacterial food poisoning are:

- **Undercooking** – for example, when the oven is not hot enough (or not used for long enough) to ensure that the inside of a chicken is completely cooked. It is essential that frozen raw meat and poultry are adequately thawed, followed by thorough cooking to ensure that any pathogenic bacteria are destroyed.
- **Food prepared too far in advance and then not refrigerated** – for example, when a ham sandwich is left out of the fridge – uncovered or covered – for several hours. Food poisoning bacteria can multiply rapidly at room temperature. All food prepared in advance must be refrigerated to ensure minimal bacterial growth. For this reason, fridges should operate below 5° C.
- **Poor personal hygiene** – for example, when a person prepares food without washing their hands properly. Poor personal hygiene can result in food becoming contaminated with bacteria. Hands must be washed as frequently as necessary, but definitely:
  a. before handling food or equipment
  b. after visiting the toilet
  c. in between handling raw and cooked food
  d. after handling waste food or refuse.

- **Cross-contamination** – for example, when a knife that has been used to cut raw meat is not washed and is then used to cut cooked or ready-to-eat food. Food poisoning bacteria may be present in raw food such as meat and poultry. If these bacteria are allowed to contaminate food which is to be eaten without further cooking, food poisoning can result. Cross-contamination from raw food may happen as a result of poor **storage**, when the juices from raw meat are allowed to drip onto cooked food, or are transferred via a chopping board or utensils used for both raw and cooked food.
- **Infected food handlers** – for example, a person who returns to work after a brief episode of vomiting and diarrhoea may still be a carrier of food-poisoning bacteria. Any person suffering from vomiting and/or diarrhoea should not prepare or serve food until totally clear of symptoms for at least 48 hours. Even then, extra attention to hand washing is essential. Septic boils and cuts are another potential source of pathogens. Uninfected wounds should be completely covered and protected by a waterproof dressing.
- **Failure to keep cooked food** hot – for example, serving food which has been allowed to stand and become cool – under 63° C – after cooking. As thorough cooking does not destroy spores, hot food kept below 63° C can allow the spores to germinate and produce food-poisoning bacteria. For this reason, it is important to keep hot food above 63° C.
- **Eating food from unsafe sources** – for example, buying food from a shop which does not properly refrigerate its products.

 REVISION QUESTIONS

1. Why are babies and young children particularly at risk of food poisoning?
2. Give five reasons why food poisoning may occur.

The prevention of food poisoning

Even healthy people carry food-poisoning bacteria on their bodies. These can be spread to the hands through touching parts of the body that contain them, such as the nose, mouth or bottom, and then from the hands to the food.

Why washing your hands is vital

Hands are the most obvious way in which a person can contaminate food because they touch utensils, work surfaces and the food itself when it is being prepared, served or eaten. Nails can also harbour dirt and bacteria and should be kept short and clean at all times.

> **Safety tip:** Hand washing is one of the most important ways you can prevent the spread of infection.

If hands are not clean they can spread food-poisoning bacteria all round the kitchen. Washing your hands *thoroughly* is a good way to reduce the chance of passing on bacteria. This should include washing the backs of hands, wrists, between the fingers and under fingernails with soap and warm water – and then drying them thoroughly.

Storing food safely

- Keep food cold. The fridge should be kept as cold as it will go without actually freezing the food (1–5° C or 34–41° F).
- Cover or wrap food with food wrap or microwave cling film.
- Never refreeze food that has begun to thaw.
- Do not use foods that are past their sell-by or best-before date.
- Always read instructions on the label when storing food.
- Once a tin is opened, store the contents in a covered dish in the fridge.
- Store raw foods at the bottom of the fridge so that juices cannot drip onto cooked food.
- Thaw frozen meat completely before cooking.

Preparing and cooking food safely

- Always wash hands in warm water and soap and dry on a clean towel: *before* handling food and *after* handling raw foods, especially meat.
- Wear clean, protective clothing that is solely for use in the kitchen.
- Keep food covered at all times.
- Wash all fruits and vegetables before eating. Peel and top carrots, and peel fruits such as apples.
- Never cough or sneeze over food.
- Always cover any septic cuts or boils with a waterproof dressing.
- Never smoke in any room that is used for food.
- Keep work surfaces and chopping boards clean and disinfected; use separate boards for raw meat, fish, vegetables and so on, to avoid cross-contamination.
- Make sure that meat dishes are cooked thoroughly.
- Avoid raw eggs. They sometimes contain salmonella bacteria, which may cause food poisoning. (Also avoid giving children *uncooked* cake mixture, home-made ice creams, mayonnaise or desserts that contain uncooked raw egg.) When cooking eggs, the egg yolk and white should be firm.
- When reheating food, make sure it is piping hot all the way through, and allow to cool slightly before giving it to children. When using a microwave, always stir and check the temperature of food before feeding children, to avoid burning from hot spots.
- Avoid having leftovers – they are a common cause of food poisoning.

Keeping the kitchen safe

- Teach children to wash their hands after touching pets and going to the toilet, and before eating.
- Clean tin-openers, graters and mixers thoroughly after use.
- Keep flies and other insects away – use a fine mesh over open windows.
- Stay away from the kitchen if you are suffering from diarrhoea or sickness.
- Keep the kitchen clean – the floor, work surfaces, sink, utensils, cloths and waste bins should be cleaned regularly.
- Tea towels should be boiled every day and dishcloths boiled or disinfected.
- Keep pets away from the kitchen.
- Keep all waste bins covered, and empty them regularly.
- Keep sharp knives stored safely where children cannot reach them.

Guidelines: food hygiene

When serving food and clearing away after meals and snacks, you should observe the rules of food hygiene:

- Wash your hands using soap and warm water and dry them on a clean towel.
- Wear clean protective clothing.
- Ensure any washing-up by hand is done thoroughly in hot water with detergent (and use rubber gloves).
- Cover cups/beakers with a clean cloth and air-dry where possible.
- Drying-up cloths should be replaced every day with clean ones.
- Never cough or sneeze over food.

 QUICK FACTS

- The number of bacteria on fingertips doubles after using the toilet.
- Bacteria can stay alive on our hands for up to three hours.
- A thousand times as many bacteria spread from damp hands than from dry hands.
- Even after thorough washing, bugs (such as E. coli) can remain under long fingernails.
- Millions of bacteria can hide under rings, watches and bracelets.
- A 1 mm hair follicle can harbour 50,000 bacteria.

 REVISION QUESTIONS

1. What is one of the most important things you can do to prevent food poisoning?
2. What is cross-contamination, and how can you prevent it?
3. Why is it important to store raw foods (such as meat and fish) at the bottom of the fridge?

 ACTIVITY

In groups, design and make a colourful poster to explain how to prevent cross-contamination.

8 Response to infection

How infection is spread

Infectious diseases are caused by both bacteria and viruses. Infection enters the body in several ways:

- **Droplet infection:** This occurs by breathing in air containing tiny droplets of infected mucus from an infected person's sneeze or cough. *For example*: Colds, flu, pneumonia and whooping cough are spread by coughs and sneezes.
- **Touching infected people:** Germs can be spread by touching (or kissing) someone who is infected, or by using the things they have used, such as towels, combs and cups. (This may also be called a contagious disease.) *For example*: Chickenpox and measles can be caught by touching infected people, and athlete's foot can be caught by walking on wet floors or mats used by infected people.
- **Infected food or drink:** Food and drink can be infected with germs by coughs and sneezes, dirty hands, flies, mice and pet animals. *For example*: Infected food and drink cause food poisoning and dysentery.

How the immune system works

The natural barriers of the immune system are the **skin** and the **mucosal membranes** that line the digestive, respiratory and genito-urinary systems, which can be accessed from outside the body. If this physical and chemical barrier is broken down by trauma or as a result of infection on the surface, the invading pathogens can enter the body, the bloodstream and the lymphatic system, and potentially find a niche elsewhere in the body tissue to multiply and form a colony.

The first line of defence: natural barriers to infection

We are all born with natural immunity, which is the ability of the body to resist infection. The body has a complex immune system which works in partnership with other protective body systems:

- **The skin** forms a physical barrier against germs entering your body. Skin is tough and generally impermeable to bacteria and viruses. The skin also secretes **antibacterial substances** – most bacteria and spores that land on the skin die quickly.
- **Nose, mouth and eyes** are also obvious entry points for germs. Tears and mucus contain an **enzyme** that breaks down the cell walls of many bacteria. Saliva is also antibacterial. Since the nasal passage and lungs are coated in mucus, many germs not killed immediately are trapped in the mucus and soon swallowed.
- **The respiratory system** uses cilia, mucus and coughing to rid the body of inhaled microbes and pollutants.
- **Acid** in the stomach and **enzymes** in the intestines destroy many pathogens.

If foreign materials enter the body in spite of these protective systems, then the immune and defence mechanisms come into play.

The second line of defence: white blood cells

All white blood cells are known as **leucocytes**. White blood cells are not like normal cells in the body – they actually act like independent, living, single-cell organisms, able to move and capture things on their own. If micro-organisms get into the body through a cut in the skin, the most important thing is to quickly

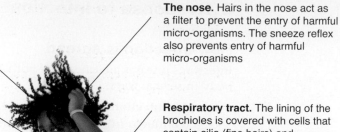

The eyes. The tears contain an enzyme called lysozyme that destroys bacteria.

The mouth. Saliva contains enzymes and other substances that destroy bacteria.

Stomach and intestine. Acid inside the stomach destroys harmful micro-organisms; in the lower intestines, friendly bacteria, or natural flora, help comtrol harmful bacteria. Vomiting and diarrhoea are also methods by which the stomach and intestines rapidly remove toxic substances.

The nose. Hairs in the nose act as a filter to prevent the entry of harmful micro-organisms. The sneeze reflex also prevents entry of harmful micro-organisms

Respiratory tract. The lining of the brochioles is covered with cells that contain cilia (fine hairs) and mucus-secreting cells. Micro-organisms are trapped by the mucus and swept by the cilia to the bronchi, where they are expelled by coughing

Genito-urinary system. The vagina and uretha contain natural flora and are protected by mucus.

The skin. Undamaged skin acts as a primary barrier against infection. The sebaceous glands secrete chemicals which are toxic to many bacteria. The constant shedding of the outermost cells of the skin also dislodges micro-organisms.

Figure 4.7 Natural barriers to infection

close the wound so more micro-organisms cannot enter. A scab does just this. The blood contains tiny structures called platelets, and a protein called fibrin. A scab is basically platelets stuck in a fibrin mesh. As a wound heals, nearby blood vessels widen to allow more blood to reach the area. This causes inflammation where the damaged area becomes swollen, hot and red. The two most important white blood cells in our immune system are phagocytes and lymphocytes:

- **Phagocytes:** These cells fight infection by surrounding and engulfing the pathogens – or germs – and then attacking them with a range of chemicals and enzymes. They are *not* effective against viruses.
- **Lymphocytes:** Once the phagocytes have attacked the invaders, the resultant parts would then be processed by other white blood cells, including the lymphocytes. If there have been similar invaders before, the lymphocytes may have a 'memory' of this and rapidly produce antibodies to set an early attack before the invading germs get a chance to multiply.

The third line of defence: antibodies

Once the lymphocytes have made a particular kind of antibody, they can make it much faster the next time; also, it may stay in your blood for a while. This makes you **immune** to the disease. You may never catch it again, or, if you do, you will only have it mildly. You can also get vaccinated against certain diseases. Specially treated germs are injected into you, to give you a mild attack of the disease. Your body responds by making antibodies, so you become immune for the future.

Antibodies neutralise pathogens in a number of ways:

- They bind to pathogens and damage or destroy them.
- They coat pathogens, clumping them together so that they are easily ingested by **phagocytes**

- They bind to the pathogens and release chemical signals to attract more phagocytes.

The lymphatic system

The lymphatic system plays an important part in our defence against infection. Lymph is a clearish liquid that contains some white blood cells and some chemicals that are also found in blood. Lymph helps to fight infections and drains fluid from body tissues back into the bloodstream. The lymph permeates the body just as blood does, but it circulates through muscle movements rather than being pumped around the body like blood. Any random bacteria that enter the body also find their way into the lymphatic system. One job of the lymph system is to drain and filter these fluids to detect and remove the bacteria. Small lymph vessels collect the liquid and move it towards larger vessels so that the fluid finally arrives at the lymph nodes for processing.

Lymph nodes contain filtering tissue and a large number of lymph cells. When fighting certain bacterial infections, the lymph nodes swell with bacteria and the cells fighting the bacteria, to the point where you can actually feel them. Swollen lymph nodes – often called swollen glands – are therefore a good indication that you have an infection of some sort. These swollen glands may be felt in the neck, in the armpits and in the groin area.

How antibiotics work

Normally our bodies are fit enough to fight an infection with all the parts of our immune system. Antibiotics are chemicals developed to help us in the fight. They reduce the risk of tissue damage while the immune system fights off the infection, and they reduce the risk of death if it is unsuccessful. There is an argument that antibiotics are used too much – for minor infections with low risks, we should wait for the body's own defences to react. One problem of giving a course of antibiotics for an infection is that, as well as killing off the harmful bacteria causing the infection, some of your harmless bacteria will die too, leaving an opportunity for others to grow. A good example is thrush, or candida infection. This yeast-like fungus normally lives on the skin and in the gut and vagina in small, well-controlled numbers, but after a dose of antibiotics it gets a chance to multiply and cause further harm. There is also a danger that people will develop resistance to antibiotics.

 KEY TERMS

Antibody: Substance the body produces to try to control or eliminate a disease.

Cilia: Tiny hairs that line the respiratory tract. They beat continuously to move mucus and dirt up the bronchii and trachea.

Pathogens: Micro-organisms that cause infectious disease. Bacteria and viruses are the main pathogens.

Phagocytes: Cells, such as white blood cells, that engulf and absorb waste material, harmful micro-organisms, or other foreign bodies in the bloodstream and tissues.

REVISION QUESTIONS

1. What are the natural defences to infection?

2. Which part of the blood protects you against infection?

3. What is the role of the lymphatic system in preventing infection?

4. What is an antibody?

9 Childhood illnesses

How to recognise signs of illness

General signs of illness in babies

Babies are not able to explain to their carers how they are feeling, so it is important to recognise some of the *general* signs that accompany illness. These include:

- crying in a 'strange' way (in a way that is different from their usual cry) – this could mean they are experiencing pain, hunger or thirst
- refusing feeds
- not smiling or playing as they normally do
- becoming unusually listless or lethargic
- cannot be comforted by the usual methods
- has a raised temperature (or fever) – indicating infection
- seeming overly clingy
- being especially sleepy at times when they are normally wide awake
- crying weakly or appearing to be in pain.

Condition	Signs and symptoms	Role of the carer
Colic	This occurs in the first 12 weeks. It causes sharp, spasmodic pain in the stomach, and is often at its worst in the late evening. Symptoms include inconsolable, high-pitched crying, drawing the legs up to the chest, and growing red in the face.	Try to stay calm. Gently massage the baby's abdomen in a clockwise direction, using the tips of your middle fingers. Sucrose solution (3 x 5 ml teaspoons of sugar in a cup of boiling water left to cool) is said to have a mild painkilling effect on small babies. Dribble 2 ml of this solution into the corner of the baby's mouth twice a day. If the problem persists, contact the doctor.
Diarrhoea	Frequent loose or watery stools. Can be very serious in young babies, especially when combined with vomiting, as it can lead to severe dehydration.	Give frequent, small drinks of cooled, boiled water containing glucose and salt, or a made-up sachet of rehydration fluid. If the baby is unable to take the fluid orally, s/he must be taken to hospital urgently and fed intravenously by a drip. If the anal area becomes sore, treat with a barrier cream.
Gastroenteritis	The baby may vomit and usually has diarrhoea as well; often has a raised temperature and loss of appetite. May show signs of abdominal pain (i.e. drawing up of legs to chest and crying).	Reassure the baby. Observe strict hygiene rules. Look out for signs of dehydration. Offer frequent, small amounts of fluid, and possibly rehydration salts.
Neonatal cold injury (hypothermia)	The baby is cold to the touch. Face may be pale or flushed. Lethargic; runny nose; swollen hands and feet. Preterm infants and babies under four months are at particular risk.	Warm *slowly* by covering with several light layers of blankets and by cuddling. Do not use direct heat. Offer feeds high in sugar and seek medical help urgently.

Table 4.4 Illness in babies

Condition	Signs and symptoms	Role of the carer
Reflux	Also known as gastrointestinal reflux (GIR) or gastro-oesophageal reflux (GOR). The opening to the stomach is not yet efficient enough to allow a large liquid feed through. Symptoms include 'grizzly' crying and excessive **possetting** after feeds.	Try feeding the baby in a more upright position and bring up wind by gently rubbing the back. After feeding, leave the baby in a semi-sitting position. Some doctors prescribe a paediatric reflux suppressant or antacid mixture to be given before the feed.
Tonsillitis	Very sore throat, which looks bright red. There is usually fever and the baby will show signs of distress from pain on swallowing and general aches and pains. May vomit.	Encourage plenty of fluids – older babies may have ice lollies to suck. Give pain relief (e.g. paracetamol). Seek medical aid if no improvement and if fever persists.
Cough	Often follows on from a cold; may be a symptom of other illness (e.g. measles).	Keep air moist. Check the baby has not inhaled an object. Give medicine if prescribed.
Croup	Croup is an infection of the voice box or larynx, which becomes narrowed and inflamed. Barking cough (like a sea lion), noisy breathing, distressed; usually occurs at night.	If severe, seek medical help. Sit the baby up. Keep calm and reassure the baby. Inhaling steam may also benefit some babies. You can produce steam by boiling a kettle, running the hot taps in the bathroom, using a room humidifier or putting wet towels over the radiator. If using steam, take care to avoid scalding.
Bronchiolitis	A harsh, dry cough which later becomes wet and chesty; runny nose, raised temperature, wheeze, breathing problems, poor feeding or vomiting. May develop a blue tinge around the lips and on the fingernails (known as **cyanosis**).	Observe closely. Seek medical help if condition worsens. Increase fluids. Give small, regular feeds. Give prescribed medicine. Comfort and reassure.
Febrile convulsions (high temperature)	Convulsions caused by a high temperature (over 39° C or 102° F) or fever are called febrile convulsions. The baby will become rigid, then the body may twitch and jerk for one or two minutes.	Try not to panic. Move potentially harmful objects out of the way and place the baby in the recovery position. Loosen clothing. Call doctor. Give tepid sponging. Comfort and reassure.
Otitis media	Will appear unwell; may have raised temperature. May vomit, may cry with pain. May have discharge from ear.	Take to doctor, give antibiotics and analgesics (or painkillers). Increase fluids; comfort and reassure.
Conjunctivitis	Inflammation of the thin, delicate membrane that covers the eyeball and forms the lining of the eyelids. Symptoms include a painful red eye, with watering and sometimes sticky pus.	Take to doctor, who may prescribe antibiotic eye drops or ointment. Bathe a sticky eye gently with cool, boiled water and clean cotton-wool swabs. Always bathe the eye from the inside corner to the outside to avoid spreading infection.
Common cold	Runny nose, sneeze; tiny babies may have breathing problems.	Keep nose clear. Give small frequent feeds. Give nasal drops if prescribed.
Meningitis	Raised temperature; may have a blotchy rash; may refuse feeds; may have a stiff neck; may have a seizure; bulging fontanelle; may have a shrill, high-pitched cry.	Seek medical help urgently. Reduce temperature. Reassure.

Table 4.4 Contin.

KEY TERMS

Colic: Persistent, unexplained crying in a healthy baby between two weeks and five months of age.

Cyanosis: A bluish discoloration of the skin and mucous membranes, resulting from inadequate oxygenation of the blood.

Hypothermia: This potentially fatal condition occurs when body temperature falls below 35° C.

Meningitis: Infection or inflammation of the membranes (meninges) that cover the brain and spinal cord.

Possetting: When a baby regularly vomits small amounts of feeds but has no sign of illness. Usually caused by a weakness of the muscle at the opening of the stomach.

General signs of illness in older babies and children up to five years old

When children feel generally unwell, you should ask them if they have any pain or discomfort and treat it appropriately. Take their temperature and look for other signs of illness, such as a rash or swollen glands. Often, feeling generally unwell is the first sign that the child is developing an **infectious disease**. Some children can also show general signs of illness if they are anxious or worried about something, either at home or at school.

Emotional and behavioural changes

Children react in certain characteristic ways when they are unwell. Some of the more common emotional and behavioural changes include:

- being **quieter** than usual
- becoming **more clingy** to their parents or primary carer
- **attention-seeking** behaviour
- changed **sleeping patterns** – some children sleep more than usual, others less
- **lack of energy**
- **crying** – babies cry for a variety of reasons (see pages 100–101); older children who cry more than usual may be physically unwell or you may need to explore the reasons for their unhappiness
- **regression** – children who are unwell often regress in their development and behaviour. They may:
  a. want to be carried everywhere instead of walking independently
  b. go back to nappies after being toilet-trained
  c. start to wet the bed
  d. play with familiar, previously outgrown toys.

When to call a doctor or call for an ambulance

If you think the child's life is in danger, **dial 999** if you are in the UK, ask for an ambulance urgently and explain the situation. Contact the **family doctor** (GP) if the child has any of the following symptoms. **If the doctor cannot reach you quickly, take the child to the accident and emergency department of the nearest hospital:**

- Has a temperature of 38.6° C (101.4° F) that is not lowered by measures to reduce **fever**, or a temperature over 37.8° C (100° F) for more than one day.
- Has severe or persistent **vomiting** and/or **diarrhoea**, seems **dehydrated** or has projectile vomiting.
- Has symptoms of **meningitis**.
- Is pale, listless, and **does not respond** to usual stimulation.
- Has bulging **fontanelle** (soft spot on top of head) when not crying.
- **Refuses** two successive feeds.
- Passes bowel motions (stools) containing **blood**.
- Has a suspected **ear infection**.
- Has inhaled something, such as a peanut, into the air passages and may be **choking**.
- Has bright pink cheeks and swollen hands and feet (could be due to **hypothermia**).
- Has **convulsions**, or is limp and floppy.
- **Cannot be woken**, is unusually drowsy or may be losing consciousness.
- Has symptoms of **croup**.
- **Cries or screams** inconsolably and may have severe pain.
- Appears to have severe abdominal pain, with symptoms of **shock**.
- Develops **purple-red** rash anywhere on body.
- Has **jaundice**.
- Has been injured, **e.g. by a burn which blisters and covers** more than 10% of the body surface.
- Has swallowed a **poisonous** substance, or an object, e.g. a safety pin or button.
- Has difficulty in **breathing**.

Common signs and symptoms of illness in children

Small children are not always able to explain their symptoms, and may complain vaguely of their 'head hurting'. Again, you are in a good position to observe if the child is ill. They may show the following signs and symptoms:

- **Loss of appetite:** The child may not want to eat or drink – this could be because of a sore, painful throat or may be a sign of a developing infection.
- **Lacking interest in play:** The child may not want to join in play, without being able to explain why.
- **Abdominal pain:** The child may rub his/her tummy and say that it hurts – this could be a sign of gastroenteritis.
- **Raised temperature (fever):** A fever (a temperature above 38° C) is usually an indication of viral or bacterial infection, but can also result from overheating.
- **Diarrhoea and vomiting:** Attacks of diarrhoea and/or vomiting are usually a sign of gastroenteritis.
- **Lethargy or listlessness:** The child may be drowsy and prefer to sit quietly with a favourite toy or comfort blanket.
- **Irritability and fretfulness:** The child may have a change in behaviour, being easily upset and tearful.
- **Pallor:** The child will look paler than usual and may have dark shadows under the eyes; a black child may have a paler area around the lips, and the conjunctiva may be pale pink instead of the normal dark pink.
- **Rash (pimples or spots):** Any rash appearing on the child's body should be investigated – it is usually a sign of an infectious disease.

Meningitis in babies

Meningitis is an inflammation of the lining of the brain. It is a very serious illness, but if it is detected and treated early, most children make a full recovery. The early symptoms of meningitis – such as fever, irritability, restlessness, vomiting and refusing feeds – are also common with colds and flu. However, a baby with meningitis can become seriously ill within hours, so it is important to act quickly if meningitis is suspected.

Symptoms of meningitis

In babies under 12 months, symptoms are:

- tense or bulging fontanelle
- high temperature
- a stiffening body with involuntary movements, or a floppy body
- the baby may be difficult to wake
- blotchy or pale skin
- the baby may refuse to feed
- a high-pitched, moaning cry
- red or purple spots (anywhere on the body) that do not fade under pressure – do the 'glass test' (see below).

In older children, symptoms are:

- headache
- neck stiffness and joint pains; the child may arch the neck backwards because of the rigidity of the neck muscles
- an inability to tolerate light
- fever.

Disease and cause	How it spreads	Incubation	Signs and symptoms	Rash or specific sign	Treatment	Possible complications
Common cold (coryza) Virus	Airborne/droplet, hand-to-hand contact	1–3 days	Sneeze, sore throat, running nose, headache, slight fever, irritable, partial deafness		Treat symptoms, Vaseline® to nostrils	Bronchitis, sinusitis, laryngitis
Chickenpox (varicella) Virus	Airborne/droplet, direct contact	10–14 days	Slight fever, itchy rash, mild onset, child feels ill, often with severe headache	Red spots with white centre on trunk and limbs at first; blisters and pustules	Rest, fluids, calamine to rash, cut child's nails to prevent secondary infection	Impetigo, scarring, secondary infection from scratching
Dysentery Bacillus or amoeba	Indirect: flies, infected food; poor hygiene	1–7 days	Vomiting, diarrhoea, blood and mucus in stool, abdominal pain, fever, headache		Replace fluids, rest, medical aid, strict hygiene measures	Dehydration from loss of body salts; shock, can be fatal
Food poisoning Bacterium or virus	Indirect: infected food or drink	1.5–36 hrs	Vomiting, diarrhoea, abdominal pain		Fluids – only for 24 hours; medical aid if no better	Dehydration, can be fatal
Gastroenteritis Bacterium or virus	Direct contact Indirect: infected food/drink	Bacterial: 7–14 days Viral: 1.5–36 hrs	Vomiting, diarrhoea, signs of dehydration		Replace fluids – water or rehydration salts; medical aid urgently	Dehydration, weight loss, death
Measles (morbilli) Virus	Airborne/droplet	7–15 days	High fever, fretful, heavy cold – running nose and discharge from eyes; later cough	*Day 1:* Koplik's spots, white inside mouth *Day 4:* blotchy rash starts on face and spreads down to body	Rest, fluids, tepid sponging; shade room if photophobic (dislikes bright light)	Otitis media, eye infection, pneumonia, encephalitis (rare)

Table 4.5 Common childhood infections

Disease and cause	How it spreads	Incubation	Signs and symptoms	Rash or specific sign	Treatment	Possible complications
Meningitis (inflammation of the meninges which cover the brain) Bacterium or virus	Airborne/droplet	Variable Usually 2–10 days	Fever, headache, drowsiness, confusion, photophobia (dislike of bright light), arching of neck	Can have small red spots or bruises	Take to hospital, antibiotics and observation	Deafness, brain damage, death
Mumps (epidemic parotitis) Virus	Airborne/droplet	14–21 days	Pain, swelling of jaw in front of ears, fever, pain when eating and drinking	Swollen face	Fluids (give via straw), hot compresses, oral hygiene	Meningitis (1 in 400) Orchitis (inflammation of the testes) in young men
Pertussis (whooping cough) Bacterium	Airborne/droplet, direct contact	7–21 days	Starts with a snuffly cold, slight cough, mild fever	Spasmodic cough with whoop sound, vomiting	Rest and assurance; feed after coughing attack; support during attack; inhalations	Convulsions, pneumonia, brain damage, hernia, debility
Rubella (German measles) Virus	Airborne/droplet, direct contact	14–21 days	Slight cold, sore throat, mild fever, swollen glands behind ears, pain in small joints	Slight pink rash starts behind ears and on forehead; not itchy	Rest if necessary; treat symptoms	Only if contracted by woman in first three months of pregnancy: can cause serious defects in unborn baby
Scarlet fever (scarlatina) Bacterium	Droplet	2–4 days	Sudden fever, loss of appetite, sore throat, pallor around mouth, 'strawberry' tongue	Bright-red, pinpoint rash over face and body – may peel	Rest, fluids, observe for complications, antibiotics	Kidney infection, otitis media, rheumatic fever (rare)
Tonsillitis Bacterium or virus	Direct infection, droplet	2–4 days	Very sore throat, fever, headache, pain on swallowing, aches and pains in back and limbs	Throat reddened, tonsils swollen and may be coated or have white spots on them	Rest, fluids, medical aid, antibiotics, iced drinks to relieve pain	Quinsy (abscess on tonsils), otitis media, kidney infection, temporary deafness

Table 4.5 Contin.

The glass test

Press the side or bottom of a glass firmly against the rash – you will be able to see if the rash fades and loses colour under the pressure. If it does not change colour, summon medical aid immediately. If spots are appearing on the child's body, this could be septicaemia, a very serious bacterial infection described as the 'meningitis rash'.

Figure 4.8 The glass test

High temperature (fever)

The normal body temperature is 36–37° C. A temperature of above 37.5° C means that the child has a fever. Common sense and using the back of your hand to feel the forehead of an ill child are almost as reliable in detecting a fever as using a thermometer.

A child with a fever may:

- look hot and flushed; may complain of feeling cold and might shiver – this is a natural reflex due to the increased heat loss and a temporary disabling of the usual internal temperature control of the brain
- be either irritable or subdued
- be unusually sleepy
- go off their food
- complain of thirst.

Children can develop high temperatures very quickly. You need to know how to bring their temperature down (see page 209) to avoid complications, such as dehydration and febrile convulsions.

 REVISION QUESTIONS

1. What is the medical name for:
   a. German measles?
   b. whooping cough?
   c. chickenpox?
2. Name four childhood infections caused by a bacterium and four caused by a virus.
3. What are the signs and symptoms of meningitis?

10 Immunisation and vaccination programmes

Immunisation is a way of protecting children against serious disease. Once children have been immunised, their bodies can fight those diseases if they come into contact with them. If a child is not immunised, they will be at risk from catching the disease and will rely on other people immunising their children to avoid becoming infected.

An immunisation programme protects people against specific diseases by reducing the number of people getting the disease and preventing it being passed on. With some diseases – like **smallpox** or **polio** – it is possible to eliminate them completely.

Age at which to immunise	Disease protected against	Vaccine *Each vaccination is given as a single injection into the muscle of the thigh or upper arm.*
2 months	Diphtheria (D) Tetanus (Ta) Pertussis or whooping cough (P) Polio (IPV) Haemophilus influenzae type B (Hib) Pneumococcal disease (PCV)	DTaP/IPV/Hib PCV
3 months	Diphtheria, tetanus, pertussis, polio and Hib Meningococcal disease (MenC)	(DTaP/IPV/Hib) MenC
4 months	Diphtheria, tetanus, pertussis, polio and Hib Pneumococcal disease Meningococcal disease	DTaP/IPV/Hib PCV MenC
Around 12 months	Hib Meningococcal disease	Hib/MenC
Around 13 months	Pneumococcal disease Measles, mumps and rubella (MMR)	PCV MMR
3 years 4 months to 5 years	Diphtheria, tetanus, pertussis and polio	DTaP/IPV or TaP/IPV

Table 4.6 Recommended immunisation schedule

Reasons for immunisation against disease

Not every disease that affects children can be immunised against. There is no routine vaccination for chickenpox or scarlet fever in the UK, although the chickenpox vaccine is offered with the MMR in some other countries. The following diseases are all included in the NHS programme of routine immunisation:

- **Diphtheria**: A bacterial infection which starts with a sore throat but can rapidly get worse, leading to severe breathing difficulties. It can also damage the heart and the nervous system.

- **Tetanus:** A bacterial infection caused when germs found in soil and manure get into the body through open cuts and burns. Tetanus is a painful disease which affects the muscles and can cause breathing problems.
- **Pertussis** (whooping cough): A bacterial infection that can cause long bouts of coughing and choking, making it hard to breathe. It is not usually serious in older children, but it can be very serious and can kill babies under one year old. It can last for up to ten weeks.
- **Polio:** A highly infectious viral disease, spread mainly through close contact with an infected person. The polio virus attacks the nervous system and can paralyse muscles permanently. If it attacks the muscles in the chest, or those that control swallowing, it can be fatal.
- **Hib** (Haemophilus influenzae type B): An infection that can cause a number of major illnesses, such as blood poisoning, pneumonia and meningitis. All these illnesses can kill if not treated quickly. The Hib vaccine protects the child against only *one* type of **meningitis**. It does not protect against any other type of meningitis.
- **Meningococcal disease:** One of the serious causes of **meningitis** (an inflammation of the lining of the brain) and serious blood infections in children. Although fairly rare now, before the introduction of the vaccine it was the most common killer of children aged one to five years. The MenC vaccine protects the child against only *one* type of meningitis (meningococcal).
- **Measles:** A highly contagious virus which causes a high fever and rash. Around 1 in 15 of all children who get measles is at risk of complications, including chest infections, fits and brain damage. In very serious cases, measles kills. In the year before the MMR vaccine was introduced in the UK (1988), 16 children died from measles.
- **Mumps:** Caused by a virus which can lead to fever, headache and painful, swollen glands in the face, neck and jaw. It can result in permanent deafness, viral meningitis (swelling of the lining of the brain) and encephalitis. Rarely, it causes painful swelling of the testicles in males and the ovaries in females.
- **Pneumococcal disease:** This is the term used to describe infections caused by the bacterium Streptococcus pneumoniae. It can cause pneumonia, septicaemia (blood poisoning) or meningitis, and is also one of the most common bacterial causes of ear infections. The bacterium is becoming increasingly resistant to antibiotics in the UK and worldwide.
- **Rubella** (German measles): Caused by a virus. In children it is usually mild and can go unnoticed. Rubella infection in the first three months of pregnancy causes damage to the unborn baby in nine out of ten cases; it can seriously damage their sight, hearing, heart and brain. In the five years before the MMR vaccine was introduced in the UK, about 43 babies a year were born with congenital rubella syndrome.

Immunisations are usually carried out in child health clinics. The doctor will discuss any fears the parents may have about particular vaccines. No vaccine is completely risk-free, and parents are asked to sign a consent form prior to immunisations being given. Immunisations are given only if the child is well, and may be postponed if the child has had a reaction to any previous immunisation, or if the child is taking any medication that might interfere with their ability to fight infection. The effects of the disease are usually far worse than any side effects of a vaccine.

The advantages of immunisation include the following:

- Children who are not immunised run the risk of catching diseases and having complications.

- Immunisation is the safest way to protect children from particular diseases that may have long-lasting effects.

- Having children immunised at an early age means they are well protected by the time they start playgroup or school, where they are in contact with lots of other children.

- Immunisation also protects those children who are unable to receive immunisation, by providing what is called herd immunity: this is a term used to describe partial uptake of immunisation, where enough people are immunised to prevent the spread of the disease.

The disadvantages of immunisation include the possibility of side effects. The possible risks that follow certain childhood immunisations must be weighed up against the possible risks of complications of the childhood illness. For example, with the MMR vaccine, there is a risk of febrile convulsions (fits) in 1 out of 1000 children. However, if a child catches the measles disease, the risk of convulsions is 1 in 200.

Alternatives to immunisation

There is no proven, effective alternative to conventional immunisation. Homeopathic medicine has been tried as an alternative to the pertussis (whooping cough) vaccine, but it was not found to be effective. The Council of the Faculty of Homeopathy (the registered organisation for doctors qualified in homeopathy) advises parents to have their children immunised with conventional vaccines.

How immunity to disease and infection can be acquired

Babies are born with some natural immunity. They are:

- able to make their own infection-fighting cells
- further protected by antibodies and other substances found in breast milk.

A child's own experiences of infection boost his/her immunity. For some infections (e.g. measles) immunity is lifelong, while for others it is short-lived. Certain illnesses, such as the common cold, are caused by one of several strains of virus, which is why having one cold does not automatically prevent another one later. Sometimes the immune system does not work properly, as in the case of HIV/AIDS infection and some other rare conditions. Sometimes it *overworks* and causes allergy. It can also be affected by emotional distress and physical exhaustion.

There are two types of immunity: active immunity and passive immunity. As discussed above, immunity can be induced by contact with an infection. It can also be induced by immunisation against certain infective agents.

Active immunity

Active immunity is when a vaccine triggers the immune system to produce antibodies against the disease, as though the body had been infected with it. This also teaches the body's immune system how to produce the appropriate antibodies quickly. If the immunised person then comes into contact with the disease itself, their immune system will recognise it and immediately produce the antibodies needed to fight it.

Passive immunity

Passive immunity is provided when the body is given **antibodies** rather than producing them itself. A newborn baby has passive immunity to several diseases, such as measles, mumps and rubella, from antibodies passed from its mother via the placenta. Passive immunity only lasts for a few weeks or months. In the case of measles, mumps and rubella, it may last up to one year in infants – this is why MMR is given just after a child's first birthday.

Herd immunity

If enough people in a community are immunised against certain diseases, it is more difficult for that disease to get passed between those who are not immunised – this is known as herd immunity. Herd immunity does not apply to all diseases because they are not all passed from person to person. For example, tetanus can only be caught from spores in the ground.

KEY TERMS

Immunisation: Immunisation protects children (and adults) against harmful infections before they come into contact with them in the community.

Immunity: A condition of being able to resist a particular infectious disease.

Lymph: A clear fluid that travels through lymph vessels, carrying immune system cells and tissue waste products.

Vaccine: A substance that stimulates the body's immune response in order to prevent or control an infection.

REVISION QUESTIONS

1. Which childhood infections can be immunised against in children under the age of five?
2. What is active immunity?
3. What is passive immunity?
4. What is herd immunity?

CHILD STUDY ACTIVITY

1. Find out if the child has had any infectious diseases and how it affected them.
2. Ask the parents how they feel about immunisation and whether they have had their child immunised.

11 Caring for sick children

How to prepare a child for a stay in hospital

Every year, one in four children under the age of five years goes into hospital, and over 2 million children are seen in accident and emergency units. How a child reacts to a hospital visit depends on:

- their age
- the reason for hospitalisation
- the tests and treatment needed
- the ambience of the ward
- their personality
- their previous experience of hospitals
- the attitude and manner of the doctors, nurses and other staff
- the carer's own anxieties and perceived ability to cope with what is often a very stressful situation.

When a child has to be admitted to hospital, either for medical treatment or for a surgical operation, it is best, if possible, to prepare them in advance. Often, the experience is stressful for parents, particularly if they have their own negative childhood memories of hospitalisation. In the event, the majority of children do enjoy their hospital stay, but adverse reactions can be avoided in younger children by careful preparation and complete honesty in all the information provided.

Guidelines for preparing children for hospitalisation

- If possible, arrange to visit the ward a few days before admission – most wards welcome such visits and are happy to talk with carers. (This helps to overcome fear of the unknown.)
- Encourage children to talk about their feelings so that you know how to help them.
- Always be honest – never say that something will not hurt if it might, and only tell them that you will be there all the time if that is your plan.
- Keep explanations simple – reading a book about a child going to hospital may help to allay fears.
- If the child is going to have an operation, explain that they will have a 'special hospital sleep' which will stop them from feeling any pain.
- Do not let the child see your own worry, as this will make him/her feel frightened.
- Play hospital games, using toys, to help the child act out any fears.
- Try to be involved in the child's care as fully as possible.
- Take the child's favourite toy or 'comforter' as a link with home – the child could even help to pack their case.
- Tell the ward staff about the child's eating and sleeping patterns, and about particular preferences or special words that may be used for the toilet and so on.
- If the child is of school age, the hospital school will provide educational activities. Play specialists, nursery nurses or teachers will provide play activities for younger children.

Isolation

Some conditions (e.g. **leukaemia**) result in damage to the child's immune system, and hospital care in such cases may involve **reverse-barrier nursing**. This technique provides the child with protection from infection that could be introduced by those people who have regular contact. In such cases, the following procedures are followed:

- A separate cubicle is used.
- Gowns and masks must be worn by any person who is in contact with the child.
- Gloves and theatre caps may be worn during certain procedures.
- Items such as toys and clothes cannot be freely taken in or out.

Children in isolation need a parent or carer to stay with them to an even greater extent than do those on an open ward, because of the strain of loneliness or boredom. Parents, in turn, need support from friends and relatives, as they are having to cope with many stressful events: the anxiety over their child's illness and treatment; the unnaturalness of being confined with their child; the lack of privacy because of the need for continuous observation by nursing staff. Some hospitals provide a parents' room where they can go to have a cup of tea and share problems with others in similar situations.

The needs of a sick child

Every child will become ill at some time during their childhood and will need to be cared for. Children who are sick have:

- **physical needs** – food and drink, rest and sleep, temperature control, exercise and fresh air, safety, hygiene and medical care
- **intellectual and language needs** – stimulation, appropriate activities
- **emotional and social needs** – love, security, play and contact with others.

The most important part of looking after sick children is to show that you care for them and to respond to all their needs.

Meeting physical needs

Bed rest

Children usually dislike being confined to bed and will only stay there if feeling very unwell. There is no need to keep a child with a fever in bed – take your lead from the child. Making a bed on a settee in the main living room will save carers the expense of extra heating and of tiring trips up and down stairs. The child will also feel more included in family life and less isolated. The room does not have to be particularly hot – just a comfortable temperature for you. If the child *does* stay in bed in his/her own room, remember to visit often so that s/he does not feel neglected.

Hygiene

All children benefit from having a routine to meet their hygiene needs, and this need not be altered drastically during illness.

Temperature control

If the child has a fever, you will need to take their temperature regularly and use tepid sponging to reduce it (see page 209).

Feeding a sick child and providing drinks

- Children who are ill often have poor appetites – a few days without food will not harm the child, but fluid intake should be increased as a general rule.

- Drinks should be offered at frequent intervals to prevent dehydration – the child will not necessarily request drinks.

Guidelines for encouraging sick children to drink

- Provide a covered jug of fruit juice or water; any fluid is acceptable, according to the child's tastes (e.g. milk, meaty drinks or soups).
- If the child has mumps, do not give fruit drinks because the acid causes pain to the tender parotid glands.
- A sick toddler who has recently given up the bottle may regress. Allow the child to drink from a bottle until they are feeling better.
- Try using an interesting curly straw.
- Give the child an 'adult' glass to make them feel special.
- Try offering drinks in a tiny glass or egg cup, which makes the quantities look smaller.
- Offer fresh fruit juices, such as pear, apple or mango; dilute them with fizzy water to make them more interesting, but avoid giving more than one fizzy drink a day; vary the drinks as much as possible.
- If the child does not like milk, add a milkshake mix or ice cream.

Guidelines for encouraging a sick child to eat

- Most children with a fever do not want to eat, so while you should offer food, you should never force a child to eat.
- Allow the child to choose their favourite foods.
- Give the child smaller meals, but more often than you would normally.
- If the child has a sore throat, give ice cream or an ice lolly made with fruit juice or yoghurt.
- If the child is feeling slightly sick, offer mashed potato.
- Offer snacks regularly and always keep the child company while they eat.
- Most children who are sick do not find ordinary food very appetising, but may be tempted to eat with 'soldiers' of fresh bread and butter, slices of fruit or their favourite yoghurt.
- Try to make food as attractive as possible; do not put too much on the plate at once; remember that sick children often cope better with foods that do not require too much chewing (e.g. egg custard, milk pudding, thick soups, chicken, and ice cream).

How to take a temperature

All family first aid kits should contain a thermometer. There are many types, but the most widely used in the home are digital thermometers and temperature strips:

- **Digital clinical thermometer:** This is battery-operated and consists of a safe narrow probe with a tip sensitive to temperature. It is placed in the mouth and is easy to read via a display panel.

- **Forehead temperature strip:** This is a rectangular strip of thin plastic which contains temperature-sensitive crystals that change colour according to the temperature measured. It is placed on the child's forehead. It is not as accurate as other thermometers but is a useful check.

Figure 4.8 Forehead temperature strip and digital thermometer

Whatever the cause of a high temperature, it is important to try to reduce it (see below). There is always the risk that a fever could lead to **convulsions** or fits.

Guidelines for taking a temperature

Using a digital thermometer:

1. Place the narrow tip of the thermometer under the child's arm, holding the arm close to the child's side.

2. Read the temperature when it stops rising (some models beep when this point is reached).

Using a fever strip:

1. Hold the plastic strip firmly against the child's forehead for about 30 seconds.

2. Record the temperature revealed by the colour change.

Guidelines for bringing down a high temperature

- **Offer cool drinks:** Encourage the child to take small, frequent sips of anything (though preferably clear fluids like water or squash, rather than milky drinks). Do this even if the child is vomiting, as, even then, some water will be absorbed.
- **Remove clothes:** Keep the child as undressed as possible to allow heat to be lost.
- **Reduce bedclothes:** Use a cotton sheet if the child is in bed.
- **Sponge the child down:** Use tepid water (see tepid sponging below).
- **Give the correct dose of children's paracetamol:** Carers should make sure they have written consent from the parents to use it in case of emergency. If not, the parents should be contacted in order to obtain consent.
- **Cool the air** in the child's room: Use an electric fan or open the window.
- **Reassure the child:** They may be very frightened. Remain calm yourself and try to stop a baby from crying, as this will tend to push the temperature higher still.
- If the temperature will not come down, **call the doctor**. Always consult a doctor if a high fever is accompanied by symptoms such as severe headache with stiff neck, abdominal pain or pain when passing urine.

Guidelines for tepid sponging to reduce a temperature

1. Make sure the air in the room is comfortably warm – not hot, cold or draughty.
2. Lay the child on a towel on your knee or on the bed and gently remove their clothes; reassure them by talking gently.
3. Sponge the child's body, limbs and face with tepid or lukewarm water – not cold; as the water evaporates from the skin, it absorbs heat from the blood and so cools the system.
4. As the child cools down, pat the skin dry with a soft towel and dress only in a nappy or pants; cover the child with a light cotton sheet.
5. Keep checking the child's condition to make sure that they do not become cold or shivery; put more light covers over the child if they are shivering or obviously chilled.
6. If the temperature rises again, repeat sponging every ten minutes.

Giving medicines

Most medicines for children are given as sweetened syrups or elixirs. They can be given with a spoon, tube or dropper.

Guidelines for giving oral medicines

1. Wash your hands before giving any medicine.
2. Always check the label on the bottle, and the instructions. If the medicine has been prescribed by the doctor, check that it is for the child in your care and follow the instructions exactly – for example, some medicines have to be taken with or after food. Generally, oral medicines are best given before meals, as they enter the bloodstream quickly.
3. Shake the bottle before measuring the dose. Always pour any medicine bottle with the label uppermost so that the instructions remain legible if the medicine runs down the side of the bottle.
4. Some medicines do not taste good (e.g. iron preparations). Always be truthful when the child asks, 'Does it taste bad?' Answer, 'The medicine does not taste good, but I will give you some juice as soon as you have swallowed it.'
5. If the child is reluctant, you should adopt a no-nonsense approach and be prepared to resort to bribery if necessary (e.g. a favourite story or a chocolate). Never punish or threaten a child who refuses to take medicine.

The medicine cabinet

Every home should have a properly stocked medicine cabinet, preferably locked, but always out of reach of children. The cabinet should contain:

- **children's paracetamol** – paracetamol elixir and junior paracetamol tablets (the doses for children of different ages should be on the bottles)
- **zinc and castor oil cream** for nappy rashes
- digital clinical thermometer or a fever strip
- **a measuring spoon**, dropper or small cup for liquid medicines
- a pack of assorted fabric **plasters** and one of hypoallergenic plasters
- blunt-edge **tweezers**, safety pins and scissors
- a small bottle of liquid **antiseptic** or mild antiseptic cream
- **calamine lotion** for soothing itchy spots and rashes
- **wound dressings** (e.g. cotton wool and gauze pad already attached to a bandage)
- a small packet of **cotton wool**
- a packet of **skin closures**
- **crepe bandages**, open-weave bandage and triangular bandages
- **surgical tape**.

Meeting children's intellectual, language, emotional and social needs

Play is an important part of recovery for a sick or convalescent child. Children who are ill often regress and may want to play with toys that they have long since outgrown. While they are ill, children will have a short attention span. You will need to be understanding and tolerant of these changes in behaviour. Never put pressure on a child to take part in an activity they do not want to do.

- Sick children often tire quickly, so toys and materials will need to be changed frequently.

- Big and complicated toys tire a child more quickly than small and simple toys, which can be changed easily.
- Use protective sheets to protect the bed covers, and supply a steady surface – a tray with legs or a special beanbag tray – for activities, as appropriate.
- If a child is ill for some time, toys and games can be borrowed from a local toy library.
- Encourage other children and adults to visit, once the child is over the infectious stage of the illness.

Ideas for activities for a sick child

- **Jigsaw puzzles:** The child could start with simple puzzles and progress to more challenging ones, with family help.
- **Board games and card games** (e.g. picture lotto, snap and happy families).
- **Drawing and painting:** Young children particularly enjoy painting with water in 'magic' painting books.
- **Play dough:** Playing with dough – either bought or home-made – is creative and also provides an outlet for feelings of frustration.
- **Making models** with Duplo®.
- **Videos, cartoons and audio tapes.**

 REVISION QUESTIONS

1. Describe five things you could do to prepare a child for hospitalisation.

2. Suggest five ways of encouraging a sick child to eat and drink.

3. What is the normal body temperature? Describe three different thermometers used to take a temperature.

4. How would you reduce a child's high temperature?

PART 5

INTELLECTUAL, SOCIAL AND EMOTIONAL DEVELOPMENT

Intellectual development

Intellectual (or cognitive) development is development of the mind – the part of the brain that is used for recognising, reasoning, knowing and understanding. Intellectual development involves:

- what a person knows and the ability to reason, understand and problem-solve
- memory, concentration, attention and perception
- imagination and creativity.

Language development is very closely linked with cognitive development, and a delay in one area usually affects progress in the other.

Language development

Language development is the development of communication skills. These include skills in:

- receptive speech – what a person understands
- expressive speech – the words the person produces
- articulation – the person's actual pronunciation of words.

Emotional, social and behavioural development

Emotional development involves the development of feelings:

- the growth of feelings about, and awareness of, oneself
- the development of feelings towards other people
- the development of self-esteem and a self-concept.

Social development includes the growth of the child's relationships with other people. Socialisation is the process of learning the skills and attitudes that enable the child to live easily with other members of the community.

Behaviour is the way we act, speak and treat other people and our environment; it is closely linked to emotional and social aspects of development.

1 Conditions for development

Children need to be in a safe, secure, loving and stimulating environment in order to develop healthily in all areas. Within their home and the wider environment, every child also needs the following conditions:

Love and security

To have friends and to feel as if they belong

New experiences and opportunities for play, praise and recognition

Responsibility

The need for love and security

This is probably the most important need, as it provides the basis for all later relationships. Research shows that children who do not get enough love and attention in early childhood are less likely to become well-adjusted adults. Every child needs to experience unconditional love from their parents or carers – this means that they are totally accepted, with no restrictions or conditions imposed on them.

Security

Babies learn about love from the words and actions of those who care for them. In their first year, their need for security may be met by having a comforter or comfort object: this is often a blanket or a favourite soft toy. Some children use their thumb or a dummy as a comfort object, while others do not have a comfort object at all. Comforters provide security for children, particularly at night; they represent something familiar for the child and help them to adjust when they are separated from their parents.

Routine

Another aspect of the child's need for love and security is the need for routine and predictability. This is why having daily routines is so important in childcare. By meeting children's need for routine, parents and carers are helping them to feel acknowledged and independent, and this increases their self-esteem.

Bonding and attachment

Bonding is a term used to describe the feelings of love and responsibility that parents have for their babies. It is a very close, two-way relationship which develops between a baby and an adult. Attachment means a warm, affectionate and supportive bond between a child and his/her carer, which enables the child to develop secure relationships. Babies quickly become emotionally attached to the person who cares for them most, such as a parent or grandparent, and those they see regularly, such as siblings, family members or carers. When children receive warm, responsive care, they feel safe and secure. Secure attachments are the basis of all the child's future relationships. Children who are securely attached in infancy have been shown to be generally more curious, to get along better with other children and to perform better in school than children who are less securely attached.

The need to have friends and to feel that they belong

Children need friends in order to develop emotionally and socially. Through interacting with friends, children learn:

- how the 'give-and-take' of social behaviour works
- how to set up rules
- how to weigh alternatives and make decisions when faced with dilemmas.

The nature of friendships changes during childhood:

- A toddler may help a friend to rebuild his tower of wooden bricks.
- A four-year-old may comfort a friend who is upset, or friends may spend time together in a joint activity.

Children and their families need an environment that is welcoming and reassuring; children need to feel that they belong. This sense of belonging can be promoted by:

- making all children feel valued for who they are – for instance, celebrating their own cultures, achievements or significant events in their lives
- encouraging a strong sense of identity, both individually and within a group
- giving children the chance to explore and talk about physical characteristics, and things they like to do or eat – these are important aspects of self-identity and also help children to learn about each other
- understanding and respecting the importance of each child's race, culture, ability and gender.

The need for new experiences and opportunities for play

Children learn best through first-hand experiences. These experiences help children to develop the skills of communication and concentration. They also provide opportunities for children to develop positive attitudes and to consolidate their learning.

We all learn best by being active learners – by 'doing'. Research shows that we remember:

- 20 per cent of what we hear
- 30 per cent of what we see
- 50 per cent of what we hear and see
- 80 per cent of what we hear, see and do

Children need stimulation in order to be able to learn. They find stimulation, wellbeing and happiness through play, which is also the means by which they grow physically, intellectually and emotionally.

The need for praise and recognition

Growing up requires an enormous amount of learning – emotional, social and intellectual. Consequently, children need strong incentives to help them cope with any difficulties that they will inevitably encounter. The most effective incentives are praise and recognition sustained over time. Praise for new achievements helps to build the child's self-esteem, and children love to be able to do things for themselves.

- **Good role models**: Children need adults as good role models. Children learn to imitate our behaviour. They learn more from how they *see us act* than they do from anything we tell them.
- **Self-fulfilling prophecy**: Children feel like failures when they cannot live up to the unrealistic hopes of their parents, and they are then less likely to repeat their efforts. The lower the expectation of the adult, the lower the level of effort and achievement of the child – sometimes called the self-fulfilling prophecy. For example, if a person thinks we are clever or stupid, they will treat us according to their idea. If we are treated as if we are clever or stupid, we will act, and even become, this way. So the person has had their prophecy about us fulfilled.
- **Intrinsic motivation**: If you make children feel anxious when they have not succeeded, they will avoid activities likely to lead to failure. It is important to praise children appropriately when they try hard or have achieved something new, however small it might seem. This will motivate children to greater effort and lead to the desire to achieve something for its own sake – this is called intrinsic motivation. For example, most people's hobbies are intrinsically motivated. People collect things or build complicated models just for the pleasure gained from doing so.

The need for responsibility

Being responsible involves knowing what is to be done and how to do it. Children have different levels of understanding at different ages. The need for responsibility is met by allowing children to gain personal independence:

- first, through learning to look after themselves in matters of everyday care
- then through a gradual extension of responsibility over other areas, until they have the freedom and ability to decide on their own actions – for example, choosing for themselves what to wear or what game to play.

Cooperation, rather than competition, allows children more freedom to accept and exercise responsibility.

 KEY TERMS

Attachment: A close relationship which babies usually develop with those who care for them (usually their parents at first).

Bonding: A term used to describe the feelings of love and responsibility which parents have for their babies.

Comfort object: An object, such as a blanket, a piece of cloth or a teddy, to which a child becomes especially attached.

Independence: Having the ability and skill to be less dependent on others.

Intrinsic motivation: The extent to which children work hard in the absence of external rewards and seem to gain pleasure from doing the work itself.

Self-esteem: The way an individual feels about themselves. Positive feelings indicate high self-esteem, while an individual's negative feelings about themselves are an indication of low self-esteem.

REVISION QUESTIONS

1. What is unconditional love?

2. What is meant by bonding?

3. What is a comfort object?

4. Why are routines important to young children?

5. Suggest three things that you could do to help a child achieve a sense of belonging.

 CHILD STUDY ACTIVITY

Observe the child's behaviour when playing with other children. What emotions does the child show?

2 Patterns of learning

There is an ongoing debate about how children develop and learn – this is often referred to as the nature–nurture debate. It centres on this question:

> **Is our ability to learn determined by our inherited genes and characteristics (nature) or by our upbringing (nurture)?**

Play and learning are inextricably linked throughout childhood, and particularly so in the first five years of a child's life. Children learn through play. Children need opportunities to learn in the following ways:

- **Learning to predict:** Children learn to predict that something is about to happen – for example, a baby learns to predict that food will soon appear if a bib is tied around his/her neck.
- **Learning the consequences of their actions:** Children understand that they can bring about a result by their own actions – for example, a baby learns that if s/he cries s/he will be picked up and comforted.
- **Asking questions:** As soon as they can talk, children ask questions to try to make sense of their world and gain information – for example, four-year-old children constantly ask the question 'Why?', whereas a child of two-and-a-half years constantly asks 'Who?' and 'What?'

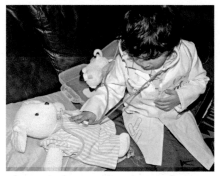

Figure 5.1 Learning through role play

- **Understanding concepts:** Experiences with real objects help young children to understand concepts and to develop problem-solving skills – for example, mathematical concepts involve understanding number, sequencing, volume and capacity, as well as weighing and measuring.
- **Repetition:** Children learn by repeating activities over and over again – for example, they can learn a song or nursery rhyme by hearing it sung to them many times.
- **Imitation:** Children learn by copying what others do – for example, they learn how to write by copying letters; and in role play children are copying the way they have observed others behaving in certain situations.

🔑 KEY TERMS

Concepts: The ways in which people make sense of and organise the information in the world around them. Concrete concepts include mathematical and scientific concepts.

Nature: The features, characteristics and abilities one is born with.

Nurture: One's upbringing, including health, emotional, social and educational factors.

Role model: An individual whose behaviour may be copied or aspired to.

Role play: A form of pretend play when children engage in, explore and learn about the everyday roles that occur in their familiar experience – the roles carried out by their parents or carers and members of their community.

3 The stages of intellectual and language development

Although each child is unique and develops in their own way and at different rates, the following tables show the *average* age for each stage of intellectual development.

Age	Stage
Birth to 6 months	<ul><li>Babies explore through their **senses** and through their own activity and movement.</li><li>They will imitate facial expressions (e.g. they will put out their tongue if you do) – if you know any very young babies, try it and see!</li><li>By 3 months, they can even imitate low- or high-pitched sounds.</li><li>By 4 months, they link objects they know with the sound (e.g. mother's voice and her face).</li><li>By 4 months, babies reach for objects, which suggests they recognise and judge the distance in relation to the size of the object.</li><li>By 5–6 months, babies can coordinate more (e.g. they can see a rattle, grasp the rattle, put the rattle in their mouth (they coordinate tracking, reaching, grasping and sucking).</li><li>By 5 months, they can develop favourite tastes in food and recognise differences.</li></ul>
6 months to 1 year	<ul><li>The baby understands signs (e.g. the bib means that food is coming). Soon this understanding of signs will lead into symbolic behaviour.</li><li>From 8–9 months, babies show they know that objects exist when they have gone out of sight, even under test conditions. This is called the concept of object permanence. They are also fascinated by the way in which objects move.</li><li>Babies are beginning to develop images. Memory develops. They can remember the past and anticipate the future. This gives them some understanding of routine daily sequences (e.g. after a feed, changing and a sleep with teddy).</li><li>They imitate actions, sounds, gestures and moods after an event is finished (e.g. they imitate a temper tantrum they saw a friend have the previous day, wave bye-bye remembering Grandma has gone to the shops).</li></ul>

Table 5.1 Stages of intellectual development

Age	Stage
1–2 years	<ul><li>Children understand the names of objects and can follow simple instructions.</li><li>They learn about things through trial and error.</li><li>They use toys or objects to represent things in real life (e.g. they use a doll as a baby, or a large cardboard box might become a car or a garage).</li><li>They begin to scribble on paper (see section on 'Learning to draw' on pages 230–231).</li><li>They often 'talk' to themselves while they are playing.</li></ul>
2–3 years	<ul><li>Children have improved memory skills, which help their understanding of concepts (e.g. they can often name and match two or three colours – usually yellow and red).</li><li>They can hold a crayon and move it up and down.</li><li>They understand cause and effect (e.g. if something is dropped, they understand it might break).</li><li>They talk about an absent object when reminded of it (e.g. they may say 'biscuit' when they see an empty plate or bowl).</li></ul>
3–5 years	<ul><li>Three-year-old children become fascinated by cause and effect; they are continually trying to explain what goes on in the world.</li><li>A three-year-old child can identify common colours, such as red, yellow, blue and green – although they sometimes confuse blue with green.</li><li>At about age four, children usually know how to count – up to 20. They also understand ideas such as 'more' and 'fewer', and 'big' and 'small'.</li><li>Five-year-old children include more detail in their drawings – for example, a house may have not only windows and a roof, but also curtains and a chimney.</li><li>They will recognise their own name when it is written down and can usually write it themselves.</li></ul>

Table 5.1 Contin.

The stages of language and communication development

Babies are born with a need and a desire to communicate with others before they can express themselves through speaking. Learning how to communicate – to listen and to speak – begins with non-verbal communication. This includes:

- body language – for example, facial expression, eye contact, pointing, touching and reaching for objects
- listening to others talking to them
- making sounds to attract attention
- copying the sounds made by others.

These skills develop as babies and young children express their needs and feelings, interact with others and establish their own identities and personalities.

Age	Stage
Birth to 3 months	*From birth*: • babies respond to sounds, especially familiar voices • they quieten when picked up • they make eye contact and cry to indicate need • they may move their eyes towards the direction of sound. *In the second month*: • babies recognise their primary carer and familiar objects • they make non-crying noises, such as cooing and gurgling • they become more expressive in their cries. *In the third month*: • babies are still distressed by sudden loud noises • they often suck or lick their lips when they hear the sound of food preparation • they show excitement at the sound of approaching footsteps or voices • they may begin to babble (e.g. 'baa', 'daa', 'maa').
3–6 months	• Babies become increasingly aware of others, so they communicate more and more; as they listen, they imitate sounds they can hear, and they react to the tone of someone's voice – for example, they might become upset by an angry tone, or cheered by a happy tone. • They begin to make sounds, whether in the company of an adult or alone. • They begin to use vowels, consonants and syllable sounds (e.g. 'ah', 'ee aw'). • They begin to laugh and squeal with pleasure.
6–9 months	• Babies' babble becomes tuneful, like the lilt of the language they can hear (except in hearing-impaired babies). • They begin to understand words like 'up' and 'down', raising their arms to be lifted up, using appropriate gestures. • They repeat sounds (e.g. 'mum mum', 'da da').

Table 5.2 Stages of language and communication development

Age	Stage
9–12 months	• When adults wave bye-bye, or say 'Show me your shoes,' for example, babies enjoy pointing and waving. • Babies can follow simple instructions (e.g. kiss teddy). • Word approximations appear (e.g. 'hee haw' = donkey, or, more typically, 'mumma', 'dadda' and 'bye-bye' in English-speaking contexts). • The tuneful babble develops into **jargon** and babies make their voices go up and down, just as people do when they talk to each other (e.g. '*Real*-ly?' '*Do* you?' '*No!*'). The babble is very expressive. • They have learnt that words stand for people and objects, what they do and what happens.
1–2 years	Children begin to talk with words or sign language. They add more and more layers to everything they know about language and communication in the first year. *By 18 months:* • they enjoy trying to sing as well as listening to songs and rhymes; action songs (e.g. 'Pat-a-cake') are much loved • books with pictures are of great interest; they point at and often name parts of their body, objects, people and pictures in books • they echo the last part of what others say (**echolalia**) • one word or sign can have several meanings (**holophrases**) (e.g. 'cat' may be used for all animals, not just cats; or the single word 'cup' may mean either 'This is my cup' or 'Where's my cup?') • they begin waving their arms up and down, which might mean 'Start again' or 'I like it' or 'More' • gestures develop alongside words (gesture is used in some cultures more than in others). *By 2 years:* • children overextend the use of a word (e.g. all animals are called 'doggie') • they talk about an absent object when reminded of it (e.g. seeing an empty plate, they say 'biscuit') • they use phrases such as 'doggie-gone' or 'daddy-car'; this is called telegraphic speech • they call themselves by their name (e.g. 'Tom up') • they spend a great deal of energy naming things and what they do (e.g. they say 'chair' when climbing on to one, and as they go up a step they might say 'up') • they can follow a simple instruction or request (e.g. 'Could you bring me the spoon?'); they are wanting to share songs, dance, conversations, finger rhymes and so on more and more.
2–3 years	• Children begin to use plurals, pronouns, adjectives, possessives, time words, tenses and sentences. They now have a vocabulary of about 300 words. • They make what are called virtuous errors in the way that they pronounce (**articulate**) things. It is also true of the way they use grammar (**syntax**). • They might say 'two times' instead of 'twice'. They might say 'I goed there' instead of 'I went there'. • Children love to converse and chat and ask questions (usually 'What?', 'Where?' and 'Who?'). • They enjoy much more complicated stories and ask about their favourite ones over and over again. • It is not unusual for children to stutter because they are trying so hard to tell adults things and to talk. Their thinking goes faster than the pace at which they can say what they want to say. They can quickly become frustrated.

Table 5.2 Contin.

Age	Stage
3–4 years	• Children begin to ask 'Why?', 'When?' and 'How?' questions, as they become more and more fascinated with the reasons for things and how things work (cause and effect). • They wonder what will happen 'if…' (problem solving and hypothesis making). • Children can think back and forward much more easily than before. • They can also think about things from somebody else's point of view, but only fleetingly. Past, present and future tenses are used more often. • They may mispronounce words or use an incorrect word ending (e.g. 'I drawed a picture'). • They can name their main body parts and they have a vocabulary of about 900–1000 words. • As they become more accurate in the way they pronounce words, and begin to use grammar, they delight in nonsense words that they make up, and jokes using words. (They also use swear words if they hear swearing.)
4–5 years	• Children try to understand the meaning of words. They use adverbs and prepositions. They talk confidently and with increasing fluency. • Children are adding to their vocabulary all the time and can now use about 1500–2000 words. • They can vocalise their ideas and feelings. • They begin to be able to define objects by their function (e.g. 'What is a ball?' 'You bounce it.'). • They enjoy jokes and riddles and continue to enjoy songs and rhymes. • Children show an interest in reading, writing and simple poetry.

Table 5.2 Contin.

KEY TERMS

Articulation: A person's actual pronunciation of words.

Babbling: Repeating single- or double-syllable sounds (e.g. 'baa', 'baaba', 'daa', 'daada', 'maa', 'maama').

Cooing: The earliest sounds made by a baby, used to express contentment.

Echolalia: The tendency of a child to echo the last words spoken by an adult.

Holophrase: The expression of a whole idea in a single word: thus 'car' may mean 'Give me the car' or 'Look at the car.'

Jargon: The child's own way of speaking, which may be understood only by those close to him or her.

Telegraphic speech: The abbreviation of a sentence such that only the crucial words are spoken, as in a telegram (e.g. 'Where Daddy going?' or 'Shut door').

Children with communication difficulties

Learning to speak is a natural process, which follows a certain pattern. Some children speak clearly but say very little; others chatter away, but in a 'language' that others may find hard to understand – there are many variations.

Some children have difficulty in communicating by speech. There are a number of possible reasons for this, including:

- **Deafness or hearing impairment**: Repeated ear infections can cause **glue ear** – a build-up of mucus that blocks hearing. If a baby suddenly stops babbling at around seven to nine months, parents should ask for the baby's hearing to be checked.
- **Emotional problems**: Stress at home, nursery or school may affect a child's speech.
- **Social/environmental**: Children whose parents talk and listen to them tend to have more advanced speech.
- **Neurological**: Sometimes late speech development may be related to a neurological disorder such as **autism**, or to specific brain damage.

Developmental reviews which assess – among other things – speech and hearing are carried out at different stages by different health authorities, but guidelines suggest that one takes place at around 18 months, and another at the age of three to four years. A health visitor can use these reviews to assess the child's emerging speech – its clarity, how well the child understands language, the range of vocabulary and the complexity of sentences.

Speech and language therapy is available on the NHS. A health visitor or GP may refer parents to a speech and language therapist, or they can contact a speech therapist directly at their local health centre or hospital.

Stammering or stuttering

Stammering is normal between two and five years, and most common around the age of three. It is four times more common in boys than girls and often runs in families. Usually, children who stammer or stutter just cannot match their words to their fast-moving brains and they think faster than they can talk. Children may repeat words or phrases or use lots of 'ums' and 'ers'.

How adults can help children's language development

All children need to be listened to, talked to, encouraged and praised.

- **Be patient**: Young children find it hard to put their thoughts and feelings into words, so listening takes patience.
- **Listen carefully** to children and allow plenty of time for them to finish what they are saying. It is very tempting to prompt children and say things for them. Instead, try nodding or saying 'Hmm…'. This gives children time to say what they want to.
- **Talk to the child** when playing together and encourage songs and nursery rhymes, especially those with actions.
- **Speak slowly and clearly**, and always make sure that you gain the child's attention before starting a conversation with them.
- **Ask questions**: Choose open-ended questions rather than ones that require a simple yes or no answer. This will encourage children to think about their response and to answer more fully. For example, you might ask, 'How did you build that big tower?'
- **Take turns to speak** and encourage other members of the family to take turns too.

- **Talk more in general**: Talk about things as they happen – for example, when out for a walk or preparing a meal.
- **Increase their vocabulary** by providing choices – for example, 'Would you like yoghurt or fruit to eat?'

The development of number skills, reading, drawing and writing

The development of number skills

Babies and young children learn about their world through their senses and by exploring objects around them. Their interaction with a wide range of objects helps them to develop the basic mathematical concepts of number, weight, size, volume and capacity. Children's number skills can be developed through a variety of methods – through songs, games, stories and imaginative play. They hear and see numbers every day: 'Would you like one biscuit or two?' and 'Look, that is our bus – number 185.' Everyday activities at home can help to promote children's understanding of numbers – for example, when measuring ingredients for cooking.

Understanding numbers

Children start to recognise numbers at an early age. They learn how to count before they know what the numbers really mean and what their relationship is to objects. Later they develop an awareness of the relationship between numbers and amounts and know that numbers can be combined to be 'added together', and can be separated by 'taking away', and that two or more amounts can be compared. They then use these skills with numbers to solve problems.

To help develop children's understanding of number, adults can:

- point out numbers that occur in everyday life: on the front door, on the bus, on clocks and in books
- help children to count items around the home, such as toys in the toy box or tins in the cupboard
- sing counting songs and nursery rhymes such as 'Ten green bottles' and '1, 2, 3, 4, 5, once I caught a fish alive'
- play games like dominoes or snakes and ladders (which involves using numbered dice)
- play counting and matching games like lotto or snap
- help children to see that the last counting word you say tells you how many things there were; this can be done by emphasising the last number you say: 'One, two, three, *four* – there are four apples'
- talk about 'more than' and 'less than': this helps children to understand, for example, that three large cars are less than six small cars in terms of quantity
- use building blocks to show children the concept that ten blocks remain constant as ten blocks, however they are arranged. This is called conservation of number and is an important concept in child development.

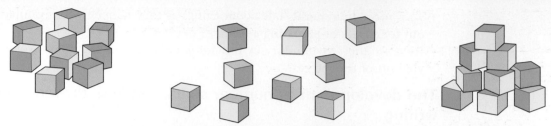

Figure 5.2 The number of objects is constant regardless of size or position

Understanding size/mass and volume

Children naturally learn to use words to compare the things they see – for example, 'big', 'bigger', 'biggest' or 'short', 'shorter', 'shortest'. They also learn naturally about the tools needed for measuring things – for example, using scales to measure weight, a tape measure or a ruler to measure length, and clocks to tell the time.

> To help develop children's measuring skills, adults can:
>
> - encourage children to weigh out ingredients when cooking
> - fill and empty containers (e.g. in sand and water play) – this encourages understanding of the concepts 'full', 'half-full', 'empty', 'nearly full' and so on
> - use non-standard measures such as hand spans, as well as tape measures, to measure everyday objects
> - compare objects to see which is heavier and which is lighter.

Reading and writing skills

Almost all children can learn to read and most really want to learn. The majority of children learn to read between the ages of four-and-a-half and six years old. Research shows that preschool children who are exposed to plenty of language (books and conversation) tend to do better at school.

In order to learn to read, children must recognise that a certain pattern of letters represents a particular sound. They need to build up a set of skills that will help them to make sense of words, signs and symbols. These 'pre-reading' skills are explored in table 5.3.

The importance of books

Unlike learning to talk, children are not born with the instinct to read. Reading must be intentionally learned, and the best place to start is in the child's home. Children who are familiar with books and stories before they start school are better prepared to cope with the demands of formal literacy teaching. Children learn by example, so if they see an adult reading, they are likely to want to join in. Reading books with children is important because:

- books contain new words that will help build children's language and understanding
- reading together is fun and helps to build relationships
- reading with children, or talking about what they have read, is a good way of showing that both reading and talking about books are valued by the family as a good way to spend their time
- children learn about make-believe worlds, true stories and folk stories, which introduces them to different cultures.

Pre-reading skill	Activities to help develop the skill
Shape recognition and matching: The ability to recognise shapes and to differentiate between them is important. Children learn to match shapes and patterns first, and this helps them to match letters and, finally, words.	• Snap • Shape sorter • Picture pairs • Lotto • Jigsaws • Dominoes
Rhyming: Research shows that children who can understand about rhyming words have a head start in learning to read and, even more, to spell.	• Rhyming games such as 'I spy with my little eye, something that rhymes with cat' (hat or mat). • Leave off the end of rhymes for the child to complete (e.g. 'Humpty Dumpty sat on a wall, Humpty Dumpty had a great...'). • Reading simple poetry.
Language skills: The more experience children have of language, the more easily they will learn to read. Children need to hear and join in conversations (with adults and children), and to listen to stories and poetry of all sorts.	• Talking. • Reading stories. • Encourage children to talk. • Share their favourite stories again and again – repeating phrases helps to build children's language.
Concepts of print: This means 'how we look at books' and includes following print the right way (from left to right), turning the pages and looking at pictures.	Children need to learn practical skills: • how to hold a book (the right way up!) • how to turn pages singly. Let the child see your finger following the print when reading.
Letter skills: Children need to learn what sounds the letters can make.	• Begin with letters with an interesting shape that makes them easy to recognise, or a letter that is important to the child, such as their own initial. • Use the letter *sounds* rather than letter *names* (e.g. 'a for ant', not 'ay for ape'). • Try a letter hunt: looking for objects which begin with a particular letter.
Motor skills: Since reading and writing are best taught together, pencil control is important.	• Encourage creativity – drawing and painting with lots of different tools and materials to encourage pencil and brush control. • Playing with small toys, especially construction sets, helps to develop fine motor skills.
Looking at a variety of printed materials – newspapers, magazines, packaging, street and shop names, etc.	• Point out words in the environment (e.g. 'Push', 'Pull', 'Open', 'Closed'). • Visit the library to encourage familiarity with the idea of books for everyone.
Memory skills: Words are made up of sequences of letters and sounds, and children need to remember this before they can read.	• Memory games (e.g. 'I went to the shops and I bought a...') and pairs (Pelmanism) all help to improve children's memory skills and increase their attention span. • Sequencing: book page layout can be reinforced by, for example, laying out the child's clothes to be selected from left to right: vest, pants, top, trousers, socks, shoes.

Table 5.3 Pre-reading skills

Figure 5.3 Sharing stories is important

Choosing books for babies and children

Books come in all shapes and sizes – big board books, squashy books, interactive books that make noises, books with 'touchy-feely' bits, 'lift-the-flap' books and so on. The variety of children's books is enormous. Babies and toddlers enjoy books that:

- are well-made and durable – babies like to really explore their favourite books, carrying them around, tugging on the pages, and even 'mouthing' them, so cloth, plastic or cardboard books are ideal
- contain bright, bold pictures, to help with focusing and identification
- may safely be left in the pram or cot, so that the baby develops a 'taste' for books (check safety labels carefully)
- have just a few words on each page or label objects in the pictures
- have rhyming verse or a repetitive theme – a great favourite for many young children is *Each Peach Pear Plum* by Allan Ahlberg and Janet Ahlberg.

Older children enjoy books that:

- have good stories, with interesting characters and a plot with lots of action
- have stories with a moral: between the ages of three and five years, children like to see rules being obeyed; they like the right to triumph
- are based on everyday experiences and use the child's vocabulary.

Children also enjoy storybooks which come with a tape, so that they can follow the pages while listening to the story. Many libraries now offer board books as well as picture books for babies and young children. Parents can set up a book exchange to avoid unnecessary expense.

Bookstart

Bookstart is a public/private partnership generously supported by children's book publishers and funded by the Department of Children Schools and Families in England and by the devolved administrations in Scotland, Wales and Northern Ireland. Bookstart is coordinated by the independent national reading charity Booktrust. It works through local organisations to give *free* packs of books to babies, as well as guidance materials for parents and carers. There are three different types of Bookstart pack available, for different age ranges:

- Bookstart pack (0–12 months): A canvas bag containing two board books and a book of nursery rhymes, advice on sharing books, information about libraries and an invitation to join.
- Bookstart+ pack (18–30 months): A bright-coloured nylon satchel including two books, a colouring pad and crayons, a 'Numbers are Fun!' bedroom frieze, a set of 'Bookplates' – colourfully illustrated stickers for children to place in their books, saying, 'This book belongs to …' thus encouraging children to build their own book collection, and guidance material for parents and carers.
- Bookstart Treasure Chest (3 years): Treasure Box with a secret compartment, two picture books, a set of 'Bookplate' stickers, a colouring pad, coloured pencils, a pencil sharpener and guidance material for parents and carers.

Figure 5.4 Bookstart packs

Learning to write

Writing and spelling are more difficult to learn than speaking and reading. The child's first word written from memory is usually his or her own name. Most of the activities shown to promote early reading skills will also help children to learn to write. Children also need to develop the following skills:

- hand–eye coordination
- pencil control (fine manipulative skills)
- the ability to sit still for some time with the correct posture for writing.

Children learn how to copy letters from as early as two years of age, and the skills of learning to write develop gradually as they become competent readers.

Learning to draw

Drawing and painting are important to children's development because they help them to:

- express their feelings and their imagination
- develop pencil or brush control and hand–eye coordination
- record significant events and people in their lives, such as holidays, birthdays, family members and pets.

Most children love to draw. They just need pencils, crayons or paint, plenty of cheap paper and a suitable chair and table or an easel. Children's drawings pass through recognisable stages as they develop manipulative skills, creativity and imagination.

Stages in learning to draw

1. Children will pick up a pen or crayon and hold it against paper, as if they are going to make a mark.
2. Children can lift the pencil from the paper and move it backwards and forwards.
3. Children are able to copy adults as they scribble round in circles, and soon after will copy as they draw a vertical or horizontal stroke.
4. The child begins to draw simple representations of objects in real life, usually drawing a person with a simple circle for the face ('big head' figures).

5. Children now add recognisable features to the face (e.g. dots and lines to represent the eyes and mouth).

6. Lines are added round the head, and gradually these are arranged to represent the arms and legs; the arms are generally shown sticking out from the circular head.

7. Children add a second circle to represent the body, with legs coming straight down from it.

8. Feet are added to the legs and there may be spiky hands coming from the arms.

9. Clothes, eyebrows and hair are often added to the drawing.

10. Other features are included (e.g. houses with windows and chimneys, trees, birds, cars).

Figure 5.5 Stages in children's drawing: Top left: 18 months; top right: 1 year; bottom left: 5 years; bottom right: 3 years

A painting that can take five to ten seconds for a three-year-old will develop by the age of four into an activity that can absorb the child for several minutes. Adults often ask a child aged three to four years, 'What have you drawn?' It is better to avoid this question, because although they may well be drawing 'something' occasionally, they may simply be enjoying expressing themselves through their pencil marks and drawings.

REVISION QUESTIONS

1. How a child develops intellectually depends on two main factors. What are they?

2. How does a child learn through:

   a. imitation?

   b. asking questions?

   c. looking at books?

3. Suggest four activities which adults can provide to help young children develop their understanding of each of the following skills:

   a. language

   b. number

   c. size, mass and volume

   d. pre-reading and writing.

 CHILD STUDY ACTIVITY

Provide a drawing and/or painting activity for the child. Observe the stage of drawing shown and relate it to the information above.

4 The development of social skills

Factors affecting the development of social skills

The development of social skills – or socialisation – is all about relating to others. How a child develops the skills to relate to others depends on many factors. These include the following:

- **Genetic inheritance**: Just as babies inherit physical characteristics, they also inherit particular temperaments and personalities, which continue to develop throughout their lives.
- **Attachment**: Secure attachments are the basis of *all* the child's future relationships. It is the expression of love that affects how a young child develops and helps to shape later learning and behaviour. They will grow to be more curious, get along better with other children, and perform better in school than children who are less securely attached.
- **Physical factors**: Poor nutrition and lack of sleep will cause a lack of energy and may result in aggressive behaviour and an inability to form relationships. Hearing impairment (even the temporary condition known as glue ear) can lead to a child lacking confidence and motivation.
- **Economic and environmental factors**: Poverty and poor housing conditions may affect children's feelings of self-esteem. For example, children who live in overcrowded homes or in temporary bed-and-breakfast accommodation may have fewer opportunities to play with other children and may feel isolated because they see themselves as different. Children whose family are travellers might not stay in one area long enough to form friendships.
- **Parental care or upbringing**: Children need consistent, loving care from their parents or carers; this helps them to feel secure and to develop self-esteem.
- **Role models**: Children need positive role models. Children are always affected by the behaviour of parents and other significant adults in their lives, such as teachers.
- **Culture and gender**: Different cultures have different expectations of their children, and child-rearing practices vary. Boys and girls are often treated differently within the family, although this is often subconscious – for example, girls may receive more cuddles than boys.
- **Size of family and the child's position in the family**: Children in large families may find it harder to gain their parents' attention, and many older children resent having to take care of younger siblings. There is a theory that all children develop certain personalities depending on whether they are born first, second, third and so on – or if they are the only child in the family. First-born or only children are more likely to be conscientious and academically ambitious. Second-born children tend to be outgoing and competitive. The youngest child in the family tends to be the most sociable and easy-going.

Developing self-esteem

The way we feel about ourselves leads to good or poor self-esteem. Our self-esteem is greatly influenced by how other people make us feel. Good self-esteem leads to a good self-image, increased self-confidence and a strong sense of identity.

The development of social and self-help skills

As early as six months of age, babies enjoy each other's company. When they are together, they look at each other, smile and touch each other's faces. As their social circle widens, they learn how to cooperate with each other when they play and they begin to make friends.

What are social skills?

Children need to develop certain social skills (or ways of behaving) in order to fit in – and to get on well – with the people around them. These social skills include the following:

Developing a sense of self and of belonging to a family

Developing confidence and self-respect

Playing with other children: sharing and taking turns

Being able to express their opinions and desires

Using words to solve conflicts and develop control of emotions

Developing skills of caring for and looking after yourself (independence)

Learning to separate from their parents

Developing trust

Learning that it is okay to make a mistake

Developing respect for others and feelings of **empathy**

What is self-image?

Our self-image is how we think about ourselves, and it involves developing a sense of identity. Children develop a self-image (or self-concept) during their first year of life, and this becomes more stable as they develop socially. Developing a sense of identity is about the following:

- **Realising you exist**: Babies gradually begin to understand that they are separate from their parents – for example, when they explore their own bodies by grasping their hands and feet, their feelings are different from when they are being held closely by their parents.
- **Who you are**: Later on during the first year of life, babies learn to respond to their own name and to understand that the people around them are separate and different from them.
- **Developing self-esteem** (or self-worth): Even before a child can understand spoken words, parents and caregivers can show approval, disappointment, anger or pleasure, by tone of voice, facial expressions and general body language.
- **A positive self-image**: When babies begin to move about, they will keep looking at the adult who is caring for them; this is called social referencing. Developing a positive self-image depends very much on the reactions from adults towards them; children need to be encouraged to feel self-confident, by receiving unconditional love and encouragement.
- **Learning to like and respect yourself**: Children need to feel valued and respected in order to develop these feelings about themselves.
- **Developing skills of caring for and looking after yourself**: Between the age of two and three years, children develop independence – with their increasing

physical skills, they are able to dress themselves, to wash their hands and to take care of their own toileting. These skills enhance their feelings of self-worth and confidence.

 KEY TERMS

Empathy: Awareness of another person's emotional state, and the ability to share the experience with that person.

Personality: The distinctive characteristics that make an individual unique.

Self-identity: A sense of who you are; liking yourself, respecting yourself and developing the skills and care to look after yourself.

Socialisation: The process by which children learn what is expected of them in terms of behaviour and attitudes within society.

Social referencing: When babies begin to move about, they will keep looking at the adult who is caring for them – just to check they are still there.

Temperament: A person's character or disposition (e.g. 'He has a happy disposition').

Stages of emotional and social development

As with all the areas of development, it is important to remember that every child is unique and will develop in their own way. The following tables provide a rough guide to the way children normally develop emotionally and socially.

Age	Stage
Birth to 8 weeks	• A baby's first smile in definite response to their carer is usually around 5–6 weeks. • They use total body movements to express pleasure at bath-time or when being fed. • Babies enjoy feeding and cuddling. • They will smile in response to an adult. • Babies turn to regard a nearby speaker's face. • They recognise the face and hands of preferred adults. • Babies may stop crying when they hear, see or feel their own carer.
2–5 months	• Babies show enjoyment at caring routines such as bath-time. • They respond with obvious pleasure to loving attention and cuddles. • Babies fix the eyes unblinkingly on the carer's face when feeding. • They enjoy attention and being with others. • They have recognisable sleep patterns.
6 months to 1 year	• Babies are more wary of strangers, showing stranger fear. • They offer toys to others. • Babies show distress when the mother leaves. • They are more aware of other people's feelings – for example, they cry if a sibling cries. They love an audience to laugh with them. They cry and laugh with others. This is called **recognition of an emotion**. It does not mean they are *really* laughing or crying, though. • They can drink from a cup with help. • Babies have and show definite likes and dislikes at mealtimes and bedtimes. • They like to look at themselves in a mirror (plastic safety mirror). • Babies imitate other people (e.g. clapping hands, waving bye-bye), but there is often a time lapse, so that they wave after the person has gone.

Table 5.4 Stages of emotional and social development

Age	Stage
1–2 years	• Children cooperate when being dressed. • They begin to have a longer memory. • They develop a sense of **identity** (I am me). • Children express their needs in words and gestures. • They enjoy being able to walk and are eager to try to get dressed – 'Me do it!' • Children are aware when others are anxious for them as they climb on and off chairs, etc.
2–3 years	• Children begin to be able to say how they are feeling. • They can dress themselves and go to the lavatory independently, but need sensitive support in order to feel success rather than frustration. • Pretend play develops rapidly when adults encourage it.
3–5 years	• Children are beginning to develop a gender role as they become aware of being male or female. • They make friends and are interested in having friends. • They learn to negotiate – give-and-take through experimenting with feeling powerful, having a sense of control, and through quarrels with other children. • Children are easily afraid (e.g. of the dark), as they become capable of pretending. They imagine all sorts of things. • Pretend play helps children to **decentre**. This means they begin to be able to understand how someone else might feel. *By 4 years*: • Children like to be independent and are strongly self-willed. • They show a sense of humour. • They can undress and dress themselves – except for laces and back buttons. • Children can wash and dry their hands and brush their teeth.

Table 5.4 Contin.

Encouraging children to recognise and deal with their strong feelings

Children feel things deeply. Feelings are hard to manage, even when we are adults. Feelings can quickly overwhelm the child and may lead to:

- sobbing and sadness
- temper tantrums that are full of anger and rage
- jealousy that makes a child want to hit out and hurt someone else
- a joy that makes a child actually jump and leap, with a wildness that is unnerving to many adults.

When children display negative emotions – such as sadness, anger, jealousy and anxiety – they are showing that they feel insecure. This feeling of insecurity may be merely temporary or it may be long-lasting.

Sadness

Young children can experience a whole range of emotions, and many will have occasional times of feeling sad or low. Such feelings are usually transient (i.e. they pass quickly), but for some children sadness can be more persistent. A child who is feeling sad may:

- be especially quiet or withdrawn
- have frequent episodes of tears and distress, perhaps in response to events with which that particular child normally has no problem
- eat excessively.

Sadness is often caused by feelings of loss. Examples include:

- a child who is just starting nursery may feel sad at the loss of the close and continuous link with familiar people
- a relative has died
- a much-loved pet has died
- the child's parents are splitting up.

How children cope with feelings of loss and sadness will depend on a number of factors, such as personality, the security of their attachment to their primary carers, and the preparation and support they are given by adults.
The moods of parents and carers are also important – for example, a sad or depressed mother can lead to a sad child.

How to help children who are sad

It is useful to try to find out why the child is sad, and to help them by:

- putting the feeling into words – even quite young children are often able to explain how they feel to an adult who is listening sensitively
- giving them plenty of love and attention
- finding an interesting activity to help distract them.

Anger

Some children become aggressive when they feel angry. They tend to be noisy and disrupt other children in their play. Young children flare up in anger for all sorts of reasons. They may respond aggressively when someone takes something that belongs to them or invades 'their space'. A child who is being ignored or feeling rejected because his/her peers will not let the child play with them may respond by pushing them or hitting out at everyone.

How to help a child who is angry

To help children cope with feelings of anger, you could:

- move the child away from the situation, if necessary
- try to distract the child by offering another activity
- give word to the feelings – try to put into words what you think the child may be feeling (e.g. 'I know you are angry because Liam took your truck, but pinching hurts and Liam is very upset now')
- stay calm – do not lose your temper with the child
- when the child has succeeded in overcoming feelings of anger, offer a few words of praise, which shows you understand that an effort has been made
- provide activities that will help children to express their feelings, such as:
  a. using malleable materials, such as dough, clay and play dough
  b. reading books and stories that feature children who have strong feelings of jealousy or fear
  c. providing music sessions using instruments such as drums, tambourines and bells
  d. encouraging children to express their feelings through drawing and painting
  e. using role play in the home corner to help children to act out their feelings of frustration.

Temper tantrums

Temper tantrums are expressions of children's feelings of anger and frustration. They start at around the age of 18 months and are the child's response to frustration. The child wants to do so much more than they are able or allowed to, and cannot yet express their anger verbally, so their feelings explode out of them in a burst of furious crying and screaming. Tantrums are a normal part of growing up and are often what parents mean when they talk of the 'terrible twos'. Tantrums are still fairly common during a child's third and fourth years. They gradually diminish as the child learns to express their feelings through words or other means.

Tantrums are often 'triggered' by the child:

- being told to do or to stop doing something
- being told 'No' or 'You'll have to wait'
- being overstimulated – often on days out or at birthday parties
- being bored or failing in an attempt to do something.

A child who is tired, hungry, unwell or coping with major changes in their life, such as a new baby sibling or starting nursery, will also be less able to handle their emotions.

How to help a child having a tantrum

Children often find their tantrums frightening and overwhelming. They feel out of control emotionally and physically, and are unable to respond to reason.

- Try to stay calm. The main thing to do is to stay calm and try not to get upset yourself.
- Reassure the child, acknowledging how they are feeling (e.g. 'You must be feeling very cross,' 'I can see that you are very angry').
- Do not smack. It never helps and only increases the level of violence and emotion in the situation.
- As soon as there are signs of the child calming down (e.g. they stop screaming), give them plenty of praise. Turn your full attention back to the child and talk to them with warmth and admiration.
- Do not give in to the child's demands during the tantrum. If the child learns that you change your mind if they have a tantrum, they will use the power of a tantrum to get their own way next time. Children are left confused by your inconsistency.
- Try to avoid tantrums – if you can anticipate them, try distracting the child with a game or another activity.
- A firm hug may help the child to feel secure and under control until s/he calms down – this is useful in situations where you cannot walk away.
- Talk about the tantrum – this may help older children to express their feelings calmly.
- Provide experiences and activities which the child finds interesting – this usually helps children to become involved in positive ways.

Jealousy

Jealousy is one of the hardest feelings to master. It often occurs when children feel insecure or unloved for some reason – the most common one being when a new baby is born into the family. This is called **sibling rivalry**. Children may react to these feelings by:

- demanding attention
- biting or hitting out at others – even a new baby sibling
- withdrawing from usual activities.

How to help a child who is jealous

- Parents should try to prepare the child if a new baby is expected.
- Give the child unconditional love and attention.
- Avoid pushing the child into the new role of 'the big boy or girl'. It probably seems to him or her that it is much more fun being the baby. (Try only to talk about the child being big when it is an obvious advantage – for instance, 'Big children can eat chocolate, and babies are not allowed.')
- Try to respect how the child is feeling and, if the child is old enough, talk these feelings through.

Anxiety

Anxiety is an instinctive response to danger. There are many common but irrational fears in childhood, such as loss of love from parents or a fear of being harmed, which leave children feeling very anxious. Young babies show fear by crying when they feel they are falling or when there is a sudden loud noise. Nursery-aged children do not always talk about their worries, often because they do not have the vocabulary to do so or because they are not really aware of what they are worried about. They may express a fear of monsters, for example, when what they are really worried about is going to nursery school and being separated from their mother for the first time. Young children have different ways of expressing their anxieties and worries. Typical signs of children's anxiety include:

- repeated tummy aches
- hitting out at other children
- becoming unusually quiet and withdrawn
- wetting themselves – having previously been dry
- fears and nightmares about the dark, monsters, spiders and animals.

These fears are very real to them and occur because of the child's developing imagination.

How to help an anxious child

- Listen patiently to their worries or their nightmares and fears. This helps them to feel that they are not on their own and that someone else shares their concerns.
- Reassure them that you believe them and that you are there to help them.
- Try to find out exactly what they are feeling and help them to express themselves.
- Avoid any frightening stories or TV programmes.

Regression

When a child feels insecure or threatened in some way, he or she might revert to an earlier stage of behaviour. This is called regression. Regression is natural and serves to help a child to adjust to a new level of development – for example, a four-year-old may temporarily enjoy a bottle for a few weeks when a new baby arrives, or a two-year-old child who has just been potty-trained will want to return to wearing a nappy. When a child reverts to 'babyish' behaviour, it is important to give extra love and attention until the child feels secure enough to go back to behaving as before.

The importance of remaining calm when dealing with children who are upset

It is often only natural to feel upset when dealing with a distressed child, but it is important to react in a positive and caring way. Children need to feel that they can express their feelings to someone they trust and who cares for them. You should:

- **always consider the needs of the child first** and think how you can best help them when they are feeling upset
- **listen to children carefully** and never dismiss their feelings as trivial – they are very important to them
- **be ready to help them** when you notice they are feeling upset – this may mean intervening in their play, providing appropriate activities or seeking advice from the child's parents.

Helping children with feelings of loss and grief

When someone whom a child loves is no longer around, it may seem to the child that the person has died. This can happen when a family experiences:

- a mother leaving home and going to hospital to have a new baby
- divorce or separation – when one parent no longer sees the child
- a parent being in hospital and unable to see the child (e.g. after a serious accident)
- a loved one who has been sent to prison
- a loved one who goes abroad
- the death of a loved one.

Children will go through a process of grieving. This process involves feeling:

- disbelief, numbness, shock and panic
- despair and anger, and yearning for the lost person
- more interest in life again eventually – but this takes time.

How you can encourage children to have good self-esteem

Above all, you need to value children for who they are, not what they do, what they look like or what you want them to be. Children need love, security and a feeling of trust. There is no single best way to give these feelings to children, as each child is unique and is strongly influenced by family and cultural background.

- **Show that you appreciate the efforts that children make:** Children do not have to achieve perfect results – the effort is more important. Avoid having unrealistic expectations about what children can manage – for example, with self-caring skills such as dressing, eating and going to the lavatory.
- **Encourage children:** When children make mistakes, do not tell them they are silly or stupid, but instead say something like, 'Never mind, let's pick up the pieces and put them in the bin. Next time, if you hold it with two hands it will be easier to work with,' and so on.
- **Offer children the opportunity to make choices and decisions** about what they do, keeping in mind the need for safety and consideration for others.
- **Provide clear, consistent boundaries:** Children need to know what is expected of them and what is not allowed; otherwise they become confused and begin to test out the boundaries to see what is consistent about them.
- **Provide children with a predictable environment** so that they can feel there is a shape to the day. There is no need to stick rigidly to routines, but children gain in confidence if they are able to take part in routine activities, such as helping to set the table or washing their hands after going to the lavatory.
- **Always talk politely and respectfully** to children and to their parents. Children need first to be *given* respect before they can feel self-respect.

• **Show interest in what children do**: Develop the skill of being a good listener so that children feel encouraged to express themselves.

How to encourage the development of social and self-help skills

Children also need to learn self-help skills. These skills include:

• being able to wash their hands
• being able to dress themselves
• being able to brush their hair
• being able to pour drinks and feed themselves.

Many of the social and self-help skills outlined above are learnt through children copying adult behaviour. All children should be allowed and encouraged to do the things that they are able to do from an early age – and to be praised and rewarded for their efforts.

Allow children to do things for themselves

Even very young children show an interest in doing things for themselves.

• Encourage independence by letting children do things for themselves as soon as they want to.
• Focus on the effort made by the child and avoid being critical of the 'end product'.
• Be patient and always praise children for doing things on their own.

Encourage children to help with challenging tasks

Facing and meeting challenges promote self-confidence.

• Encourage children to try to do new things and to face new challenges – this will promote self-confidence.
• Remember to choose tasks that children can accomplish.

Encourage children to make decisions

Children learn to make good choices by being given choices.

• At first, choices should be kept simple, like allowing children to choose what to wear out of two outfits.
• As children get older, encourage them to make increasingly complex decisions.

Be a good role model for responsibility and independence

Children learn by watching adults.

• Let children see you making decisions without wavering and taking care of responsibilities in an appropriate manner.

Help and encourage children to solve their own problems

Problem solving is a skill that must be learned.

• Encourage children to come up with their own solutions to problems. The ability to problem-solve is a skill that will be useful throughout children's lives. It will also help in the development of confidence and independence.

Encourage children to take risks

Taking risks involves facing potential failure.

- Many parents – and other adults – try to shield children from the disappointment of failure. However, children need to take risks to grow.
- Children must experience failure in order to learn how to cope with it.

Be there to provide support, when needed

Even the most independent-minded children need adult support on certain occasions.

- Make an effort to be available to the children in your care and to provide support when needed. Children who are secure in their relationships will have the confidence needed to explore the world.

Praise children

Children should receive praise when they display responsible and independent behaviour.

- Adults who praise such behaviour are letting children know that they notice and appreciate their efforts.

Give children responsibilities

One of the best ways for children to learn how to behave responsibly is to be given responsibilities.

- Make sure that the tasks assigned to the children match their capabilities.
- Take the time to show them how to carry out their assigned tasks properly.
- How well children perform a task is not as important as what they are learning about responsibility.

From birth, babies and children need to be encouraged to 'have a go', even if their early efforts are not always successful. You have an important role in helping to develop self-reliance at all stages of children's development.

Promoting self-reliance skills throughout childhood

In babies

- Encourage babies to cooperate when getting them dressed and undressed – for example, by pushing their arms through sleeves and pulling off their socks.
- Provide finger foods from about eight months and tolerate mess when babies are feeding themselves.
- Set out a variety of toys to encourage them to make choices.

In children aged two to five years

- Provide a range of activities – both indoors and outdoors.
- Encourage children to help tidy away toys.

Figure 5.6 Helping to serve drinks to other children is a social skill

- Allow children to have a free choice in their play.
- Encourage children in self-care skills – washing hands, brushing hair and getting dressed; be patient and provide them with adequate time.
- Build choice into routines such as mealtimes and snack-times.
- Encourage children to enjoy simple cooking activities.

It also helps if you break down tasks and activities into easy, manageable steps – for example:

- cutting food up into bite-size pieces
- having well-defined places to pack away toys
- using a non-slip mat under a baby's bowl when feeding
- using child-size cutlery and a drinking cup that has a lid to avoid spills
- using a footstool to reach the bathroom basin
- using small steps and a toilet seat to make the child feel more secure when going to the 'big' toilet
- choosing clothing with bigger buttons and shoes with Velcro® fastenings.

REVISION QUESTIONS

1. What is meant by self-image and self-identity? Why is the development of a positive self-image so important?
2. How can you encourage children to have good self-esteem?
3. What is meant by the term 'regression'?
4. At what age are temper tantrums most common? How would you help a child who is having a temper tantrum?
5. What are self-help or self-reliance skills?
6. Suggest six ways in which you can help children to develop self-help skills.

 CHILD STUDY ACTIVITY

Describe the child's stage of social and emotional development. What self-help skills has the child learnt?

5 Behaviour and approaches to discipline

Behaviour is observable – that is, it can be seen and/or heard. It is the way we act, speak and treat other people and our environment. It does not include our thoughts, although these usually prompt what we do.

Behaviour is influenced by:

- the customs and practices of the society or culture
- the rules, standards and expectations of the family
- copying others – with children, particularly through play
- receiving rewards or treats, or respect from others
- being punished or penalised, or feeling humiliated
- the actions and attitudes of a peer group
- the desire to be useful to others and achieve satisfaction for doing something worthwhile.

Patterns of behaviour

The following patterns of behaviour are, of course, only loosely linked to the ages shown. As with any normative measurements, they only serve as a rough guide to help in understanding children's behaviour and how best to respond to it. Much will depend on children's experiences and the way they have been helped to develop good relationships.

One to two years

At this age, children:

- have developed their own personalities and are sociable with close family and friends
- still become shy and anxious when parents or carers are out of sight
- are developing their speech and can attract attention by calling out or crying
- can become possessive over toys but can often be distracted by something else
- are discovering that they are separate individuals
- are self-centred (see things from their own point of view)
- are gaining mobility, improving their ability to explore their surroundings – this results in conflicts, often regarding safety
- begin to understand the meaning of 'no' and firm boundaries can be set
- can be frustrated by their own limitations but resist adult help (perhaps saying 'me do it').

Two to three years

At this age, children:

- are not yet able to share easily
- are developing greater awareness of their separate identities
- are developing their language abilities, which help them to communicate their needs and wishes more clearly and to understand 'in a minute'
- can still be distracted from the cause of their anger
- have tantrums (usually when parents or main carers are present) when frustrated – possibly caused by their efforts to become self-reliant (e.g. feeding or dressing themselves) or having ideas which the adult does not want them to carry out
- experience a range of feelings – being very affectionate and cooperative one minute and resistant the next
- are aware of the feelings of others and can respond to them.

Three to four years

At this age, children:

- are very aware of others and imitate them, especially in their play; with developing speaking and listening skills they tend to repeat swear words they hear
- are more able to express themselves through speech and, therefore, there is often a reduction in physical outbursts; however, they are still likely to hit back if provoked
- can be impulsive and will be less easily distracted
- become more sociable in their play and may have favourite friends
- can sometimes be reasoned with and are just becoming aware of the behaviour codes in different places or situations
- like, and seek, adult approval and appreciation of their efforts.

Four to five years

At this age, children:

- can behave appropriately at mealtimes and during other 'routine' activities, and may begin to understand why 'please' and 'thank you' (or their equivalent) are important
- are able to share and take turns, but often need help
- are more aware of others' feelings and will be concerned if someone is hurt
- are becoming more independent and self-assured, but still need adult comfort when ill or tired
- will respond to reason, can negotiate and be adaptable, but can still be distracted
- are sociable and becoming confident communicators, able to make more sense of their environment; there will continue to be conflicts which they cannot resolve on their own and with which they will need adult help
- can sometimes be determined, may argue and show aggression.

Linking behaviour to child development

When assessing children's behaviour it is important to bear these patterns in mind and to view it in the context of overall development.

For example, it is well known that tantrums are a common, even expected, feature of a two-year-old child's behaviour. There is bound to be some cause for concern if tantrums are a *regular* feature of a six-year-old child's behaviour. However, some adults have unrealistic expectations of children and express surprise when unwanted behaviour occurs.

A five-year-old might become fidgety and whine during a Christmas pantomime, for instance. The adults may view the occasion as a treat and could feel resentment that their child is complaining. However, it is reasonable that a five-year-old should lose concentration, be unable to sit still for a lengthy period or understand all of what is going on.

When trying to understand behaviour, it is useful to observe whether there are particular incidents or situations that seem to **trigger** unwanted behaviour. Some of these can be avoided altogether by minor changes in routine or approach, but others, such as siblings teasing each other, will occur frequently, so children need to be given some strategies and support to be able to cope with them effectively. It is important never to reject the child, but only what the child has done – for example, 'That was an unkind thing to say' rather than 'You are unkind.'

The ABC of behaviour

- Antecedent: What happens before, or leads up to, the observed behaviour.
- Behaviour: The observed behaviour – what the child says and how s/he acts (this is any behaviour – positive or negative).
- Consequence: What happens following the observed behaviour.

Behaviour is very closely linked to self-esteem. Children who feel bad about themselves may not behave well. The poem in figure 5.7 sums up the ways in which adults can contribute positively to children's development and behaviour.

CHILDREN LEARN WHAT THEY LIVE
If children live with criticism, they learn to condemn.
If children live with hostility, they learn to fight.
If children live with fear, they learn to be apprehensive.
If children live with pity, they learn to feel sorry for themselves.
If children live with ridicule, they learn to be shy.
If children live with jealousy, they learn to feel envy.
If children live with shame, they learn to feel guilty.
If children live with encouragement, they learn confidence.
If children live with tolerance, they learn patience.
If children live with praise, they learn appreciation.
If children live with acceptance, they learn to love.
If children live with approval, they learn to like themselves.
If children live with recognition, they learn it is good to have a goal.
If children live with sharing, they learn generosity.
If children live with honesty, they learn truthfulness.
If children live with fairness, they learn justice.
If children live with kindness and consideration, they learn respect.
If children live with security, they learn to have faith in themselves and in those about them.
If children live with friendliness, they learn the world is a nice place in which to live.

Figure 5.7 *Children learn what they live* by Dorothy Law Nolte

Factors affecting behaviour

It is well known that behaviour is commonly affected by certain factors. There are some factors that stem from the children themselves:

- illness
- accident and injury
- tiredness.

Other factors result from the situations they might find themselves in:

- arrival of a new baby
- moving house
- parental separation or divorce
- change of carer – either at home or in a childcare setting
- loss or bereavement
- change of setting (e.g. transition from home to nursery or nursery to school).

Individual children will respond to these situations differently, but regression is common (usually temporary) – this is when they revert to behaviour that is immature for them. Events that they do not understand will leave them confused, leading to frustration and aggressive outbursts; or they may blame themselves, which could result in withdrawn behaviour and the development of unwanted habits through anxiety.

Generally, any factor that causes stress may result in the child:

- needing more comfort and attention
- being less sociable
- being unable to cope with tasks that they would normally manage
- being subject to mood swings
- being unable to concentrate (this includes listening to instructions) and less able to cope with challenging situations and difficulties.

How to manage behaviour: setting goals and boundaries

If children are to understand what is regarded as acceptable behaviour at home, in the work setting and in society, they must be given very clear guidelines. Work settings will have a policy relating to behaviour and discipline that all staff should follow and which is reviewed regularly. The policy will explain the rules that are applied and how children will be helped to understand and learn to keep to them. In most cases, the rules are simple and reflect concerns for safety and for children to be considerate of others and their environment. They should be appropriate for the age and stage of development of the children and for the particular needs of the work setting.

Goals are the forms of behaviour that are encouraged; they cover physical, social and verbal aspects. They should be set realistically for the child's age and stage of development.

Examples of goals for a child aged four to five years are:

- to say 'please' and 'thank you'
- to share play equipment
- to tidy up
- to be quiet and listen for short periods (e.g. storytime or register time).

Boundaries are the limits within which behaviour is acceptable – they identify what may, and may not, be done or said. Children need to understand the consequences of failing to act within those boundaries. It is important that the boundaries are appropriate for the age and stage of development.

Examples of boundaries for children aged four to five years are:

- they may play outside, but must not tread on the flowerbeds
- they may watch television, but only until tea is ready
- they may use the dressing-up clothes, if they put them away when they have finished.

Promoting positive behaviour

- It is helpful to set 'positive' rules rather than 'negative' rules.
- Negative rules tend to begin with the words 'Do not' and tell children what they must not do, but give them no guidance as to what they may or should do.
- Consistency in applying the boundaries is important, especially in the work setting, where children need to relate to several adults. They will check that the rules have not changed and that they still apply, whichever adult is present.
- If you are supervising an activity, the children will expect you to apply the same rules as other adults. It undermines your own position if you allow unacceptable behaviour and another staff member has to discipline the children you are working with.

Discipline: managing behaviour

First, it needs to be agreed in a group setting what sort of behaviour is unwanted, and then some decisions need to be made as to how staff will manage such behaviour if and when it does arise. These decisions should take account of individual needs, as children will respond in their own ways.

For example, in a school setting, staying in at playtime can be a form of punishment for some children, but for those who have poor social skills and find the playground rather intimidating, it can be a relief. Some children enjoy tidying up and helping the teacher – maybe because they might receive more individual attention – while for others this is a chore.

Theories about behaviour

Albert Bandura developed a 'social learning' theory, which states that children learn about social behaviour by watching and imitating other people, especially those they admire. Children will learn negative behaviour as well as positive behaviour, so the presence of good role models is very important.

B.F. Skinner developed a 'behaviourist' theory, which states that children's behaviour is shaped by adults – through positive and negative reinforcement. These two theories have influenced current practice for managing and modifying (shaping or reforming) behaviour.

There are three main aspects of behaviour modification:

1. Identifying positive and negative behaviour – deciding what behaviour is to be encouraged and what is to be discouraged.
2. Rewarding positive behaviour – encouraging and promoting it through reward. There are different forms of reward:
   - verbal praise ('Well done')
   - attention (this could be non-verbal – e.g. smile of approval, a nod)
   - stars or points (for older children), leading to certificates or for group/team recognition
   - sharing success by having other staff and parents told about it
   - own-choice activity or story
   - tangible rewards such as stickers.

   These work on the principle of positive reinforcement – based on the idea that if children receive approval and/or a reward for behaving acceptably, they are likely to want to repeat that behaviour. If one child is praised (e.g. for tidying up), others are often influenced to copy or join in, so that they too will receive praise and attention. For young children, the reward must be immediate, so they understand the link between the reward and the positive behaviour. It is of little value to promise a treat or reward in the future. Similarly, star charts and collecting points are not always appropriate for children younger than five years old.
3. Discouraging negative behaviour (negative reinforcement):
   - whenever possible such behaviour should be ignored (bearing in mind safety or injury), although not if attention is drawn to it (perhaps by another child), as the message sent then is that it is acceptable
   - giving attention and praise to another child who is behaving acceptably
   - distracting the child's attention (particularly appropriate with younger children) or removing him/her to another activity or group
   - expressing disapproval – verbally and/or non-verbally, through body language, facial expression (frowning) and shaking of the head
   - imposing a punishment – withdrawal of a privilege (e.g. watching a favourite TV programme).

These work on the principle of negative reinforcement – based on the idea that children will avoid repeating an unpleasant experience. If they behave unacceptably and earn the disapproval of an adult or receive some sort of punishment, they will be less likely to repeat that behaviour. As they learn from watching others, older children may be deterred (put off) from behaving unacceptably by seeing someone else receive discipline. This approach requires the adult to act immediately so that young children understand the link between the unacceptable behaviour and the adult's response to it.

> **Remember:** Physical, or corporal, punishment is illegal in work settings and never allowed under any circumstances. This includes pulling a child by his/her elbow or arm, or grabbing him/her by the wrist. Intervention, to protect the child, others or property, should involve *minimal* physical restraint.

Using rewards

There are problems associated with rewards in that some children may behave in a particular way purely to receive the reward, rather than from an understanding of the need to consider safety, others and their environment, or enjoying what they have achieved for its own sake.

The type of reward also needs to be considered – for example, is it desirable for children to be given sweets as rewards? Some parents may have strong views about this.

Rewards might work in the short term, but do not always succeed in the long term. They might even undermine lifelong learning by encouraging children to seek reward, rather than be disposed to learn because something is interesting.

Problem – or unwanted – behaviour

Attention-seeking behaviour, aggression (physical and verbal) towards others, and self-destructive behaviour need to be dealt with calmly.

Attention-seeking behaviour

Children will do just about anything to get the attention they crave from parents and carers. This is often shown through disruptive (making noises, not responding to an instruction) or aggressive behaviour, and needs managing, as identified above. Sometimes children who are trying to please can be just as disruptive. Those who desperately want adults to notice them will call out, interrupt, ask questions and frequently push in front of other children to show something they have made or done. Children who seek attention challenge one's patience, but with a bit of reminding about turn-taking, and the clear expectation that they will do so, they can learn to wait for their turn. It is important to give them attention when they have waited appropriately, so that they are encouraged to repeat this behaviour.

Physical aggression

This usually results from strong feelings that are difficult to control. Whatever the cause – and it may be provocation – the adult should deal with it calmly and ensure that the needs of all the children involved are met. A child who has lost control frightens him/herself and other children. Some parents and work settings favour a time-out approach:

- the aggressive child is taken to an identified place, away from the incident – a corner or a chair

- time-out allows for a calming-down period for the child, and for other children to be reassured.

This method can work, but needs positive follow-up by a staff member to explain that the behaviour was unacceptable, and why, and to suggest how the child might have behaved instead – for example, asking instead of snatching, listening to the apology for the model being broken and so on. Unless this is done, there is a danger that the chair or area becomes known to the children as the 'naughty chair', and staff begin to use it as a way of 'grounding' a child who is causing annoyance, without addressing the issues. Many adults do not like to use this approach for this reason.

Self-destructive behaviour

This includes head banging and forms of self-mutilation (e.g. tearing out hair, excessive nail biting, causing pain and bleeding). It usually signals some emotional difficulty that needs expert intervention. Staff and parents need to discuss their concerns and agree a common approach, based on the advice they are given.

Unacceptable language

This includes swearing and name-calling that often result from children repeating what they have heard from other people. Sometimes they are unaware that it is unacceptable in certain settings. In these cases, they need to be told firmly not to say those words 'here' – you cannot legislate for language they may use at home, or criticise their families.

- Some children will deliberately use unacceptable language to shock or seek attention. In these cases, you should state the rule calmly and firmly.
- Name-calling, particularly if it is discriminatory (regarding race, creed, disability, family background, appearance, etc.) must always be challenged and dealt with firmly. Explain that it is hurtful and that we are all different. This behaviour is best combated through good example and through anti-discriminatory practices in the work setting, which will help children to value other people as individuals.

Sometimes the behaviour management strategies outlined above fail to be effective or are effective for only a short period of time. So when behaviour is inappropriate for the child's stage of development or is persistently challenging, there are other professionals who may be called on to help all those involved (see part six, pages 278–281).

 REVISION QUESTIONS

1. List five factors that might affect children's behaviour.
2. Why is it important for children to have goals and boundaries?
3. What is positive reinforcement? Give two examples.
4. What is negative reinforcement? Give three examples.

DISCUSSION TOPIC

'In the UK it is illegal for a teacher to smack another person's child. It is also against the law for a parent or carer to smack their child, except where this amounts to "reasonable punishment".'

In class, discuss the following statements:

- Parents have a right to discipline their children in any way they choose.

- Being smacked does not damage children – it is a momentary sensation that is gone as quickly as it happens, but it does serve a valuable purpose, if your children respond to it.

- It is up to any citizen to intervene when they think a child is being mistreated.

- All smacking is an abuse of the child's rights.

6 Learning through play

What is play?

Through play, children bring together and organise their ideas, feelings, relationships and their physical life. It helps them to use what they know and to make sense of the world and people they meet. Play brings together:

- ideas and creativity
- feelings
- relationships
- physical coordination
- spiritual development.

During play, children:

- get things under control so that they can face the world and deal with it
- get ready for the future
- think about things that have happened.

There are different ideas about how to develop play, but although there are wide cultural variations, all children seem to develop and learn through play, including children with severe disabilities.

Children who do not have opportunities for play find it difficult to learn – for example, children in the Romanian orphanages were held back in learning about objects, ideas, feelings, relationships and people.

The UN 'Convention on the Rights of the Child' (1989) says that every child in the world should have the right to play.

7 The different types of play

There are many different types of play, but these are the four main types:

- creative play
- imaginative or pretend play
- physical play
- manipulative play.

Creative play

In creative play, children must not be expected to 'make something'. Creative play is about **experimenting** with materials and music. It is not about producing things to go on displays or to be taken home – for example, when children are involved with messy finger play with paint, nothing is left at the end of the session once it has been cleared away.

Adults can encourage creative play by offering children a range of materials and play opportunities, including:

- dance
- music
- drawing
- collage
- painting
- model making and woodwork
- sand (using small-world scenarios)
- water (using small-world scenarios).

Creative play helps children to express their feelings and ideas about people, objects and events. It helps children to:

- be physically coordinated
- develop language
- develop ideas (concepts)
- develop relationships with people
- be more confident
- boost their self-esteem.

Figure 5.8 Painting and drawing are a form of creative play

Imaginative or pretend play

Imaginative play is also called **dramatic play** or **pretend play**. Children make play scenarios – for example, about a shop or a boat, a garage, an office, a swimming pool. In pretend play, children:

- use **play props** – for example, they pretend a box is a fridge, or a stick is a spoon
- **role play** and pretend that they are someone else, such as a shopkeeper
- pretend-play **everyday situations**, such as getting up, going to sleep, eating (just as the Teletubbies™ do)
- **act out situations** that they have definitely experienced, like going to the supermarket
- develop **superhero play** when they use unreal situations, like Superman, Power Rangers or cartoon characters
- gradually develop their play scenarios to include situations that are not everyday events and which they may only have heard about and not experienced – this is called **fantasy play**; they might pretend to

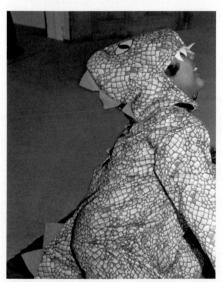

Figure 5.9 Dressing up is a form of pretend play

go to the moon or go on an aeroplane – it is not impossible that they will experience these things one day.

The important thing to remember about pretend play is that there will be nothing left to show anyone when the play comes to an end.

Figure 5.10 A running game is a form of physical play

Physical play

Physical play promotes a child's health. Physical play links with all other areas of a child's development. The brain works better if children have plenty of fresh air and exercise. This is why both indoor and outdoor play are very important. Through physical play, children learn to challenge gender stereotypes. Boys *and* girls can enjoy playing ball games – for example, football play scenarios – running and climbing. Children need to be encouraged in these activities. It helps if children wear clothes and shoes that allow freedom of movement.

They also:

- learn through their senses
- coordinate their movements
- develop their muscles
- learn about pace and keeping going (stamina)
- learn how to use space in a coordinated way
- learn to challenge gender stereotypes.

Manipulative play

Children need plenty of opportunities to play using manipulative skills. This particularly encourages children to use their hands, which is very important in human development. Manipulative play involves children using their hands to move, turn or screw items to make them fit.

The following toys and activities all provide children with opportunities for manipulative play:

- puzzles – all varieties
- construction toys, such as wooden blocks, Duplo® and Meccano®
- beads and cotton reels for threading activities
- sewing cards
- musical instruments
- drawing and painting equipment
- water
- sand
- materials for cooking, dough, clay
- ball play – throwing and catching and so on.

Figure 5.11 Playing with wooden blocks is a form of manipulative play

8 The benefits of play

Play is fundamental to the healthy development of children. When children play, there is a benefit to all areas of their development.

Physical development	Intellectual development
Play helps children to: • develop gross motor skills • develop fine motor skills • be physically coordinated • exercise their muscles • develop their senses: sight, sound, hearing, touch and taste.	Play helps children to: • be creative and imaginative • develop communication and language skills • think, have ideas and learn concepts • count and solve problems • learn about cause and effect • develop memory and concentration.
Emotional development	Social development
Play helps children to: • feel happiness and joy • have a sense of control • achieve a sense of wellbeing and increase their self-esteem • deal with setbacks by acting out their feelings • feel confident and more independent.	Play helps children to: • understand and care about others • learn about sharing and taking turns • make good relationships • test their boundaries and challenge themselves • develop social and self-care skills.

Table 5.5 The benefits of play to children's development

KEY TERM

Gender stereotype: A set of common beliefs and judgments concerning the existing position of men and women in society – for example, girls/women play with dolls and can be nurses; boys/men play with cars and can be firefighters.

9 The development of the stages of play

Children discover and learn about their world when they play. Play gives them the opportunity to practise their social skills. By playing with one another, children learn social rules such as waiting, taking turns, cooperation and sharing things. Children go through certain developmental stages of play as they grow. These stages are:

- solitary play
- parallel play
- associative play
- cooperative play.

Recent research demonstrates that children do not develop as if they are climbing up a ladder. Instead, brain studies show that their play develops like a network. Sometimes they will play alone (solitary play); sometimes they will play with others (in parallel, associative or cooperative form). This will depend partly on their age, but it will also depend on their mood, others around them, where they are, and whether they are tired, hungry or comfortable.

It is certainly easier for toddlers and young children to play together in parallel, associatively or cooperatively if they are with one other child. Larger groups are more of a challenge for young children. Gradually, three or four children might play cooperatively together. This tends to develop from around three or four years of age.

Developmental stages of play

Stage 1: Solitary play (from six months onwards)

Solitary play is play that is undertaken alone, sometimes through choice and at other times because the child finds it hard to join in, or because of his/her developmental stage.

In this first stage of play, beginning at about six months, babies play alone. Babies and toddlers need time and space to play alone, but often appreciate having others around them as they do so.

Figure 5.12 Baby playing alone

- Solitary play provides personal space and time to think, get to know yourself and like yourself.
- When toddlers play alone, they seek interesting experiences, but need support when frustrated.
- Children of all ages engage in solitary play sometimes; playing alone enables older children to concentrate and practise their skills (e.g. when constructing a model).
- It is important to protect the child's play space and toys from interference by other children.
- Children should be allowed to experience 'ownership' of toys and not be pushed to share before they are ready.

Example: A child might play alone – for instance, with a doll's house – because they want to play out a story that they have in their head. Having other children join the play would stop them being able to do this.

Stage 2: Onlooker 'play' (from about eight months to three-plus years)

Onlooker 'play' is the passive observation of the play of others, without actual participation.

Before children begin to play with each other, they go through a brief stage of looking-on behaviour.

- Children will stop what they are doing to watch and listen to what other children are doing.
- Older children may also watch others play if they are new to the group and do not yet feel ready to enter into the play.
- Even a child who is already secure in a group may engage in onlooker behaviour – taking a passive interest in what their friends are doing, but not joining in.

Stage 3: Parallel play (from two to four-plus years)

Figure 5.13 Parallel play

Parallel play is when children play alongside each other but quite separately, and without communicating with each other.

- Children in this stage of parallel play may comment on what they are doing or imitate what another child does, but they rarely actively cooperate in a task.
- During this stage, children like to have exactly the same toys as their peers, but their own play space.
- They are no longer content to play alone, but they are also not ready for the demands of sharing toys or taking turns.
- Older children also enjoy parallel play with their friends.

Example: Two children might both put dolls to bed in the home area. They do not take much notice of each other.

Stage 4: Associative play (between three-and-a-half and five-plus years)

Figure 5.14 Associative play

Associative play is when two or more children actively interact with one another by sharing or borrowing toys, while not doing the same things.

Children playing at the **parallel** stage will begin to become aware of other children. They will often begin to communicate through talking to each other or by becoming aware of each other's games and explaining to each other what they are doing.

Gradually, one child will become involved in the other child's play. This is known as **associative** (or partnership) play.

Language becomes much more important, imagination increases and dramatic themes begin to come into the play. (This category of play may seem to be cooperative, but this is not the case – at this age, children are still too egocentric to have true cooperation.)

Example: Two children might play so that one is the cook in the cafe and the other is the waitress. They do not seem to care that they have no customers.

Stage 5: Cooperative play (from four-and-a-half years onwards)

Cooperative play is when children begin to play together – to share their play. They become more sociable and take on roles in the play.

- Children begin to be aware of the needs and the roles of their peers, and gradually the play can become complex.
- Rules are sometimes devised and some cooperative play will be revisited over several days.

- Cooperative play continues throughout middle childhood, where it evolves into more stylised games with rules.
- In the early stages of cooperative play, the rules are not as important as the sense of belonging to a group and working towards a common goal.

Example of early (or simple) cooperative play: One child might be the baby and the other might be the parent, as they play going to the shops. They talk about their play ideas: 'You say "Mum" and I say "Yes, darling."'

Example of later (or complex) cooperative play: A group of children aged between three and five years have been on an outing to the local market. When they return, the adult sets up a market stall. Some children become customers and buy things. Others sell things and they talk as they play.

Figure 5.15 Cooperative play

? REVISION QUESTIONS

1. What are the four main categories of play?

2. When children act out different roles (e.g. one child is 'Mummy' and the other is 'the baby'), what is the category of play?

3. What is a gender stereotype?

4. List the four main developmental stages of social play.

10 Selection of toys

There are various factors to consider when selecting toys for children. The main questions to ask are:

1. **Is it safe?** Inspect toy packaging for safety symbols and age-appropriate guidance (see pages 153–154). Also watch for sharp corners and small pieces that could be swallowed.
2. **Is it developmentally appropriate?** Toys need to be suitable to a child's age, interests and abilities (see table 5.6).
3. **Will it stimulate a child's imagination?** Often, toys that are simple in design allow for more creative, useful options. Toys that are too complicated may frustrate a young child.
4. **Can it be used in many different ways and by children of different ages?** If so, the toy may have lasting benefits.
5. **Will it withstand the active play of young children?** Or is it a toy that may break after a couple of uses? Saving money to invest in a more durable toy may be worthwhile.
6. **Does it allow the child to assemble, stack pieces or connect pieces together?** From these processes, children learn how our world is put together and have opportunities to try their hand creating something.
7. **Is it exciting and stimulating?** Children should actively want to play with the toy, rather than be given one that the parent has chosen simply for its educational value.

Age	Stage of development	Suitable toys	Examples of toys

Birth to 1 year	• Young babies learn through the five senses: smell, taste, sound, touch and sight.
	• Newborn babies like to gaze at mobiles and pram toys.
	• A baby who is sitting up is ready to play with a rolling ball and stacking and nesting toys.
	• Babies use their hands and mouths to explore.
	• They enjoy handling their first sturdy picture books, showing familiar objects.
	• They love listening to stories being read.
		Toys for babies should:
		  – have pieces that are too large to swallow
		  – be lightweight for handling and grasping
		  – have no sharp edges or points
		• be non-toxic.
		• Rattles
		• Baby gyms
		• Stacking toys
		• Floating bath toys
		• Wooden blocks
		• Strings of big beads
		• Activity centre
		• Nested boxes or cups
		• Card/fabric books
		• Beanbags
		• Soft toys
		• Foam balls	

Table 5.6 Selection of toys for different stages of development

Age	Stage of development	Suitable toys	Examples of toys
1–2 years	• By 13 months, about half of all babies walk, but most still fall over if they lose momentum. • They are more purposeful in the way they explore objects. • They start to treat objects in appropriate ways (e.g. cuddling teddy bears and pressing the button on a jack-in-the-box). • By 21 months, they are usually very mobile. • They can pull a toy on a string or manage a push-along toy. • They can use their feet to move along on a tricycle or pedal-car.	• Push- and pull-along toys • Shape sorters/posting boxes • Building bricks • Simple books • Simple jigsaw puzzles • Sit-and-ride cars • Sand and water play • Painting and drawing • Matching games • Action rhymes and puppet play • Cuddly soft toys	

Table 5.6 Contin.

Age	Stage of development	Suitable toys	Examples of toys
2–3 years	• Children jump and hop, and walk up and down stairs one foot at a time. • They have good hand–eye coordination and can build quite elaborately. • They enjoy rolling and cutting play dough. • They imitate those they know and like to copy them. • They can follow simple instructions and can remember what to do.	• Books • Music-making toys • Crayons, poster paints and finger paints • Hammer-and-peg toys • Play dough • Balls, slides and swings • Tricycles • Basic counting, number and shape-matching toys • Jigsaw puzzles • Dressing-up toys	
3–4 years	• Children love running and chasing. • They rarely fall and are reluctant to be still. • They can throw a ball for a short distance and catch a large ball thrown directly into their arms. • They often play at being someone else and enjoy dressing up. • They begin to show sympathy and empathy for characters in stories.	• Construction toys (e.g. Duplo®) • Small-world toys (e.g. Playmobil® Play People) • Simple hand-puppets • Dressing-up clothes and props • Picture books and storybooks • Activity books • Intermediate jigsaw puzzles • Simple board games • Sand- and water-play toys • Pedal tricycles	

Table 5.6 Contin.

Age	Stage of development	Suitable toys	Examples of toys
4–5 years	• Children have good balance and coordination. • They can climb up the steps of a slide, use a climbing frame skilfully and ride a bicycle. • They are starting to add details to drawings (e.g. windows to houses and fingers on hands). • They may print their own name on their paintings. • They understand that other people have thoughts, experiences and feelings that are different from their own. • They move in a more grown-up way, although they lack an adult's strength and foresight.	• Storybooks • Modelling and craft materials • Musical instruments • Complex jigsaw puzzles • Construction toys • Board games • Two-wheeled bike with stabilisers and helmet • Skipping ropes • Bats and balls • Climbing frames with slides and ladder	

Table 5.6 Contin.

Non-commercial toys

There is a lot of pressure on parents to buy expensive toys for their children, especially just before Christmas. Toy manufacturers spend vast amounts on advertising their products, and many parents do not want their child to miss out on what everyone else seems to be playing with. The truth is that children can get just as much satisfaction and more creativity from things like empty boxes and tins – although, of course, parents must ensure that they are safe to play with. Examples include the following:

- Shakers can be made from cardboard rolls or plastic bottles, securely sealed at each end and filled with rice, lentils or similar.
- Empty cardboard boxes can be used to play shops, to provide a doll's bed or simply to climb in and out of.
- Provide bubble play using a bowl of washing-up liquid and water, with plastic cups and funnels.
- Make some play dough and provide a rolling pin and cutters.
- A children's den or playhouse can be made using a table and an old sheet or blanket.
- Make some stilts – use two identical strong tins (e.g. coffee or powdered milk); thread strong string through holes made near the bottom of the tin. The string should form a loop and be taut when the child is standing upright with arms held straight against their body.
- Make some simple puppets – for example, decorate a wooden spoon by drawing faces on both sides (e.g. happy or sad); glue wool on top for hair and tie material around the spoon as a cape or dress. Or use a child's sock: sew on buttons or felt for eyes, wool for hair, and felt or material for the tongue and nose.
- Make some dressing-up clothes – capes can be made easily from any material, with a stocking threaded through the hem and gathered to loosely tie around the child's neck.
- A dressing-up box – provide old clothes for dressing up (e.g. hats, scarves, dresses, jewellery and handbags).
- Buy cheap rolls of lining wallpaper and cut into large sheets for painting and drawing.
- Outdoors, children love to paint with water on a hot day: provide a bowl of water and some large brushes.

Safety points

Supervise children closely while making toys, especially if using knives and scissors, or glue, paint, staplers and so on. Be aware of choking hazards and toxic materials.

Any sand- or water-play must be carefully supervised, as young children can drown in just a few inches of water.

REVISION QUESTIONS

1. Certain toys remain popular throughout a child's life. Name two such toys.
2. List five safety points to consider when buying toys for young children.

 DISCUSSION TOPIC

Discuss the toys you remember playing with in early childhood – both indoors and outdoors. Which were your favourites?

 CHILD STUDY ACTIVITY

Which toys does the child prefer? Observe the child playing with a favourite toy and list the ways in which the toy promotes the child's development.

COMMUNITY SUPPORT

1 The need for day-care provision

There are several reasons why there is a greater need for day-care provision for young children in the UK today. The main reason is the increase in the numbers of families in which both parents work, but there is also much more importance given to the benefits of early education for children under the age of five – or before they start formal schooling.

Many parents choose or have to go out to work when their children are young. This means that they need to arrange suitable daytime care for their children. Some families rely on grandparents or other relatives to provide this care, in which case it is usually provided within the child's own home. It may be paid or unpaid. This sort of childcare is known as **informal care**. When children are looked after *outside* the family unit it is known as **formal care**.

Parents and guardians can choose childcare from the following options:

- **Crèches** provide occasional care for children under the age of eight. Crèches are often provided at a subsidised rate at the parent's work-place.

- **Preschools and playgroups** provide opportunities for play and often also early education to children under five years.

- **Day nurseries** provide care for children from birth to four or five years and beyond, often integrated with early education and other services.

- **Sure Start Children's Centres** offer early learning, childcare, health advice and family support for families with children up to age five.

- **Out-of-school or kids' clubs** are open before and after school and all day long during school holidays, giving children aged 3–14 years (and up to 16 years for children with special needs) a safe and enjoyable place to play, meet and sometimes catch up on homework.

- **Childminders** usually look after children under the age of 12 in the childminder's own home, and often collect school-aged children from a nearby school.

- **Nannies** provide childcare in the child's own home and can look after children of any age.

Figure 6.1 A day nursery

2 The types of preschool provision

The regulation and control of day-care provision

All childminders and day-care providers caring for young children – including playgroups, preschools, private nurseries, crèches and out-of-school clubs for children under eight years – must be registered by **Ofsted** (the Office for Standards in Education, Children's Services and Skills) on the Early Years Register (or, in Wales, by the Care Standards Inspectorate). Registration includes a criminal records check on anyone involved in providing childcare, and an inspection of the premises to look at health and safety and educational welfare issues.

In order to become registered, day-care providers have to meet a set of **National Standards** relating to quality. These cover the following areas:

- staff experience and qualification requirements
- staff-to-child ratios
- the quality of toys and equipment
- behaviour management
- health and safety and general care
- play and learning.

Childcare services that *must* be registered with Ofsted are:

- full day care
- childminding
- workplace crèches
- out-of-school care
- sessional care (this includes playgroups, nurseries and preschools).

Nannies

Nannies look after a child in the family home. They do not have to be centrally registered. Although many nannies *do* have nursery nurse or childcare training, they do not *have* to hold any qualifications. Parents are responsible for interviewing and checking all the relevant references of nannies. Some nannies live in with the family, while others come to the family home each day and parents take over the childcare in the evenings and at night. There are three main types of nanny:

- **A daily nanny** comes to the house each day, at hours agreed between the nanny and the employer.
- **A live-in nanny** lives in the family home. They therefore need their own bedroom and their meals provided. Around 20 per cent of nannies in the UK live in.
- **A nanny share** is when the nanny works for more than one family. The nanny looks after one family's child on certain days and other people's children on other days, or may look after more than one set of children together. (If there are more than two families nanny-sharing, the nanny will need to be registered as a childminder.)

A new scheme enables nannies to become approved or registered if they wish, but it is not compulsory. Parents can only claim help with childcare costs if their nanny is approved under the **Childcare Approval Scheme** or registered on the new **Voluntary Ofsted Childcare Register**.

The advantages and disadvantages of using a nanny

Advantages

Nannies:

- often have a professional childcare qualification and at least two years' experience
- offer one-to-one care and attention
- enable the child to be looked after in familiar surroundings
- provide a tailor-made service to suit the parents' schedule
- tidy the kitchen and children's rooms and look after their laundry; some do general housework too
- may do evening babysitting at short notice
- look after your children when they are ill
- receive a fixed wage rather than an amount per child
- can be shared with another family, reducing the costs.

Disadvantages

Nannies:

- are the most expensive form of childcare (when not shared with another family)
- involve extra costs: heating, phone and food costs, use of a car, insurance (particularly for nannies under 21 or from non-EU countries)
- need a separate bedroom and usually bathroom (for a live-in nanny)
- may compete with parents for the child's affection
- do not have to be monitored or registered with social services, so may cause safety concerns
- provide fewer opportunities for the child to socialise
- cause distress to the child if they leave suddenly.

Childminders

Childminders are often the childcare of choice for working parents. **Registered childminders** work in their own home and are registered and inspected by Ofsted, demonstrating the quality and standards of their care. Ofsted ensures that every registered childminder meets the National Standards, such as:

- ensuring that they are suitable to be with children
- checking that they provide a safe, stimulating and caring environment, giving children opportunities for learning and play
- making sure they work in partnership with parents and carers.

In addition, in order to become registered, a childminder must undertake police and health checks, have a regular inspection of their home and take an introductory childminding course and first aid training. Registered childminders can only look after a certain number of children at any one time, which allows them to focus more on each child:

- **In England and Wales**, childminders are not allowed to care for more than three children under the age of 5 and a further three children under 8. Their own children are included in these numbers.
- **In Scotland**, childminders may care for no more than six children under 12; of these six, no more than one may be under 1 year old, and no more than three who are not yet attending school. Their own children are included in these numbers.

Childminders can:

- provide consistent, one-to-one care, tailored to the individual needs of a child
- form a stable, ongoing relationship with the child, continuing from infancy through to when they need care around schooling
- provide care for siblings together
- be very flexible over the hours of care provided, as well as picking up or delivering children to and from other forms of care
- provide care in a home that can include involvement in activities such as cooking, shopping, gardening and family mealtimes.

The advantages and disadvantages of using a childminder

Advantages

Childminders:

- tend to be mothers themselves, so are usually experienced and confident
- provide a homely atmosphere
- have been on a childminders' training course
- are inspected by Ofsted every two years, to ensure high standards and to check that the home is safe and well-equipped
- are relatively affordable
- use their own home, so there is no disruption in your own home
- usually look after more than one child, which provides company for all the children
- may have a reciprocal arrangement with another childminder to provide sickness and holiday cover
- can care for all the children from one family together
- know the local area well and will take your child out and about to playgroups and activities.

Disadvantages

Childminders:

- often have a high turnover of children
- may live some distance away and the parents have to get the children ready and out of the house in the morning
- may refuse to look after children who are ill, which means parents have to find a suitable alternative
- set their own activities and plan their day, meaning that the parent has less control
- charge fees *per child* – that is, fees are double for two children
- may not provide alternative care if they are ill or away on holiday
- are not provided through an agency, so parents have to do the fact-finding and interviewing
- may have several children in their care who need to be collected and dropped off at nurseries and schools – this can be quite tiring for young children.

Au pairs

An au pair is an overseas visitor – male or female – who comes to the UK primarily to learn to speak English and to help out in a family home. She, or he, will live in the child's home as part of the family and will need their own bedroom. An au pair is normally expected to work 25–30 hours a week, depending on their country of origin, and must have time off to attend language classes. They should not be expected to take on heavy housework, but are generally expected to help with light household tasks and caring for the children. Au pairs do not have to be registered with any official body in the UK; nor do they need any qualifications in childcare.

 REVISION QUESTIONS

1. Registered childminders are subject to various checks. Describe what these are and how the system helps to safeguard children.

2. What are the advantages (a) for the child and (b) for the parents of the children being looked after by a nanny?

3. What are the advantages (a) for the child and (b) for the parents of the children being looked after by a childminder?

 RESEARCH ACTIVITY

Individually or in a group, find out about the range of day-care provision for children under five years in your area and produce a leaflet for parents.

 CHILD STUDY ACTIVITY

Find out how the child's parents feel about different types of day care. Have they used any formal childcare provision? If so, how do they think their child has settled in?

3 Community provision: the statutory services available for children and families

A wide range of organisations exists to provide services for young children and their families. These include statutory services, voluntary services, self-help agencies and private services.

Statutory services are those which are funded by government and which have to be provided by law (or statute). Some services are provided by *central* government departments – for example:

- National Health Service (NHS)
- Department for Children, Schools and Families (DCSF)
- Department for Education and Skills (DfES).

These large departments are funded directly from **taxation** – income tax, VAT and National Insurance.

Other **statutory services** are provided by *local* government – for example:

- housing department
- Local Education Authority
- social services department/Children and Young People's Services.

These are largely funded through **local taxation** (council tax) and from grants made by central government.

Social services for children

Social services departments are a statutory service, organised at a local level. Social workers provide a range of care and support for children and families. This includes:

- families where children are assessed as being in need (including disabled children)
- children who may be suffering 'significant harm' – for example, from violence in the home or from some form of child abuse (this aspect of social work is known as **child protection**)
- children who require looking after by the local authority (through fostering or residential care)
- children who are placed for adoption
- families experiencing housing or financial problems.

Financial help for families with young children

Every parent is entitled to receive **Child Benefit**. This is a *universal*, tax-free payment that can be claimed for each child under the age of 16 years. Other benefits include free prescriptions and dental care during pregnancy and childhood.

There are also *targeted* benefits for families to help with the extra costs of childcare. The family's income is assessed (by means testing) to find out if they are in need of financial support. These **means-tested** benefits include:

- **Sure Start Maternity Grant:** This is a one-off payment to help pay for things needed for a new baby if the parent or parents are on a low income.
- **Working Tax Credit:** This includes a specific element to support the cost of registered or approved childcare for working parents. The childcare element can help with up to 80 per cent of childcare costs.
- **Time off (parental leave):** A working parent can take up to 13 weeks' parental leave for each child until his or her fifth birthday (they get more than this if they have a disabled child). The parent's employer does not *have* to pay the parent when they take this leave, but they might do so as part of the employment package.

- **Flexible working**: Parents, foster parents and guardians have a right to request a flexible working pattern if they have a child aged under 6 or a disabled child under 18. Various conditions apply – such as the length of time already spent working for the employer – but the employer has to consider seriously any request for flexible working.
- **Child maintenance**: The Child Support Agency (CSA) is part of the Department for Work and Pensions (DWP). The CSA's role is to make sure that parents who live apart from their children contribute financially to their children's upkeep by paying child maintenance. Child maintenance is money paid to help cover the child's everyday living costs. The parent with whom the child does not normally live (the non-resident parent) is responsible for paying child maintenance to the parent or other person, such as a grandparent or a guardian, with whom the child normally lives (the parent with care).
- **New Deal for Lone Parents**: This is a government programme that gives people on benefits the help and support they need to look for work, including training and preparing for work.

Education services for children

The **Department for Education and Skills (DfES)** is headed by the Secretary of State for Education and is responsible for deciding the policies and funding for Local Education Authorities.

All children aged three and four years are now entitled to free early education for 12.5 hours per week for 38 weeks of the year. Many children under the age of five attend one of the following:

- **maintained (or state) nursery school**
- **nursery class** attached to a primary school
- **playgroup or preschool** in the voluntary sector
- **privately run nursery**
- **Children's Centre**
- **home learning environment (HLE)** – many young children are cared for by childminders (in the childminder's home) or by nannies or grandparents.

The Early Years Foundation Stage (from birth to five years old)

All schools and early years providers have to follow a structure of learning, development and care for children. This is called the Early Years Foundation Stage (EYFS) and it enables children to learn through a range of activities. The main principles of the EYFS are as follows:

- children learn through play
- providers work closely with parents
- the child's learning at home is taken into account
- parents and guardians are kept up to date on the child's progress
- it is **inclusive** – it ensures the welfare, learning and all-round development of children with different backgrounds and levels of ability, including those with special educational needs and disabilities.

The EYFS applies to all schools and registered early years providers in the maintained, private, voluntary and independent sectors attended by children from birth to five years. This includes:

- reception and nursery classes in maintained and independent schools
- day nurseries
- childminders

- playgroups
- after-school and breakfast clubs
- holiday play schemes
- Children's Centres.

The following groups do not have to use the EYFS:

- mother-and-toddler groups
- nannies
- short-term, occasional care (e.g. crèches).

Statutory integrated provision for children

Children's Centres

Children's Centres serve children and their families from the antenatal period until children start in reception or year one at primary school. They also offer a base within the community, linking to other providers of day care – such as childminder networks and out-of-school clubs.

Each centre offers the following services to families with babies and preschool children:

- good-quality early learning, integrated with full day-care provision (a minimum of ten hours a day, five days a week, 48 weeks a year)
- family support services
- a base for a childminder network
- child and family health services, including antenatal services
- support for children and parents with special needs
- links with Jobcentre Plus, local training providers and further and higher education institutions.

Children's Centres may also offer other services, including:

- training for parents (e.g. parenting classes, basic skills, English as an additional language)
- benefits advice
- toy libraries.

Local authority day nurseries

Local authority day nurseries are funded by social services and offer full-time provision for children under school age. They cater mainly for families who may be facing many challenges and who need support. They provide care from 8 a.m., often until 7 p.m., and are registered and inspected every year. Staffing levels are high, the usual ratio being one staff member for every four children. Some local authority day nurseries also operate as family centres, providing advice, guidance and counselling to families with difficulties.

 REVISION QUESTIONS

1. Describe three means-tested benefits that may be paid to families needing financial support to help with childcare costs.
2. What is the New Deal for Lone Parents?
3. What is the Early Years Foundation Stage?

4 Community provision: the voluntary services and self-help agencies for children and families

These are health, education and social care services which are set up by **charities** to provide services which local authorities can buy in, benefiting from their expertise. Voluntary organisations are:

- non-profit making
- non-statutory
- dependent on donations, fund raising and government grants.

For example, Children England (www.childrenengland.org.uk), the new name of the National Council of Voluntary Child Care Organisations (NCVCCO), is an organisation whose members are all registered charities that work with children, young people and their families. They range from very large national organisations (such as **Barnardo's**) to small, locally based charities.

Within any local authority in the UK, there are childcare and education settings which come into the category of **voluntary** or **self-help provision**. Two examples are:

1. Community nurseries

   Community nurseries exist to provide a service to local children and their families. They are run by local community organisations – often with financial assistance from the local authority – or by charities such as Barnardo's and Save the Children. Most of these nurseries are open long enough to suit working parents or those at college. Many centres also provide, or act as a venue for, other services, including:
   - parent-and-toddler groups
   - drop-in crèches
   - toy libraries
   - after-school clubs.

2. Pre-School Learning Alliance community preschools

   Pre-School Learning Alliance community preschools (playgroups) offer children aged between three and five years an opportunity to learn through play.
   - They usually operate on a part-time, sessional basis. Sessions are normally two-and-a-half hours each morning or afternoon.
   - Staff plan a varied curriculum that takes into account children's previous experiences and developing needs.
   - The Early Years Foundation Stage is adapted by each group to meet the needs of their own children, and to allow them to make the most of a variety of learning opportunities that arise spontaneously through play.
   - At many preschool playgroups, parents and carers are encouraged to be involved, and there are often parent-and-toddler groups meeting at the same sites.

Leisure activities and recreation services

These services provide children and their families with activities and opportunities for recreation and sport. Some of these are provided by the local authority, either free or at a subsidised cost; others are privately owned and run. They include:

- sports centres, children's gyms
- music groups

- parks
- adventure playgrounds and soft play areas
- holiday schemes and activities
- lessons (e.g. dance and drama)
- clubs (e.g. Beavers, Cubs and Scouts; Rainbows, Brownies and Guides; Woodcraft Folk)
- libraries.

Local provision for children

Most local authorities have a special department to coordinate all the services to children within their locality. These departments are often called Early Years Services and deal exclusively with the needs of young children and their families. The range of services provided varies greatly from one local authority to another, but typically will include the following services (those marked * must be provided by law):

- **Housing**: Children and their families in need (e.g. homeless families and those seeking refuge) are a priority. Services include providing bed-and-breakfast accommodation or council housing.*
- **After-school clubs**: These offer supervised play opportunities in a safe, supportive and friendly environment. They usually cater for children 5–11 years, but some centres have facilities for children under five.*
- **Nursery education**: Most authorities are not able to offer full nursery education to all children within the borough. Nursery classes are usually attached to maintained primary schools. Nursery schools are separate.
- **Community places for families with low incomes**: Most local authorities keep a number of full-day nursery places at Children's Centres, specifically for children in families with low incomes.
- **Regulation and registration of services**, such as childminders, private fostering and private or voluntary day care and family centres.*
- **Social workers**: They work with families where children are assessed as being *in need*; they give practical support and advice on a wide range of issues, including adoption and foster care.*
- **Infant or primary education**: Children must attend full-time school from the age of 5 years, and must follow the National Curriculum.*
- **Residential holidays**: These provide opportunities for children to develop self-reliance, as well as providing a break for many children who otherwise would not have the chance of a holiday.
- **Holiday play schemes**: Full-day programmes of activities during the school holidays.
- **Advice, information and counselling**: Local authorities have a duty to provide information and counselling to families where there is a child in need.*
- **Children's Centres**: These include early learning, parent information services and support for children and parents with special needs.*
- **Respite care**: Families where a child has special needs may be offered a residential holiday for their child so that they can have a break – or respite – from caring full-time for them.*

These services are usually listed and coordinated by a local **Council for Voluntary Service**. Voluntary organisations sometimes also provide some of the statutory services and will receive payment from the local authority or government for these services – for example, after-school clubs.

KEY TERMS

Jobcentre Plus: The agency within the Department for Work and Pensions (DWP) which is responsible for the assessment and payment of social security benefits.

Means testing: The method of assessing the amount to be paid in social security benefits (e.g. income support and housing benefits), which takes into account all sources of personal or family income.

Statutory service: Any service provided and managed by the state or government (e.g. the NHS or a local authority day nursery).

Voluntary organisation: An association or society which has been created by its members rather than by the state (e.g. a charity).

5 Children with special or additional needs

What are special or additional needs?

Children with additional needs have needs which are 'in addition' to the general needs of children. Some children have a very obvious and well-researched **disability**, such as Down's syndrome or cerebral palsy; others may have a specific **learning difficulty or difference**, such as dyslexia or giftedness. What defines them as children with additional needs is the fact that they need *additional help* in some area of development, care or education, compared with other children.

It is important to remember that children are more alike than they are different. *Every* child needs:

- to feel welcome
- to feel safe, both physically and emotionally
- to have friends and to feel as if they belong
- to be encouraged to live up to their potential
- to be celebrated for their uniqueness.

In other words, children are always **children first** – the special or additional need is secondary.

Additional needs is a broad term to cover children and young people who need **extra support**, long-term or temporarily. This might be because they have:

- a physical disability
- a learning disability
- sight and/or hearing problems
- specific behaviour problems
- some other condition needing treatment over a long period.

Sometimes a child might have a *temporary* or short-term need. Examples include:

- when a child's parent or sibling is seriously ill or has died
- when the child is a victim of bullying or abuse
- when the child has temporary hearing loss after a common cold.

Categories of special needs

It is often difficult to categorise special needs neatly. This is because some conditions – such as Down's syndrome – cause difficulties in more than one area. However, broadly speaking, children's special needs can be grouped into the following categories:

- **Physical disability:** Needs related to problems with mobility or coordination, such as cerebral palsy, spina bifida or muscular dystrophy.
- **Speech or language difficulties:** Needs related to communication problems, such as delayed language, difficulties in articulation or stuttering.
- **Specific learning difficulties (SLD):** Needs related to problems usually confined to the areas of reading, writing and number skills. Dyslexia is a term often applied to difficulty in developing literacy skills.
- **Chronic illness:** Needs related to medical conditions, such as cystic fibrosis, diabetes, asthma or epilepsy.
- **Giftedness:** Needs related to being highly academically or artistically gifted.
- **Sensory impairment:** Needs related to problems with sight or hearing.
- **Complex needs:** Needs related to problems, many of which result from a genetic defect or from an accident or trauma.
- **Behavioural difficulties:** Needs related to aggression, challenging behaviour,

hyperactivity, attention deficit hyperactivity disorder (ADHD) or antisocial behaviour.

- **Life-threatening illness:** Needs related to a serious or terminal illness (e.g. childhood cancer, HIV/AIDS and leukaemia).
- **Emotional difficulties:** Needs related to conditions such as anxiety, fear, depression and autistic spectrum disorder (ASD).

 RESEARCH ACTIVITY

1. Choose *one* from the following list of disabilities:
   - autism (autistic spectrum disorder)
   - cerebral palsy
   - cystic fibrosis
   - Down's syndrome.

Find out:

   a. what it is

   b. possible cause – if known

   c. signs and symptoms and effects on the individual

   d. support groups.

2. Produce *either* a leaflet or fact file *or* a Microsoft PowerPoint® presentation for your chosen disability.

(Contact a Family is a UK charity for families with disabled children. They offer information on specific conditions and rare disorders – with useful links to other websites. Go to: www.cafamily.org.uk).

6 Statutory services for children with additional needs and their families

Most families in an area use statutory services – that is, the services provided by their local authority for *all* families and children, including all the **health**, **education** and **social services** described above.

Local authorities provide some services directly – for example, benefits, schools and short-break or respite care are all schemes funded by social services.

The Early Support programme

The **Early Support programme**, started in 2002, is the central government device for achieving better coordinated, family-focused services for young disabled children and their families in England.

Features of Early Support include the following:

- It is for families with a baby or young child who has **additional support needs** because of a disability or an emerging special educational need. It is particularly relevant where families are in contact with a number of different agencies, because the programme facilitates better **coordination of support**.
- Each family is given a **Family File** – a family-held record that supports better coordination of services provided for a child and family, and more effective exchange of information between professionals working for different agencies.
- A range of **Information for Parents** booklets on particular conditions or disabilities which provide standard 'first step' information for families where a particular factor has been identified as significant for a child.
- **Coordination/multi-agency support for families** – families receive coordinated support through **keyworker** systems, better sharing of information between agencies, family support plans and family-held records.
- **Partnership across agencies** and geographical boundaries – access to good services for families does not depend on where they live.

The role of specialist professionals

All local authorities are obliged by law to keep a register of local disabled children. This is to help the local authority to plan services more effectively. How many professionals are involved with one disabled child will vary greatly. Some children may have a temporary special need – for example, a child who is in hospital for several weeks will need help from a hospital play specialist. Others may need support from a range of professionals – for example, a child with cerebral palsy may need help from a physiotherapist, a speech therapist and a portage worker (see below).

The following professionals are all involved in the care and education of children with special needs:

Family doctors (GPs)

Family doctors are independent professionals who are under contract to the National Health Service, but who are not employed by it. They are the most available of the medical profession, and are also able to refer patients to specialist doctors and paramedical services.

Health visitors

Health visitors are qualified nurses who have undertaken further training, including midwifery experience. They work exclusively in the community, and can be approached either directly or via the family doctor. They work primarily with children up to the age of five years; this includes all children with disabilities, and they carry out a wide range of developmental checks.

Physiotherapists

The majority of 'physios' are employed in hospitals, but some work in special schools or residential facilities. Physiotherapists assess children's motor development and skills, and provide activities and exercises that parents and carers can use to encourage better mobility and coordination.

Occupational therapists

Occupational therapists ('OTs') work in hospitals, schools and other residential establishments. Some OTs specialise in working with children (paediatric OTs); they assess a child's practical abilities and advise on the most appropriate activities and specialist equipment to encourage independent life skills.

Community nurses

Most community nurses work closely with family doctors and provide nursing care in the home. They also advise parents and carers on specialist techniques – for example, how to lift, catheter care.

School nurses

School nurses may visit a number of mainstream schools in their health district to monitor child health and development – by checking weight, height, eyesight and hearing, and by giving advice on common problems such as head lice. They may also be employed in special schools to supervise the routine medical care of disabled children.

Speech therapists

Speech therapists may be employed in schools, in hospitals or in the community. They assess a child's speech, tongue and mouth movements, and the effects of these on eating and swallowing. They provide exercises and activities to develop all aspects of children's expressive and receptive communication skills, and to encourage language development.

Play specialists

Play specialists are employed in hospitals and are often qualified nursery nurses who have additional training. They may prepare a child for hospitalisation and provide play opportunities for children confined to bed or in a hospital playroom.

Play therapists

Play therapists also work in hospitals and have undertaken specialist training. They use play to enable children with special needs to feel more secure emotionally in potentially threatening situations.

Clinical psychologists

Clinical psychologists usually work in hospitals. They assess children's emotional, social and intellectual development, and advise on appropriate activities to promote development.

Dieticians

Most dieticians work in hospitals and can advise on a range of special diets – for example, for those with diabetes, cystic fibrosis or coeliac disease.

Social workers

Most social workers now work in specialised teams dealing with a specific client group – for example, a Disability and Learning Difficulties Team. They are employed by social services departments ('social work departments' in Scotland) and initially their role is to assess the needs of the child. They may refer the family to other departments, such as the Department for Work and Pensions (DWP) or the National Health Service (NHS), or to voluntary organisations. A social worker may also act as an advocate on behalf of disabled children, ensuring that they receive all the benefits and services to which they are entitled.

Technical officers

Technical officers usually work with people with specific disorders – for example, audio technicians or audiologists monitor the level of hearing in children as a developmental check; and sign-language interpreters translate speech into sign language for deaf and hearing-impaired people.

Nursery officers

Nursery officers are trained nursery nurses who work in day nurseries and family centres. Such staff are involved in shift work, and they care for children under five years when it is not possible for those children to remain at home.

Family aids

Family aids (or home care assistants) used to be called 'home helps'; they provide practical support for families in their own homes – shopping, cooking, looking after children and so on.

Special educational needs coordinator (SENCO)

Special educational needs coordinators liaise with colleagues in special schools and with the parents of children with special needs. They are responsible for coordinating provision for children with special educational needs, for keeping the school's special education needs (SEN) register and for working with external agencies – for example, educational psychology services, social service departments and voluntary organisations.

Educational psychologists

Educational psychologists are involved in the educational assessment of children with special needs, and in preparing the statement of special educational needs. They act as advisors to professionals working directly with children with a range of special needs, particularly those with emotional and behavioural difficulties.

Portage worker

Portage is an educational programme for children who have difficulty in learning basic skills due to either physical or behavioural problems. Home portage advisors are specially trained in understanding child development and come from a variety of professions, ranging from nurses or other health professionals to schoolteachers.

Orthoptist

An orthoptist works with people who have visual problems and abnormal eye movements.

Special needs teachers

Special needs teachers are qualified teachers with additional training and experience in teaching children with special needs. They are supported by:

- **special needs support teachers** or **specialist teachers**, who are often **peripatetic** – that is, they visit disabled children in different mainstream schools – and who may specialise in a particular disorder – for example, vision or hearing impairment

- special needs support assistants, who may be qualified nursery nurses and who often work with individual statemented children, under the direction of the specialist teacher.

Educational welfare officers

As in mainstream education, educational welfare officers will be involved with children whose school attendance is irregular. They may also arrange school transport for disabled children.

 KEY TERMS

Attention deficit disorder (ADD): A behavioural disorder characterised by an inability to concentrate on tasks. In **attention deficit hyperactivity disorder (ADHD)**, inability to concentrate is accompanied or replaced by hyperactive and impulsive behaviour.

Autism (autistic spectrum disorder): A rare developmental disorder which impairs a child's understanding of and ability to relate to the environment.

Cerebral palsy: A general term for disorders of movement and posture resulting from damage to the child's developing brain.

Down's syndrome: A genetic disorder resulting from the presence of an extra chromosome; children usually, but not always, have learning difficulties.

Keyworker or key person: A member of staff (usually in a nursery setting) who spends more time with a small number of identified children, builds a close relationship with them and is the main contact person for their families.

Spina bifida: This occurs when the spinal canal in the vertebral column is not closed (although it may be covered with skin). Individuals with spina bifida can have a wide range of physical disabilities. In the more severe forms, the spinal cord bulges out of the back, the legs and bladder may be paralysed, and obstruction to the fluid surrounding the brain causes hydrocephalus.

---

7 Voluntary and independent support for children with additional needs and their families

In the independent sector, some services are provided by **charities** or commercial organisations with a particular interest in special needs or particular disabilities. Sometimes these services are funded by local authorities. For example, children with **autistic spectrum disorder (ASD)** might attend a nursery run by a local voluntary organisation with particular experience of supporting children with ASD, but with their Local Education Authority or social services department paying for them to attend.

Problems occur when children are not recognised as having additional needs until their development begins to look different from that of other children. This is especially true for children with ASD or attention deficit hyperactivity disorder (ADHD). Diagnosis of a disorder or disability is not always straightforward and is often ambiguous.

Extra help or support in the preschool years is provided at different levels, depending on how severe a child's need for extra help is, and on the approach taken by each individual local authority.

How to access available information to support children and their families

Parent partnership services

The Parent Partnership Scheme (PPS) is a statutory service which offers the following support:

- information, advice and support for parents of children and young people with special educational needs (SEN)
- putting parents in touch with other local organisations
- making sure that parents' views are heard and understood, and that these views inform local policy and practice.

Some parent partnerships are based in the voluntary sector, although the majority of them remain based in their local education authority (LEA) or Children's Trust. All parent partnerships, wherever they are based, work separately and independently from the LEA; this means that they are able to provide impartial advice and support to parents.

(For more information, visit the National Parent Partnership Network (NPPN) website at www.parentpartnership.org.uk)

The Every Disabled Child Matters campaign (EDCM)

The EDCM campaign was launched in 2006 to achieve rights and justice for every disabled child. Every Disabled Child Matters wants:

- families with disabled children to have ordinary lives
- disabled children and their families to be fully included in society
- all disabled children and their families to get the right services and support – no matter where they live
- poverty among disabled children and their families to be cut by 50 per cent by 2010 and eliminated by 2020
- an education system that meets the needs of each child and enables them to reach their full potential.

8 The impact on families of having a child with special or additional needs

Each family will respond in its own way when they find out that their child has a disability or a special need. Common reactions of parents to having a child with disabilities include the following:

- **A sense of tragedy**: Parents who give birth to a child with a disability experience complex emotions. They may grieve for the loss of a 'normal' child, but they have not actually been bereaved – they still have a child with a unique personality and identity of his/her own. Relatives and friends can be embarrassed if they do not know how to react to the event, and their awkward response can leave parents feeling very isolated at a time that is normally spent celebrating.
- **Feelings of isolation**: Parents with a disabled child often describe feelings of isolation. They might struggle to come to terms with the news of a child's disability and may find that they have a lack of time for themselves and each other. This can put a strain on their relationship.
- **A fear of making mistakes**: Sometimes there is an over-reliance on professional help. If the disability seems to be the most important aspect of the child's personality, parents may believe that only a medical expert can advise on the care of their child. The reality is that the parent almost always knows what is best and what is required for their child.
- **Being over-protective**: A desire to cocoon the child – or to 'wrap them in cotton wool' – can be counterproductive. The child needs to be equipped for life and can only learn by making mistakes. In addition, siblings may resent the disabled child who is seen as being spoilt or never punished.
- **Exercising control**: Parents may take away freedom of choice from the child, which will disempower the child. Parents and carers often dictate where and with whom the child plays, depriving them of an opportunity for valuable social learning.
- **Achieving a balance**: Negotiating which parent will take time off work and use up holiday entitlement, and which parent will keep everything else going at home, can be difficult. Also, there might be unforeseen costs, such as travelling to and from hospital, loss of income, telephone calls and possibly paying for additional childcare for other children.

There are other factors that can have an impact on family life. These include:

- **financial worries**, especially when parents have to juggle work commitments with childcare
- **feeling guilty** that other children in the family are missing out on family fun because of one child's special needs
- **parents feeling tired and stressed** because of the extra attention required by their child, especially during bouts of illness.

The impact on siblings

Having a child with special needs in the family can have a range of positive and negative effects on the everyday life of other children in the family. For example, siblings may experience:

- stronger bonds with other family members if they choose to help and work together
- acceptance of others as they are
- a wider range of friends/specialist clubs/groups
- how to be more tolerant of others

- more awareness of disabilities
- an example from their parents of how to integrate with others in the wider community
- limited time and attention from parents; siblings often feel that their needs come second to those of the child with special needs
- being excluded from activities that their disabled brother or sister can't do – or maybe doesn't even want to do.
- anxiety about bringing friends home, and stresses of home life
- guilt about feeling angry with their situation
- teasing and embarrassment in public
- feelings of isolation – they may feel that no one else is in their position and may feel misunderstood.

Sibs is the UK charity for people who grow up with a disabled brother or sister. They offer information and support (www.sibs.org.uk).

The importance of avoiding labelling and stereotyping

Many years ago, people who were obviously *different* – that is, those who might be unable to walk or talk, or who seemed a bit 'simple-minded' – were believed to be in some way evil; some were even burnt to death as witches. Today, we are more aware of individual differences and have greater knowledge about diverse needs and abilities. It is very important that we do not apply labels to anyone.

Disabled children are often stereotyped *and* labelled. This *always* has a negative effect on the child and their family. Table 6.1 shows which terms are appropriate to use and which should be avoided.

Avoid	Use instead
The handicapped	Disabled people
The disabled	Disabled people or people with an impairment
The deaf	Deaf people/hard-of-hearing people (depending on which group) or hearing-impaired people
The blind	Blind people or partially sighted people (depending on which group), or visually impaired
(Using the collective noun – 'The . . .' – implies that all disabled people have the same needs and issues, and reinforces their supposed separateness from the rest of society.)	
Able-bodied, healthy, normal	Non-disabled
Handicapped, cripple, invalid	Disabled or disabled people/person, or, if appropriate, a person with a mobility impairment
Victim of or suffering from	Has . . . (an impairment – e.g. epilepsy or diabetes), or a person with . . . (an impairment) and avoid using medical labels which define people by their disability, such as 'she is epileptic' or 'he is Down's syndrome'
Wheelchair-bound or confined to a wheelchair	Wheelchair user or a person who uses a wheelchair
An epileptic	A person with epilepsy
A spastic	A person with cerebral palsy
Mentally ill, insane, crazy, psycho, schizo, etc.	A person with mental health problems
Mental handicap/retarded	Learning difficulties/a person with learning disabilities
Dwarf or midget	Restricted growth or short stature
Fits, spells, attacks	Seizures

Table 6.1 Terms to use and not to use in order to avoid labelling and stereotyping

The importance of having realistic expectations of children's development

Having positive, realistic expectations for children's achievements and behaviour is something that both parents and carers should strive for. When expectations for children are set at the right level – not too high and not too low – children can expect to have high self-esteem and to fulfil their potential.

A good understanding of child development is vital to working with children. Parents and carers need to have realistic expectations for each child, based on:

- **the child's stage of development**
- his or her **temperament**
- any **special or additional needs**.

It is very important to **promote the strengths** of children, as well as assisting with their difficulties. This can be achieved by choosing some of the activities that you know the child is good at. For example, a child may have difficulty tying their shoelaces, but may be very skilled at cutting out shapes; therefore, do some cutting-out sessions and always offer plenty of praise and encouragement, both for **achievement** and for the **effort** the child has made.

How to use specific methods of communication

Most children with **special educational needs** have difficulties with language and communication. Many preschool children benefit from learning a 'sign language', such as Makaton®, PECS or Signalong.

Makaton®

The Makaton® vocabulary is a list of over 400 items with corresponding signs and symbols, with an additional resource vocabulary for the UK National Curriculum. The signs are based on British Sign Language (BSL), but are used to support spoken English. The Makaton® Charity publishes a book of illustrations of the Makaton® vocabulary. Most signs rely on movement as well as position, so you cannot really learn the signs from the illustrations. Also, in many signs, *facial expression* is important. If a child at a school or nursery is learning Makaton®, the parents should be invited to learn too. The Makaton® Charity will support schools and parents in this, as they know that everyone involved with the child must use the same signs.

Signalong

Signalong is a sign-supporting system which is also based on British Sign Language. It is designed to help children and adults with communication difficulties (it is mostly associated with learning disabilities) and is user-friendly for easy access. The Signalong Group has researched and published the widest range of signs in Britain.

Picture Exchange Communication System (PECS)

PECS begins with teaching children to give their teacher a picture of an object that they want; the teacher immediately gives them the object. For example, if they want a drink, they will give a picture of 'drink' to an adult, who directly hands them a drink. Verbal prompts are not used; this encourages spontaneity and avoids children being dependent on the prompts. The system goes on to teach recognition of symbols and how to construct simple 'sentences'. Ideas for teaching language structures, such as asking and answering questions, are also incorporated. It has been reported that both preschool and older children have begun to develop speech when using PECS. The system is often used as a communication aid for children and adults who have an **autistic spectrum disorder**.

REVISION QUESTIONS

1. List eight professionals who might be involved with children with special needs.
2. What does a portage worker do?
3. What does a hospital play specialist do?
4. What is Makaton®?
5. What does PECS stand for?

 RESEARCH ACTIVITY

Find out what support is available for children with special needs and their families in your area.

COURSEWORK AND EXAM PREPARATION

About the coursework (controlled assessment)

As part of your OCR Child Development course for GCSE, you have to complete the following pieces of coursework for controlled assessment:

- *three* short tasks
- *one* Child Study Task.

The three short tasks form 30 per cent of the total GCSE marks.
The Child Study Task forms 30 per cent of the total GCSE marks.
(The remaining 40 per cent is assessed by examination.)

Unit B011: the three short tasks

Choosing your short tasks

All tasks are set by OCR and should be chosen from the list of OCR set task titles. *One* task must be chosen from the Investigative Task list and *two* tasks must be chosen from the Practical Task list. Your teacher will give you the OCR list of tasks from which to make your choices. (The specimen tasks below have been provided by OCR to give you an idea of what is expected.)

Specimen investigative task

Undertake an investigation (experiment) into baby-changing provision available in your area. Compare the baby-changing facilities available to both men and women, highlighting any differences that are evident. Choose a range of baby-changing units to investigate. Plan and visit a range of establishments. Collect and present information and evaluate your work.

Specimen practical tasks

1. Produce a magazine article comparing the advantages and disadvantages of breastfeeding and bottle-feeding, to help young pregnant women to be able to make an informed choice. Evaluate your work.
2. You have been asked to babysit for two children aged three and five years old, for five hours during the day on a Saturday. Plan the lunch, activities and routine required to give them an interesting and safe experience. Evaluate your work.

Each short task can be divided into four areas, involving different skills:

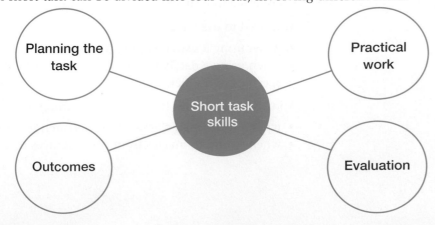

Planning the task

In this section of the short task, you need to show that you can:

- make and justify suitable choices in response to your short task title
- produce accurate plans and identify suitable resources for implementing your choices for carrying out the task
- plan and produce (or select, if appropriate to the task) methods for recording your results (e.g. questionnaire, testing, comparison charts, costing).

Practical work

In this section of the short task, you need to show that you can:

- follow your plans, making good use of the time available
- organise your resources effectively
- use any equipment safely and independently
- demonstrate a range of skills, which might include ICT skills (producing a leaflet, use of graphic data), costing and comparisons/testing.

Outcomes

In this section of the short task, you need to show that you can:

- produce one appropriate, well-presented outcome, linked to the area of study
- accurately carry out and record results of findings or other recording methods used.

Evaluation

In this section of the short task, you need to show that you can:

- identify strengths and weakness in all aspects of the short task
- suggest and/or justify improvements to your work
- draw conclusions from your work.

Using ICT when planning the short tasks

When preparing for these internally assessed tasks, you must plan to use a variety of formats or methods to present them:

- when providing visual images of analysis – for example, a flow diagram or a pie chart
- when selecting, organising and presenting information collected from research
- when preparing action plans and time plans for practical activities.

You also need to use software to present data in an appropriate form:

- when producing recording sheets to collect evidence
- when setting up tables/charts to record results of research
- when using ICT to handle data – for example 'the costs of children's clothing' collected in a survey.

You need to use a research tool when seeking sources of information:

- when using a search engine to find relevant information
- when using a database – for example, to calculate the nutritional value of a specific child's diet.

You also need to use ICT to produce images:

- when presenting evidence from research in a variety of formats
- when scanning images from other sources to use in the presentation of work.

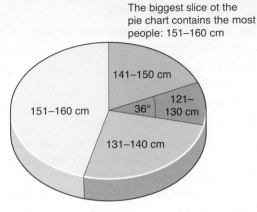

The biggest slice ot the
pie chart contains the most
people: 151–160 cm
141–150 cm
121–
130 cm
36°
151–160 cm
131–140 cm

Figure 7.1 A sample pie chart showing different people's heights

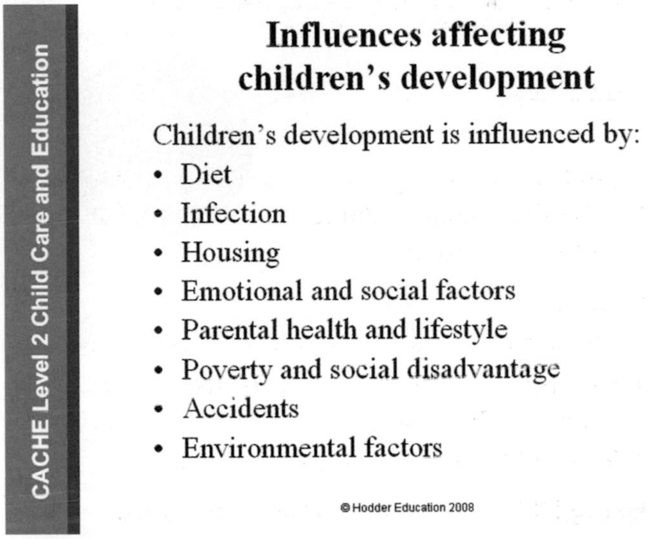

CACHE Level 2 Child Care and Education
Influences affecting
children's development
Children's development is influenced by:
• Diet
• Infection
• Housing
• Emotional and social factors
• Parental health and lifestyle
• Poverty and social disadvantage
• Accidents
• Environmental factors
© Hodder Education 2008

Figure 7.2 A sample Microsoft PowerPoint® presentation slide

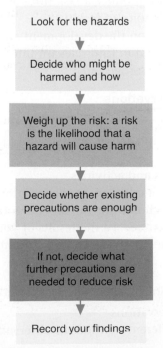

Look for the hazards
Decide who might be harmed and how
Weigh up the risk: a risk is the likelihood that a hazard will cause harm
Decide whether existing precautions are enough
If not, decide what further precautions are needed to reduce risk
Record your findings

Figure 7.3 A sample flow chart for risk assessment

Unit B012: Child Study Task

The theme for the Child Study Task must be selected from the themes set by OCR. These are broad themes such as:

- children learn through play
- physical development
- the development of social skills
- creative play.

Your teacher will give you the list of OCR themes and you need to be able to give clear reasons for choosing to research the theme and also to develop a suitable task title for your Child Study Task.

The Child Study Task can be divided into five areas, involving different skills:

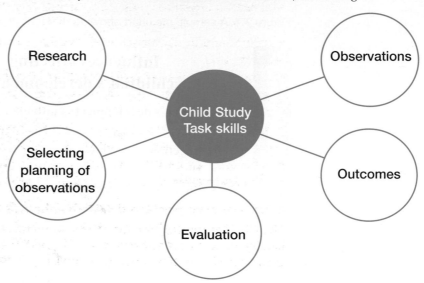

Research

In this section of the Child Study Task, you need to show that you can:

- choose a set OCR theme and produce a task title for research
- give clear reasons for your choice of task title
- carry out secondary research on the development area chosen
- explore the child's background to find relevant information
- explain how the task will be carried out.

Selecting planning of observations

In this section of the Child Study Task, you need to show that you can:

- recommend possible ideas and activities that would be suitable for the age of the chosen child
- select and justify your ideas and activities
- consider suitable methods of carrying out observations
- select and justify methods chosen for the observations
- show a variety of methods to record the results of your observations
- produce a clear plan for the observations that you intend to carry out.

Observations

In this section of the Child Study Task, you need to show that you can:

- carry out the planned observations
- demonstrate a range of different methods of observations.

Outcomes

In this section of the Child Study Task, you need to show that you can:

- review the observations undertaken
- show your understanding of the areas of development identified
- relate information gained to earlier research
- offer original thoughts and opinions about what you have observed
- explain how the child compares to the norms
- compare the child's progress with that of other children.

Evaluation

In this section of the Child Study Task, you need to show that you can:

- review all aspects of your work, identifying strengths and weaknesses in each area of the Child Study Task
- refer to and justify any changes you have made while carrying out the Child Study Task
- draw conclusions, referring back to your task title; you should also include your own personal views about what you have learned from completing the task
- recommend improvements to your work *or* recommend further work that could be completed to develop your Child Study Task
- demonstrate your written communication skills
- record results clearly and include ICT where appropriate.

A step-by-step guide to the Child Study Task

The Child Study Task involves the systematic observation and recording of the behaviour and/or development of the child over a period of weeks or months. It is useful to break this down into smaller steps.

Step 1: Information about the child to be studied

- Age and position in the family
- Type of house (whether it is semi-detached, detached or terraced)
- Whether they live in the town or in the country
- Structure of family – for example, lone-parent family or nuclear family
- Likes and dislikes
- Current stage of physical, intellectual, language, emotional and social development

NB: Do not use the child's surname or address.

Step 2: Choose an OCR theme and a broad area to research

- Consider all the areas of development, using the PIES framework in part three of the book (pages 106–107).
- Decide which area to focus on in relation to the child.

Step 3: Choose a more focused area to research

- The area chosen will depend on the age and developmental stage of the child.
- Decide which area of development will yield relevant information – for example, intellectual development would be a more appropriate focus for a child of three or four than for a baby of six or nine months. Similarly, choosing physical development in a child under two would be more appropriate than in a five-year-old who has already mastered most of the physical skills.

Step 4: Carry out research into your chosen area

- Study the appropriate sections on normative child development. (Remember: Normative development – often referred to as stages or milestones – indicates a typical range of what children can and cannot be expected to do and learn at a given time.)
- Link the information on development to the age of the child. For example, if the child is 18 months old, select only information relating to children aged one to two-and-a-half years; this will enable you to compare the child's development with the 'average' or normative development charts.
- Use whatever method of presenting your research you feel happiest with – for example, spidergrams, flow charts or bullet points.

Step 5: Choose a relevant Child Study Task title

- The title chosen should be relevant to the child and to the area of development chosen.
- The title may be expressed as a question (to be answered) or as a statement (to be evaluated).
- Explain how you intend to carry out the task.

Some samples of Child Study Task themes and titles are:

OCR theme: Children learn through play
Title: How does a three-year-old child develop physically and socially through play?
OCR theme: Physical development
Title: How an 18-month-old child develops fine motor and manipulative skills
OCR theme: The development of social skills
Title: The development of social skills in a four-year-old child
OCR theme: Creative play
Title: How does a three-and-a-half-year-old child demonstrate creative skills?

Step 6: Develop an action plan

- Use a timetable, diary or planner to make an action plan for the Child Study Task. Mark on it all the things you intend to do and when – for example, organising your visits to the child's home, researching the individual activities.
- Produce an overview of the activities and observations you intend to carry out, including a variety of different methods – you can always amend the plan if other things get in the way. NB: Make sure you make a note of any changes to your plan to record in the evaluation section of the task.
- Plan each observation *in detail*, including the following factors:
  a. which method of observation will be used
  b. a description of the planned activity and what you intend to observe
  c. the length of time needed to carry out the observation
  d. any resources required, such as paper, paints and brushes or a camera or video recorder.
- Think ahead. Try to anticipate problems that could prevent you from carrying out the activity – for example, if the child is unwell or if bad weather prevents an outdoors activity. Record any necessary changes to your plan and suggest possible solutions in the evaluation section.

Step 7: Observations

- There are no rules stating how many observations should be carried out, but you should ensure that you have enough information to be able to answer the task title.

- Record your observations. Always include essential details such as date, time, place and length of observation.
- Written accounts – or narrative method – should link closely to your chosen area of development.
- Try to use a variety of methods in order to gain more marks, and also get used to writing a conclusion at the end of each observation. This will make it easier when you come to the evaluation task.

Step 8: Applying understanding to the observations

- Interpret your observations to show that you have a good understanding of the areas of development identified.
- What have you learnt about this particular child, and how has this helped you to understand children's development more widely?
- Look back at the background research you did in steps 2 and 3. Use relevant books to help you, and make reference to them – or quote directly from them – if you can find a statement or section that relates to what you are saying or the point you are making.
- Compare the child's development to the norms of child development.

Step 9: Evaluation – reviewing and assessing your performance

- Check the original requirements of the Child Study Task. Have you met them all?
- Check that you have written conclusions for each observation and that you have clearly interpreted the evidence gained.
- Was the task title you selected appropriate and relevant to the child? Have you found out what you needed to know to answer the task title?
- Consider whether the way in which you tackled the work was appropriate. Could you have done the work differently? What could you have done to improve the work?
- What approaches to the task did you consider and actually use? Which worked well and which did not? Why?
- Review the whole Child Study Task and record any changes you made to your original plan. If, for example, you substituted a different activity, you must write this up and explain your reasons for the change.

Methods for observations

Your teachers will have their own preferences for how they want you to present your work, but, generally, each observation should include the following sections:

- title or aim
- introduction
- actual observation
- evaluation
- bibliography.

Title or aim

Your **aim** should be identified at the start of your work, and can be used as the observation title. For example:

Aim: To see what fine manipulative skills Child K uses when eating a meal.
A clear aim explains what you want to find out and the activity or context that

you have decided will best show you. This is better than simply saying that you will watch Child K eating. The aim you identify should affect what information you write in your introduction and in the actual observation.

Introduction

In this section you must explain where the observation is taking place – for example, in the kitchen of the family home – and give some information about what is happening – for example, Child K has just returned from nursery school. The introduction to your observation should include the following:

- date carried out
- start and finish times/length of observation
- who gave permission
- where it took place (setting)
- number of children present
- number of adults present
- age(s) of child(ren)
- names or identification of children (remember confidentiality).

Include only information that is relevant to your aim. For instance, it may be important to know whether Child K is of average build if you are observing gross motor skills, such as running and jumping, but not particularly relevant if you are dealing with imaginative play or with fine manipulative skills.

Actual observation

There are many different methods of recording and your teacher will help you to decide which one is best – perhaps a chart format, a checklist or a written record describing what you see as it happens. (Try to include a variety of methods to gain extra marks.)

- Remember only to write what you see and, if appropriate, hear. Do not write your judgements, opinions and assessments in this section. Make sure you include information about other children or adults involved if this is relevant.
- When recording your observation, remember to maintain confidentiality by only using a child's first name or initial, or some other form of identification – for example, Child K. You may use 'T' or 'A' for 'teacher' or 'adult'.

Evaluation

An evaluation is an assessment of what you have observed. This section can be dealt with in two parts:

1. You need to look back at your recorded information and summarise what you have discovered into a conclusion:
   Example: Child K was eating his lunch at the kitchen table. He was using a spoon and a fork and managed to eat everything on his plate. He was very chatty and seemed to be enjoying his lunch.
   This is a brief review – or summary – of what you have observed. The observation itself will be much more detailed and will include a description of, for example, how Child K held the spoon and fork, which hand he used, how he managed to transfer the food to his mouth, any difficulties he experienced and so on.
2. You then need to consider what you have summarised and compare your findings to the 'norm' or 'average' or 'expected' for a child of this age and at this stage of development. What have you learnt about this particular child and how has this helped you to understand children's development more

widely? Use relevant books to help you and make reference to them – or quote directly if you can find a statement that is particularly relevant. (Your teacher or assessor wants to know what *you* understand – not information that he or she could read in a book, so use references carefully.) In this section, you may also give your opinion as to reasons for the behaviour and so on. But take care not to jump to conclusions about the role of the child's background, and *never* make judgements about the child or the child's family.

Guidelines for research using the internet

1. Always have a notebook handy to write down website, date and topic researched. If a site proves not to be useful it can be crossed through. Otherwise a note can be made indicating whether or not material was copied/pasted.
2. If you print off information you should highlight the website information and date at the bottom of the page.
3. If copying and pasting into your own Microsoft® Word documents (only for notes) you should also copy and paste the website address.
4. Material you intend to use should be printed out and relevant sections highlighted so that you are selecting appropriate information. Remember to write the information in your own words. If you do take any text or images directly from the internet they must be properly acknowledged within the body of your work.

Exam preparation

Unit B013: The examination

Revision

Start the process of revision and review well in advance of the exam date, using your weekly planner to assign short but regular chunks of time to exam preparation.

1. Plan: Make a revision timetable, and try to stick to it:
   - Make sure that coursework deadlines are also included on the timetable. You will not be able to do much revision when you are working hard to complete coursework.
   - Plan for 30-minute sessions, or an hour at most. Any longer and it is likely that nothing more will sink in.
   - Allow short breaks in between for a glass of water or something similar to drink.
   - In the evenings after school, plan to revise one or two GCSE subjects only. Plan to revise specific topics in each subject – not everything at once.

2. Have all the books you need to hand so you do not get distracted by having to go off looking for information.

3. Choose a revision style that suits you. Simply reading through is not usually effective. Instead, try:
   - reading and writing your notes out over and over again
   - drawing diagrams or spider diagrams of key issues
   - using mnemonics (rhymes or word lists) to prompt you
   - working through past exam papers
   - revising with someone else.

4. Too much study is not helpful, so plan some time for fun too. Try to plan it at the end of a section of study, so that taking time out will not make you lose the thread of your revision. For example, you could promise yourself an evening out with friends on Friday if you study hard on Wednesday and Thursday evenings.

5. Sometimes it is better to study with a friend or 'study buddy'. Working with a friend can be useful because it allows you to test each other and to talk about the work. Try to explain something you have just learned to your study buddy. If your friend can follow your explanation then you will be able to produce a good answer to an exam question on that topic.

6. If there are any parts of your work that you do not understand, ask for help from your subject teacher. Do not be afraid to be persistent until you do understand a subject: this is your last chance to master it before the exams.

The exam

When the day of the exam arrives, give yourself plenty of time to check everything and have a last look at any brief notes or summaries you have made.

Top exam tips

1. Have a relaxing night before your exams: Have an early night, and try to have a healthy breakfast.
2. Have all necessary material with you: You cannot borrow items such as pens, pencils, rulers or special equipment while in an examination.
3. Read the entire paper: The OCR exam requires you to answer all the questions.

4. **Make sure you understand the instructions**: Underline key words and note down any key facts you know you will have to use at some point but may forget as the exam proceeds.

5. **Look at the number of marks awarded for each question**: This will often indicate how much detail is needed in your answer.

6. **Jot down ideas as they come to you**: When you are answering one question, information about another may suddenly occur to you. Jot it down somewhere because when you come to that question, perhaps an hour later, you may have forgotten it.

7. **Start with the questions** you feel most confident with and then tackle the rest.

8. **Answer all the questions**: Never omit an entire question. No matter how well you answer other questions, you must leave time for all questions. A perfect answer can still only earn a certain number of marks. If you write nothing, you cannot receive any marks and you will have lost all your marks for a particular question. Write something – it may at least give you a few points.

9. **Keep an eye on the clock or a watch**: Be strict about keeping within the time limits for the questions. If you are short of time, use note form. Remember, you can only be marked on the answers you give.

10. **Never leave the room early**: If you have time at the end, go over your work and add information (e.g. in the margin). After you have left the room, you cannot return if you suddenly remember a fact you want to include.

GLOSSARY

alpha-fetoprotein (AFP)   A protein, produced by the foetus's liver, which can be detected in the mother's blood most accurately between the 16th and 18th weeks of pregnancy. High levels of AFP may be associated with a neural tube birth defect called spina bifida; low levels may be associated with Down's syndrome.

amenorrhoea   The absence of menstrual periods.

amniotic sac   Often called 'membranes' or the 'bag of waters', the amniotic sac is the bag of amniotic fluid that surrounds and cushions the foetus.

anaemia   A condition in which the concentration of the oxygen-carrying pigment, haemoglobin, in the blood is below normal.

anterior fontanelle   A diamond-shaped soft area at the front of the head, just above the brow. It is covered by a tough membrane; you can often see the baby's pulse beating there under the skin. The fontanelle closes between 12 and 18 months of age.

areola   The areola is the dark area on the breast surrounding the nipple, which may spread or darken further during pregnancy.

attachment   A close relationship – at first with their parents – which babies usually develop with those who care for them.

attention deficit disorder (ADD)   A behavioural disorder characterised by an inability to concentrate on tasks. In **attention deficit hyperactivity disorder (ADHD)**, inability to concentrate is accompanied or replaced by hyperactive and impulsive behaviour.

autism (autistic spectrum disorder)   A rare developmental disorder that impairs a child's understanding of, and his/her ability to relate to, the environment.

babbling   Repeating single- or double-syllable sounds (e.g. baa, baaba, daa, daada, maa, maama, etc.).

barrier method   A device that will not allow semen or sperm to come into contact with the cervix.

blood pressure   The pressure exerted by the flow of blood through the main arteries.

bonding   A term used to describe the feelings of love and responsibility that parents have for their babies.

Braxton Hicks contractions   The irregular 'practice' contractions of the uterus that occur throughout pregnancy, but can be felt especially towards the end of pregnancy.

They can sometimes be uncomfortable and intense, but are not usually painful.

breech position   A baby is said to be breech presentation, or breech position, when it is 'bottom-down' rather than 'head-down' in the uterus just before birth. Either the baby's bottom or feet would be born first. Around 3–4 per cent of full-term babies are positioned this way.

Caesarean (C-)section   When the baby is delivered through an incision in the mother's abdomen and uterus. It is used when a woman cannot give birth vaginally or if the baby is in distress or danger.

central nervous system (CNS)   The brain and the spinal cord, which are the main control centres of the body.

cerebral palsy   A general term for disorders of movement and posture resulting from damage to the child's developing brain.

cervix   The lower end or neck of the uterus which leads into the vagina and gradually opens during labour.

chromosome   A threadlike structure in the cell nucleus that carries genetic information in the form of genes.

cleft palate   A hole or split in the palate (the roof of the mouth).

coeliac disease   A condition in which the lining of the small intestine is damaged by gluten, a protein found in wheat and rye.

cognitive/intellectual development   These words both refer to the ideas and thinking of the child. Cognition emphasises that children are aware, active learners, and that understanding is an important part of intellectual life. Intelligence is about the ability to profit from experience.

coitus   Another name for sexual intercourse.

colic   An attack of acute abdominal pain caused by spasms in the intestines as food is being digested; sometimes called 'three-month colic'.

colostrum   Colostrum is the first 'milk' the breasts produce, as a precursor to breast milk. It is rich in fats, protein and antibodies, which protect the baby against infection and kick-start the immune system. Most women produce colostrum a few days before and after childbirth; some women produce small amounts of it from the fifth or sixth month of pregnancy. It is gradually replaced by breast milk over the first week or so of breastfeeding.

conception   The start of pregnancy, when a male sperm and a female egg unite to form a new cell, and the start of a new baby.

contraception The prevention of conception by the use of birth control devices.

convulsions Uncontrolled movements of the muscles which may be accompanied by loss of consciousness.

cooing The earliest sounds made by a baby, used to express contentment.

cystic fibrosis A condition that affects certain organs in the body, especially the lungs and pancreas, by clogging them with thick, sticky mucus. New treatments mean that people with cystic fibrosis can live relatively healthy lives.

dehydration The loss of fluid or water from the body.

development The general sequence in the way that the child functions in terms of movement, language, thinking, feelings, etc. Development continues from birth to death and can be linked to a web or network.

diabetes A disorder in which the body does not produce enough insulin (the hormone which converts sugars into energy), resulting in too much sugar in the bloodstream. It can usually be controlled with appropriate treatment, diet and exercise.

diphtheria An acute bacterial illness that causes a sore throat and fever; it was responsible for many childhood deaths until mass immunisation against the bacillus was introduced.

Down's syndrome A genetic disorder resulting from the presence of an extra chromosome; children usually, but not always, have learning difficulties.

dyslexia A specific reading disability, characterised by difficulty in coping with written symbols.

echolalia The tendency of a child to echo the last words spoken by an adult.

eclampsia Eclampsia is a rare but serious condition that affects women in late pregnancy. If pre-eclampsia is not treated, it can develop into eclampsia, which can cause convulsions and coma. It may require emergency delivery of the baby.

ectopic pregnancy An ectopic pregnancy occurs when a fertilised egg implants outside the uterus, usually in a Fallopian tube, although it can be anywhere in the abdominal cavity. There is not enough room for a baby to grow, so the foetus must be surgically removed to prevent rupture and damage.

eczema A skin condition that can give rise to cracked and sore patches of skin.

egocentric Self-centred, or viewing things from one's own standpoint.

ejaculation The process of ejecting semen from the penis; it is usually accompanied by orgasm as a result of sexual stimulation. It may also occur spontaneously during sleep (a nocturnal emission or 'wet dream').

embryo The unborn child during the first eight weeks after conception.

empathy Awareness of another person's emotional state, and the ability to share the experience with that person.

endometriosis The endometrium is the tissue which lines the uterus. Endometriosis is a disease where endometrial cells grow outside the uterus, most often on the ovaries, Fallopian tubes or the exterior of the uterus. The condition can cause pain and damage, although some women have no symptoms at all; it is also associated with infertility.

endometrium The lining of the womb.

enuresis The medical term for bed-wetting.

epididymis A storage chamber in the male's body which is attached to each testicle. This is where sperm cells are nourished and mature.

epidural A form of pain relief for labour in which anaesthetic is injected into the dural space around the spinal cord. An epidural numbs the lower body, decreasing or eliminating pain, and enabling the woman to save her strength for pushing. It can completely numb the lower body, however, so she may be unable to feel the contractions when it is time to push the baby out.

episiotomy A small surgical cut made in the perineum during labour to allow the baby's head to be delivered.

erection The penis becomes stiff and hard due to increased blood flow. Erections may happen in response to physical or emotional stimulation, or sometimes for no reason at all.

failure to thrive A term which refers to the slow growth and development of a baby, characterised by failure to gain weight, delayed development, unwillingness to interact and gastrointestinal problems. Failure to thrive is sometimes called 'faltering growth' and is almost always the result of inadequate nutrition.

Fallopian tubes There are two Fallopian tubes, one on each side of the uterus, leading from the area of the ovaries into the uterine cavity. When an ovary releases an egg, the nearest Fallopian tube draws it in and transports it down to the uterus.

family A group of people living together or apart who have strong emotional relationships and who are significant to each other through blood or other links.

fertilisation The moment when sperm and egg meet, join and form a single cell. It usually takes place in the Fallopian tubes. The fertilised egg then travels into the uterus, where it implants in the lining before developing into an embryo and then a foetus.

fine manipulative skills Skills involving precise use of the hands and fingers in pointing, drawing, using a knife and fork or chopsticks, writing, doing up shoelaces, etc.

fine motor skills These use the smaller

muscles and include manipulative skills involving precision in finger and hand movements.

foetal alcohol syndrome Babies born to mothers who drink large amounts of alcohol throughout the pregnancy may be born with foetal alcohol syndrome; these babies have characteristic facial deformities, stunted growth and mental retardation.

foetal distress Signs of foetal distress – including slowed heartbeat or absence of foetal movement – are watched for throughout labour. If a foetus's life is believed to be in danger, usually because of lack of oxygen, the immediate delivery of the baby is called for.

foetus The unborn child from the end of the eighth week after conception until birth.

fontanelles The soft spots on the top of the newborn baby's head; when the fontanelles are sunken, it is a sign of dehydration.

fundal height The distance between the top of a pregnant woman's uterus (called the fundus) to her pubic bone. It is measured to determine foetal age.

fundus The upper, rounded portion of the uterus.

gastroenteritis Inflammation of the stomach and intestines, often causing sudden and violent upsets – diarrhoea, cramps, nausea and vomiting are common symptoms.

gender role The way that boys learn to be male and girls learn to be female in the culture they grow up in. The gender role might be narrow or broad, according to the culture.

gene Unit of the chromosome containing a pattern which is passed on through generations. (Genes influence hair and eye colour, blood group, etc.)

genetic counselling Guidance given (usually by a doctor with experience in genetics) to individuals who are considering having a child but who are concerned because there is a blood relative with an inherited disorder.

gestation The period of time a baby is carried in the uterus; full-term gestation is between 38 and 42 weeks (counted from the first day of the last menstrual period).

glue ear A build-up of sticky fluid in the middle ear which usually affects children under eight years old.

gross motor skills These use the large muscles in the body, as in walking, climbing and running.

haemolytic disease of the newborn Also called rhesus disease, haemolytic disease results when a woman who is rhesus negative has a foetus who is rhesus positive and the mother's immune system makes antibodies against the foetus's blood. The disorder is treated with a compound which prevents the woman's immune system from making antibodies.

haemophilia An inherited bleeding disorder caused by a deficiency of a particular blood protein.

health visitor A health visitor is a registered nurse with qualifications in obstetrics and midwifery, who visits mothers and babies at home.

hearing impairment A loss of hearing, ranging from slight, through moderate and severe to profound, because of damage to the nerve endings of the inner ear.

hepatitis B Inflammation of the liver, caused by a virus. A mother can unknowingly pass the infection to the child she carries in her womb.

Hib vaccine A vaccine given to protect against Haemophilus influenzae type B (Hib), a serious bacterial infection which causes ear and airway infections and is the leading cause of meningitis in children under two years of age.

holistic Seeing a child in the round, as a whole person, emotionally, socially, intellectually, physically, morally, culturally, spiritually and in terms of their health.

holophrase The expression of a whole idea in a single word: 'car' may mean 'Give me the car' or 'Look at the car.'

hydrocephalus An excessive accumulation of cerebrospinal fluid under increased pressure within the skull. Commonly known as 'water on the brain', hydrocephalus occurs in more than 80 per cent of babies born with spina bifida.

intrinsic motivation The extent to which children work hard in the absence of external rewards and seem to gain pleasure from the work itself.

jargon The child's own way of speaking, which may only be understood by those close to him/her.

jaundice Yellow coloration of the skin and the whites of the eye, caused by interference with the production of bile.

Jobcentre Plus The agency within the Department for Work and Pensions (DWP) that is responsible for the assessment and payment of social security benefits.

keyworker or key person A member of staff (usually in a nursery setting) who spends more time with a small number of identified children, builds a close relationship with them and is the main contact person for their families.

lanugo Downy, fine hair on a foetus. Lanugo can appear as early as 15 weeks of gestation, and typically begins to disappear some time before birth.

learning difficulty A learning difficulty may be moderate to severe and often leads to low attainment and/or poorly developed social and mobility skills.

listeria A bacterial infection resulting from eating chilled foods, particularly soft cheeses and meat pâté. It causes a flu-like illness, can also cause miscarriages and is sometimes fatal in babies and elderly people.

means testing The method of assessing the amount to be paid in social security benefits (e.g. income support and housing benefits), which takes into account all sources of personal or family income.

meconium The dark, sticky substance released from a newborn's intestines into his first bowel movements. If visible in amniotic fluid prior to delivery, it can be a sign that the foetus is in distress.

menopause The stage at which menstrual activity ends.

menstruation When the lining of the womb or uterus breaks down and there is a small flow of blood from the vagina; usually referred to as a 'period'.

motherese When adults (often mothers) talk to babies in a high-pitched tone about what is happening.

nature The features, characteristics and abilities one is born with. (See also nurture.)

neural tube defects These include anencephaly, encephalocoele and spina bifida. These conditions occur if the brain and/or spinal cord, together with the protecting skull and spinal column, fail to develop properly during the first month of embryonic life.

non-verbal communication Everything that is not actual words; it can include body language, posture, tone of voice, etc.

norm An average or typical state or ability, used with others as a framework for assessing development. Norms are the result of observations by many professionals in the field of child development.

nurture An individual's upbringing, including health, emotional, social and educational factors. (See also nature.)

nutrients Essential dietary factors, such as carbohydrates, proteins, certain fats, vitamins and minerals.

oedema Swelling caused by fluid retention in the body's tissues; it is very common during pregnancy. It can also be a sign of kidney or urological problems.

ovary Female sex gland.

ovulation When a female egg is released from an ovary.

ovum A single female egg.

paediatrician A doctor who specialises in treating babies and children.

penis The male reproductive organ, involved in sexual intercourse and elimination of urine.

perinatal The period just before, during and immediately after birth.

perineum The skin between the vagina and the rectum.

personality The distinctive characteristics which make an individual unique.

placenta An organ which develops in the uterus during pregnancy, providing nutrients for the foetus and eliminating its waste products. It is also referred to as the afterbirth because it is delivered after the baby in a vaginal birth.

placenta praevia A pregnancy-related condition where the placenta is placed abnormally low in the uterus, possibly covering the cervix, usually necessitating a Caesarean section.

plaque A rough, sticky coating on the teeth that consists of saliva, bacteria and food debris.

possetting The regurgitation (or bringing back) of small amounts of milk by infants after they have been fed.

posterior fontanelle A small, triangular-shaped soft area near the crown of the head; it is much smaller and less noticeable than the anterior fontanelle.

post-natal The first days and weeks after the birth of the baby (post = after, natal = birth).

preconceptual care When both partners work to reduce known risks before trying to conceive, in order to create the best conditions for an embryo to grow and develop into a healthy baby.

pre-eclampsia A condition that a mother may develop late in pregnancy, marked by sudden oedema, high blood pressure and protein in the urine. It can lead to eclampsia, where the mother has convulsions, so antenatal care staff monitor women carefully for the warning signs.

premature baby A premature baby is one who is born before 37 weeks of gestation.

prescription drugs Medicines that are only available on the authorisation of a doctor because they may be dangerous or habit-forming, or are used to treat a disease that needs to be monitored.

primary health care team (PHCT) The health care professionals working as part of a GP practice team who are responsible for an individual's overall health. The GP and other members of the primary health care team will suggest and authorise referrals to specialists or clinics where required.

progestogen A synthetic version of the natural hormone progesterone.

puerperium The period of about six weeks which follows immediately after the birth of a child.

salmonella Salmonellosis is an infection caused by the *Salmonella* group of bacteria, generally by ingesting infected food; the organisms can be found in raw meats, raw poultry, eggs and dairy products.

screening test A test that assesses the risks of having a baby with an abnormality.

self-esteem This refers to the way individuals feel about themselves. Positive feelings indicate high self-esteem, while negative feelings are an indication of low self-esteem.

self-identity A sense of who you are; liking yourself, respecting yourself and developing the skills and care to look after yourself.

self-image/self-concept How you see yourself and how you think others see you.

semen A milky, white fluid made by the seminal vesicles and prostate gland. This fluid mixes with the sperm cells during an ejaculation. About a teaspoon of semen comes out of the penis during an ejaculation.

sensation Being aware that you are having an experience through seeing, smelling, hearing, touching, tasting and moving.

sensorimotor Using the senses and your own movement/actions.

six-week check Both mother and baby will have a thorough medical examination and check-up approximately six weeks after the birth to monitor their overall progress and ensure their good health.

socialisation The process by which children learn what is expected of them in terms of behaviour and attitudes within society.

social referencing When babies begin to move about, they will keep looking at the adult who is caring for them – just to check they are still there.

special care baby unit (SCBU) A unit in a hospital which provides specialised care to premature babies and babies with serious illnesses.

sperm The microscopic cells produced by a male that contain the genes from the father. A sperm cell from the father must join with an egg cell from the mother for a baby to be created.

sperm duct (vas deferens) A muscular tube that passes upwards alongside the testicles and transports the sperm-containing semen.

spina bifida This occurs when the spinal canal in the vertebral columns is not closed (although it may be covered with skin). Individuals with spina bifida may have a wide range of physical disabilities. In the more severe forms, the spinal cord bulges out of the back, the legs and bladder may be paralysed, and obstruction to the fluid surrounding the brain causes hydrocephalus.

statutory service Any service provided and managed by the state or government (e.g. the NHS or a local authority day nursery).

stepping reflex Newborns have a stepping reflex: they will lift one leg and then the other – taking what may appear to be steps – if they are held upright on a table or other flat surface and supported under the arms.

stereotype A limited image of someone and what they can do or be.

stillbirth If a foetus dies *in utero* (in the womb) before delivery, usually after the 24th week, it is called a stillbirth. The loss of a pregnancy before 24 weeks of gestation is called a miscarriage.

surrogate mother A surrogate mother carries and gives birth to a baby for a couple who cannot have a baby themselves. She hands the baby over to the couple after the birth.

telegraphic speech The abbreviation of a sentence such that only the crucial words are spoken, as in a telegram (e.g. 'Where daddy going?' or 'Shut door').

temperament A person's character or disposition (e.g. he has a happy disposition).

testes (singular = testis) The medical name for testicles, the main male reproductive glands in which sperm are produced. The testicles also produce the main male hormone testosterone.

testosterone The hormone that causes boys to develop deeper voices, bigger muscles and body and facial hair; it also stimulates the production of sperm.

transitional object A transitional object is any toy, stuffed animal or blanket to which a child becomes attached and which s/he uses for comfort as s/he gradually makes the transition to self-comfort rather than being dependent on parents for comfort.

trimester A period of three months; pregnancy is divided into the first, second and third trimesters.

tuberculosis (TB) An infectious disease, caused by the tubercle bacillus, which commonly affects the lungs. It used to be a major killer in childhood and early adult life.

ultrasound In ultrasound procedures, high-frequency sound waves are used to create a moving image, or sonogram, on a television screen. Often carried out at various stages of pregnancy, ultrasound scans can help to identify multiple foetuses and to detect anomalies.

umbilical cord The cord connecting the foetus to the maternal placenta. It contains blood vessels that carry nutrients to the placenta and remove waste substances.

urethra *In the male*: the tube through which urine and semen exit.
In the female: the tube through which urine exits.

uterus Another name for the womb.

vaccination A type of immunisation in which killed or weakened microorganisms are introduced into the body, usually by injection.

vagina A muscular, hollow tube that extends from the vaginal opening to the uterus.

vas deferens (pl. = vasa deferentia) One of two tubes through which sperm travel from the epididymis and combine with seminal fluid ready for ejaculation. (The two vasa deferentia are severed in a vasectomy.)

vernix A protective, white, greasy substance that often covers the skin of the newborn baby.

viable Able to maintain an independent existence – to live after birth.

voluntary organisation An association or society that has been created by its members rather than by the state (e.g. a charity).

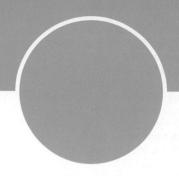

INDEX